AFRICAN DEVELOPMENT REPORT
2007

NATURAL RESOURCES FOR SUSTAINABLE
DEVELOPMENT IN AFRICA

PUBLISHED FOR THE AFRICAN DEVELOPMENT BANK
BY
OXFORD UNIVERSITY PRESS

OXFORD
UNIVERSITY PRESS

Great Clarendon Street, Oxford OX2 6DP
Oxford University Press is a department of the University of Oxford.
It furthers the University's objective of excellence in research, scholarship,
and education by publishing worldwide in

Oxford New York
Auckland Cape Town Dar es Salaam Hong Kong
Karachi Kuala Lumpur Madrid Melbourne
Mexico City Nairobi New Delhi Shanghai Taipei Toronto

With offices in
Argentina Austria Brazil Chile Czech Republic France Greece
Guatemala Hungary Italy Japan Poland Portugal Singapore
South Korea Switzerland Thailand Turkey Ukraine Vietnam

Oxford is a registered trade mark of Oxford University Press
in the UK and in certain other countries

Published in the United States
by Oxford University Press Inc., New York

The African Development Report 2007 is produced by the staff of the African Development Bank,
and the views expressed therein do not necessarily reflect those of the Boards of Directors
or the countries they represent. Designations employed in this Report do not imply the expression
of any opinion, on the part of the African Development Bank, concerning the legal status of any
country or territory, or the delineation of its frontiers.

British Library Cataloguing in Publication Data
Data available
Library of Congress Cataloging-in-Publication Data
Data available
ISBN 978–0-19-923886-6

Typeset by Hope Services, Abingdon, Oxon
Printed in Great Britain
on acid-free paper by
Ashford Colour Press Limited, Gosport, Hampshire

FOREWORD

The theme of the *African Development Report 2007 — Natural Resources for Sustainable Development in Africa —* is motivated by the need to deepen current understanding of natural resource management practices in Africa. The rekindled interest in Africa's resources is largely driven by global economic growth, especially in Asia, and the related demand for fossil fuels and minerals. This situation raises questions; how the continent can best leverage its resources for its own development given the complexities and trade-offs. Indeed, the market demand for Africa's natural resources is strong and growing; but Africa needs these resources too for its own development.

It is within this spirit that the African Development Bank and the United Nations Economic Commission for Africa (ECA) jointly organized the Big Table 2007 Forum to deliberate on the challenges and strategies for managing Africa's natural resources for growth and poverty reduction. The *African Development Report 2007* leverages and complements the knowledge generated by the Big Table 2007. The Report clearly sets the stage for a more proactive stakeholder engagement in the effective management of Africa's natural resource wealth. Indeed, collaborative efforts between key stakeholders — governments, companies, civil society organizations and local communities — is needed to ensure that Africa's natural resource wealth translates into broad-based socio-economic development, taking into account the lessons and impact of past experience of commodity booms and busts. This is important, given the paradox of the so-called natural resource curse. It underscores the crucial need for synergies to be created and strengthened between the public, the private sector, civil society, and external development partners. Initiatives such as the Extractive Industries Transparency Initiative, the Kimberly Process, and the African Peer Review Mechanism, among others, need to be strengthened and vigorously supported.

The African Development Bank, in cooperation with other stakeholders and development partners, is scaling up financial assistance for governance and institutional reforms in the natural resources sector. It is providing technical assistance, capacity building, knowledge and advisory services for appropriate fiscal systems and regulatory institutions, among others. It is prepared to do more.

The *African Development Report 2007* sets the stage for a re-thinking of the role of natural resources in economic development and poverty reduction in Africa. It articulates the crucial issues behind this relatively untapped potential and offers a rich discussion on ways to reverse the current trends. We hope that the Report will serve as an important catalyst for change, and the starting point of a broader process that will elicit action by all stakeholders to ensure efficient natural resource management for sustainable development in Africa.

Donald Kaberuka
President
African Development Bank

ACKNOWLEDGEMENTS

The *African Development Report 2007* has been prepared by a staff team in the Development Research Department of the African Development Bank under the direction of Temitope Waheed Oshikoya (Director, Development Research Department).

The research team comprised Abdul B. Kamara (Manager, Research Division), John C. Anyanwu (Task Manager), Michael Juel (Technical Assistant) and research assistants in the Research Division. Valuable statistical inputs from the Statistics Department were provided by Beejay Kokil, Maurice Mubila, and Fetor Komlan. Further statistical/research assistance was provided by Lobna Bousri and Magidu Nyende (Intern) from the Development Research Department.

Rhoda R. Bangurah and Afef Chihi provided production services, Felicia Avwontom editorial services, Lassaad Lachaal translation coordination, and Abiana Nelson administrative services.

Preparation of the Report was aided by the background papers listed in the bibliographical notes. The contributors of these background papers (and text boxes) include Peter Veit (Institutions and Governance Program, World Resources Institute, Washington, D. C., USA), MINTEK (Randburg, South Africa), Tony Venables (DFID and Department of Economics, London School of Economics and Political Science, London, UK), Rick (Frederick) van der Ploeg (Robert Schuman Centre, European University Institute, Italy), ElWathig Mohamed Kameir (Private Consultant, Tunis, Tunisia), Adeniyi Sulaiman Gbadegesin (Department of Geography, University of Ibadan, Nigeria), Paul Collier (Department of Economics, Oxford University, Oxford, UK). Ejeviome Eleho Otobo (Strategic Planning, Peacebuilding Support Office, United Nations) contributed a Text Box in his private capacity. Comments from outside the Bank added a great deal to the thorough-ness of the Report, and are highly appreciated.

We are also grateful to staff of the African Development Bank who provided critical inputs, review comments, guidance and support at various stages of the Report preparation. These include Abou-Sabaa, Aly; Afrika, Philibert; Barnett, Douglas; Bedoumra, Kordje; Black, Frank; Bocoum, Brigitte; Chakroun, Lofti; Darbo, Suwareh; Gadio, Kalidou; Garbi, J. Mohammed; Gaye, Diarietou; Goldstein, Ellen; Issahaku, Abdul-Nasirou; Johm, Ken; Kromer, Jean-Louis; Kandil, Hesham; Kayizzi-Mugerwa, Steve; Kwesiga, Freddie; Litse, K. Janvier; Lonsway, Kurt; Moussa, Sami Zaki; Mousseau, Louis P.; Mwaikinda, Jackson; Negatu, Gabriel; Ojukwu, Chiji C.; Olanrewaju, Stephen; Omoluabi, Charles O.; Ordu, Aloysuis Uche; Outaguerouine, Abderrahmane; Rakotobe, Razanakoto; Roberts, Thomas; Santiso, Carlos; Sering, Jallow; Strauss, Tove; Shalaby, Hany R.; Traore, Modibo; Ponzi, Danielle; and Vyas, Yogesh K.

Overall guidance to the preparation of this Report was provided by Louis Kasekende, Chief Economist.

CONTENTS

LIST OF BOXES, FIGURES AND TABLES

BOXES

TEXT FIGURES

TEXT TABLES

ACRONYMS AND ABBREVIATIONS

ADF	African Development Fund
AEO	African Economic Outlook
AfDB (ADB)	African Development Bank
AMCOW	African Ministers Council On Water
AOAD	Arab Organization for Agricultural Development
APRM	African Peer Review Mechanism
ARWR	Annual Renewable Water Resources
AU	African Union
AWF	The African Water Facility
BGS	British Geological Survey
BIC	(1) Bushveld Igneous Complex; (2) Bank Information Center
BOP	Base Of the Pyramid
BP	British Petroleum
Btu	British thermal unit (energy content of fuels)
CBOs	Civil Based Organizations
CCD	Convention to Combat Desertification
CEC	Commission of the European Communities
CGD	Center for Global Development
CGS	Council for Geoscience
CO_2	Carbon Dioxide
DFID	Department For International Development
DLA	Department of Land Affairs (South Africa)
DME	Department of Minerals and Energy (South Africa)
DRC	Democratic Republic of Congo
DTI	Department of Trade and Industry (South Africa)
ECA	Economic Commission for Africa (UN)
ECOWAS	Economic Community of West African States
EEA	European Environmental Agency
EEA/EEPRI	Ethiopian Economic Association / Ethiopian Economic Policy Research Institute
EI	Extractive Industry
EIA	(1) Energy Information Administration; (2) Environmental Impact Assessment
EITI	Extractive Industry Transparency Initiative
EPFIs	Equator Principles Financial Institutions
EU	European Union
FAO	Food and Agriculture Organization (United Nations)

FD	Fiscal Deficit
FDI	Foreign Direct Investment
FGF	Future Generations Fund
GBS	General Budget Support
GDP	Gross Domestic Product
GEF	Global Environment Facility
GHG	Green House Gases
GNI	Gross National Income
GNP	Gross National Product
Ha	Hectares
HDI	Human Development Index (UNDP)
HIPC	Heavily Indebted Poor Countries
IAI	International Aluminium Institute
ICMM	International Council on Mining and Metals
IFA	International Fertilizer Industry Association
IFC	International Finance Corporation
IFIs	International Financial Institutions
IISD	(1) International Iron and Steel Institute; (2) International Institute for Sustainable Development
ILRI	International Livestock Research Institute
ILZSG	International Lead Zinc Study Group
IMF	International Monetary Fund
IPCC	Intergovernmental Panel on Climate Change
IRLI	International Research Livestock Institute
IRR	Internal Renewable Resources (water)
ITCZ	Inter-Tropical Convergence Zone
IWRM	Integrated Water Resource Management
KP	Kimberly Process
KPCS	Kimberly Process Certification Scheme
LNG	Liquified Natural Gas
LVEMP	Lake Victoria Environmental Management Program
MDGs	Millennium Development Goals
MDRI	Multilateral Debt Relief Initiative
MECs	Multinational Extractive Companies
MFIs	Multilateral Financing Institutions
MII	Mineral Information Institute
MMSD	Mining, Minerals and Sustainable Development (Project)
MNCs	Multinational Corporations
NBI	Nile Basin Initiative
NDP	National Development Plan

NEITI	Nigerian Extractive Industries Transparency Initiative
NELSAP	Nile Equatorial Lakes Subsidiary Action Program
NEPAD	New Economic Partnership for Africa's Development
NEPAD-WSP	NEPAD Water and Sanitation Program
NGOs	Non Governmental Organizations
NORAD	Norwegian Agency for Development Cooperation
NRM	Natural Resource Management
NSA	Nubian Sandstone Aquifer
OECD	Organization for Economic Co-operation and Development
OMVS	Senegal River Development Organizations
OPEC	Organization of Petroleum Exporting Countries
PES	Payment for Ecosystem Services
PGM	Platinum Group Metals
PPP	Public-Private Partnerships
PRSPs	Poverty Reduction Strategy Policies
PSOs	Private Security Organizations
PWYP	Publish What You Pay (Campaign)
RBOs	River Basin Organizations
RMC's	Regional Member Countries (AfDB)
RWSSI	Rural Water Supply and Sanitation Initiative
SADC	Southern African Development Community
SANE	South Africa, Algeria, Nigeria and Egypt
SEA	Strategic Environmental Assessment
SSA	Sub-Saharan Africa
TFP	Total Factor Productivity
TWRM	Transboundary Water Resource Management
UAE	United Arab Emirates
UK	United Kingdom (of Britain)
UN	United Nations
UNCBD	United Nations Convention on Biological Diversity
UNCCD	United Nations Convention to Combat Desertification
UNCHR	United Nations Commission on Human Rights
UNCTAD	United Nations Conference on Trade and Development
UN COMTRADE	United Nations Commodity Trade (Online Database)
UNDP	United Nations Development Program
UNECA	UN Economic Commission for Africa
UNECE	UN Economic Commission for Europe
UNEP	United Nations Environmental Program
UNESCO	United Nations Educational, Scientific and Cultural Organization
UNFCCC	United Nations Framework Convention on Climate Change

UNICEF	United Nations International Children's Emergency Fund (now United Nations Children's Fund)
USAID	United States Agency for International Development
USD	United States Dollars ($)
USGS	United States Geological Survey
WB	World Bank
WBO	Water Basin Organizations
WCED	World Commission on Environment and Development
WGC	World Gold Council
WHO	World Health Organization
WMO	World Meteorological Institute
WRI	World Resource Institute
WSSD	World Summit on Sustainable Development
WTO	World Trade Organization
WWC	World Water Council

EXECUTIVE SUMMARY

Africa's natural resources and the wealth they generate are more important than ever before as developing nations on the continent strive towards achieving the Millennium Development Goals (MDGs). Considering the continent's significant resources — and the decades of resource exploitation — economic growth has been disappointing. In other words, resource abundance has not translated into improved livelihoods and increased welfare. This is largely attributable to Africa's poor management of its natural resources — a recurring theme in recent debates on the 'natural resource curse' associated with many resource-rich countries. Yet, there is also strong evidence that natural resource wealth can make an important contribution to *economic growth* and *poverty reduction* in the continent. Such a scenario is contingent upon the fulfillment of critical conditions, chiefly, improving governance and transparency, eliminating corruption and strengthening the macroeconomic framework.

Natural resource management is a broad concept that involves the integration of efficient resource use and the prevention of adverse environmental impacts. It also concerns distribution for sustainable economic development, management of resource extraction and the resultant financial resources, wastes, and emissions. Given the broad scope of natural resources, the analyses in the 2007 African Development Report focus on a selection of natural resources: fossil fuels, minerals, water, forestry, and land use. The main objectives of the Report are grouped around the following four areas:

1. Define, in operational terms, the contextual meaning of natural resources and how they relate to sustainable development and social outcomes.
2. Examine and analyze good and poor management practices with respect to Africa's natural resources.
3. Advance and analyze the thesis that better natural resource management, in particular, better use of natural resource wealth, is the most direct route to reversing Africa's poverty and economic malaise.
4. Propose concrete suggestions on how stakeholders involved in natural resource exploitation (at the local, national, and international levels) can help improve public policies and governance in natural resource-endowed countries in Africa.

Renewable Natural Resources

Water resources are a key component of Africa's natural resource endowments, but water is becoming increasingly scarce. By the year 2025, almost 50 percent of Africans will be living in areas of water scarcity or water stress. Consequently, one of the current challenges facing Africa is how to take comprehensive stock of its water resources, and how to use these resources optimally to sustain an acceptable standard of living.

Average annual rainfall in Africa is about 678 mm per year, albeit with high spatial and temporal variability. About 86 percent of water resources withdrawal is used for agriculture, 10 percent for domestic consumption, and 4 percent for industrial use. However, in Africa as a whole, the amount of water withdrawn for these three major uses amounts to only 5.5 percent of internal renewable resources, reflecting the low level of development and of water resource use on the continent. Altogether, very few African countries have at present developed all the available water reserves (mainly countries in Northern Africa) and for the majority, the main obstacle is lack of resources and means to exploit and develop the resources. Thus, the need for more investments in water resource development remains as critical as ever.

Forest ecosystems play multiple roles at global as well as local levels and provide a range of important economic, social, and environmental goods and services. Forests help regulate the climate, protect coastlines, preserve the land, and improve the environment. The acknowledgment of competing interests in reaping the benefits of forest resources and woodlands has led to more holistic thinking and approaches in achieving sustainable forest management.

Africa's total forest cover was estimated at nearly 650 million hectares in 2000, equivalent to 17 percent of global forest cover, and to approximately 22 percent of Africa's land area. Forest areas can change in terms of nature, extent (dimension), and bio-ecological characteristics, due to both human and natural causes. Recent estimates of forest extent, management, and character-istics conclude that the situation in Africa is of particular concern, as very limited progress seems to have been made towards sustainable forest management over the past 10–15 years. Deforestation, forest degradation, and the associated loss of forest products and environmental services are some of the serious challenges facing African countries today. The most intensive pressures stem from deforestation for commercial timber sales, clearance for agricultural and urban developments, and over-harvesting of wood for fuel, medicinal products, and construction materials.

Land is a critical natural resource in Africa and the basis of survival for the majority of Africans. Land use concerns the products and benefits obtained from use of land and from land management actions (activities) carried out by humans to produce these products and benefits. With a total land area of more than 3,025.8 million hectares, Africa is the second largest continent in the world after Asia. If sustainably managed, the African landscape, a rich and dynamic mosaic of resources, holds vast opportunities for the development of human well-being. The economies of most African countries depend heavily on land-based activities such as agriculture, mining, and tourism. Agriculture is perhaps one of the most challenging factors that influence land use dynamics in Africa. It contributes about 40 percent to the regional gross domestic product and employs more than 60 percent of the labor force.

Access to land and the ability to exchange it with others and to use it effectively, including as collateral in access to finance, are of great importance for poverty reduction, economic growth, and private sector investment as well as for empowering the poor. In Africa, land can either be purchased or inherited. This largely determines patterns of land accessibility and ownership. Land issues in Africa remain largely political and the challenge of addressing land access is largely embedded in ensuring good governance and continues to be a critical factor in the development of African economies, natural resources, and related policies.

Management of Renewable Natural Resources

Africa's renewable resources are fundamental to its commercial and subsistence-activities. The Report clearly indicates that the resources are fragile and susceptible to degradation. Consequently, proper management of the resources and of the wealth they generate is a key component of the future development of Africa.

In conformity with the global approach to **water resources management**, Africa manages its scarce water resources through various partnership arrangements among riparian countries (for example, water basin organizations). However, in spite of the formal steps taken to create relevant organizations, most of them have been ineffective. Furthermore, despite the fact that numerous water resources in Africa are shared by many countries, issues of water rights and ownership of international waters remain largely unresolved. As a result, national interests tend to prevail over shared interests. There is general consensus that integrated water resources management is a prerequisite for enhanced water resource development in Africa. Also gaining recent popularity in several African countries are public-private partnerships (PPP) in water resources management and water supply programs.

Several African governments are currently shifting emphasis from passive to active involvement in **forestry** and are progressing, to varying degrees, towards sustainable utilization of forest and woodland resources. Overall, a more holistic approach is gaining traction, reflecting the recognition that effective resource conservation and management must involve strong local participation (the concept of integrated conservation and development).

Access to land remains critical for the survival of the population in most African countries where land is the primary means of generating a livelihood. Proponents of land reform typically argue that equity, poverty reduction, economic development, political stability, and land reforms are important contributors to human freedoms, civil liberties, and sustainable democracies. Owing to the diverse history and conditions in different African countries, land rights have evolved along different pathways and thus require different reform options. Many countries in Africa are clearly struggling to implement the laws and policies they have formulated in recent years. The reasons for these difficulties include over-ambition, lack of capacity, and scarcity of financial resources. Moreover, land has always been an object of policy intervention from colonial times to the present. Any new policy must therefore take into account previous policies and their effects, in addition to the socio-economic conditions of land tenure they aim to alter.

Climate Change is emerging as one of the most important international development challenges of the 21st Century. Africa has the lowest green house gas emissions of any continent, yet it is prone to be hardest hit by climate change. Africa is particularly vulnerable to climate change because of its overdependence on natural resources and rain-fed agriculture, land degradation, and the ongoing deforestation process — compounded by widespread poverty and weak capacity for planning, monitoring and adaptation to the changes.

Adaptation to climate change should be understood as a continuous process which addresses current climate variability and extremes and future climate risks. Consequently, natural resource management policies and strategies should adequately incorporate climate change issues — present and anticipated future risks. Adaptation approaches based on better management of natural resources, such as "no regrets" options, i.e., those measures that are expected to generate benefits even without long-term climate change, are an important avenue to pursue. Actions by local communities that are most directly affected play a very important role.

Non-Renewable Natural Resources

The Report includes a comprehensive analysis of Africa's *non-renewable* natural resources: fossil fuels (coal, gas and oil) and other minerals (metals and non-metals).

Mineral exports contribute significantly to the economies of resource-rich African countries. In fact, Africa's top five exports are mineral-related (crude oil, other petroleum oils, natural gas, diamonds, and coal). Although Africa ranks high in terms of resources, its share of world base metal and mineral fuel *consumption* is very modest, a consequence of the continent's low level of industrialization, economic status, and per capita consumption patterns.

The majority of Africa's **coal resources** are located in southern and western Africa. By a large margin, South Africa holds the majority of the continent's estimated recoverable coal reserves, being the sixth-largest holder of coal reserves in the world. The outlook for African coal exploration and production is relatively bright.

Africa's major known deposits of **crude oil** are located towards the north of the continent in the states of Algeria, Chad, Egypt, Libya, Morocco and Tunisia; and in the countries of Nigeria and Angola in the south. Africa produces about 10 million barrels of oil per year, bringing its share of world crude petroleum production to about 12 percent. Nigeria accounts for more than a quarter of the continent's production, which rose by nearly 18 percent from 2004 to 2007. Further expansion is expected in the future.

Africa's largest deposits of **natural gas** are located in Algeria and Mozambique, with other significant deposits in Libya, Niger, Morocco, Nigeria, Rwanda, Ghana, Egypt, Tunisia, and off the coasts of South Africa, Tanzania, and Namibia. Liquified Natural Gas (LNG) accounted for 79 percent of natural gas production, giving Africa an 18 percent share in world LNG trade. From 2004 to 2007, African natural gas production rose nearly 28 percent; it is expected to rise by an additional 5 percent from 2007 to 2011.

The African continent is endowed with a diverse mix of precious, ferrous, non-ferrous, and industrial minerals (metals and non-metals). For example, it is the top producer of platinum and gold and has very large shares of world reserves. This notwithstanding, its production of minerals is comparatively small and the trend has been negative for some minerals.

Management of Non-renewable Natural Resources

To create and sustain wealth in the long term, mineral resources have to be converted into other forms of capital and into more sustainable livelihood opportunities. Between 2000 and 2005, the world trade value of minerals grew 17 percent per year, while production rose 2.5 percent. The growing interest in African resources is largely about its non-renewable resources.

Fiscal Regimes for fossil fuels and other minerals in Africa are by no means uniform, as is the case in the rest of the world. A multitude of royalties, taxes, resource rents, incentives, state equity levels, and so on, have been developed to foster interest in exploration and investments, on the one hand, and capture some of the benefits for the state and the public, on the other hand. A review of key issues and analysis of selected case countries reveals that most countries in Africa have taken important steps to formulate policies and legislation and to adopt fiscal terms for extraction of minerals. However, more coherent principles, structures and, above all, due diligence in enforcement would considerably increase the benefits and sustainability for all countries.

Some concrete sustainable development issues need to be improved — for instance, incorporating environmental concerns into the full extraction cycle, including rehabilitation and mine closures. The natural resource management track record of African countries certainly varies a lot, and policy- and decision-makers need to learn from both good (for instance Botswana) and bad experiences. Implementation of formulated principles and legislation is often insufficient since the key constraints are more related to lack of enforcement, weak capacity and institutions, and poor governance.

The Paradox of Plenty — The Natural Resource Curse

The resource curse refers to a situation in which a country has an export-driven natural resources sector that generates large revenues for the state but leads, paradoxically, to economic stagnation and political instability. It is commonly used to describe the negative development outcomes associated with non-renewable extractive resources (petroleum and other minerals).

However, historical accounts indicate that natural resource booms do not always worsen economic performance and can indeed catalyze economic transformation. A resource boom can therefore lead to growth expansion, and the so-called natural resource curse can be avoided with the right knowledge, institutions, capacity, and policies.

This Report includes a comprehensive analysis of the key features of resource wealth in Africa. In this light, it categorizes African countries into the following groups: (1) Resource-rich (oil and mineral exporters);

(2) Resource-scarce countries;

(3) Land-locked (resource-rich and resource-scarce) countries;

(4) Coastal (resource-rich and resource-scarce) countries, and

(5) The SANE group (Africa's four largest economies: South Africa, Algeria, Nigeria and Egypt).

The following trends and conclusions emerge from the data, tables and figures presented in the Report:

- Resource-rich African countries are richer (in terms of revenues, GDP, and GDP per capita) than their resource-scarce peers. The gap narrowed during the 1980-2000 period but is widening again on account of the recent resource boom.

- Cumulatively, resource-rich countries only experienced an average growth rate of 2.4 percent from 1981-2006, considerably lower than the 3.8 percent average for resource-scarce countries.

- Resource-scarce coastal countries, where almost a quarter of Africa's population is found, have experienced an average growth rate of 4.1 percent, much higher than the 2.3 percent recorded by resource-rich coastal countries.

- These findings indicate that being resource-rich does *not* make a significant difference for coastal countries. Indeed, resource-scarce coastal countries have a somewhat higher GDP per capita.

- The four SANE countries are by far the wealthiest in terms of GDP and have sustained a significant growth rate since 1995.

- Land-locked resource-scarce countries are the poorest — they are five times

poorer than resource-rich countries and almost six times poorer than resource-scarce coastal countries. Furthermore, from 1981-2006 the growth rate in this group of countries averaged only 2.5 percent. In other words, the most important determinant of poverty is whether a country is land-locked or not. This is even more important than being resource-rich or resource-scarce or any other aspect reviewed in the analysis.

- Over the long-term, both accumulation and factor productivity are significantly higher in resource-scarce countries than in resource-rich countries.

A common feature of many countries endowed with abundant natural resources is that, despite the rents obtained from extracting and selling natural resources, they generally save less than what is expected. The analysis in the Report shows that most resource-rich countries in Africa indeed have negative genuine savings. These countries are therefore using their natural resource wealth at the expense of future generations, without investing sufficiently in other forms of intangible or productive wealth.

One of the dilemmas of natural resource abundance is that it *may* pervasively cause a country to neglect human capital development. High levels of natural resource revenues can divert attention from the diversification of the revenue base and wealth creation, and from institutional and human development. In this regard, Africa ranks low on the UNDP's Human Development Index: 29 of the 31 countries in the world considered to have a low human development index are African. A detailed analysis of the HDI data indicates that the primary determinant of human development status seems to be *geography* and not resource abundance — that is, whether a country is landlocked or not — as landlocked countries as a group score very low on this index.

This Report offers a comprehensive analysis of the role of the state in natural resource management. It reviews policy failure aspects, including poor decision-making by governments, enhanced corruption and rent seeking, revenue misallocation, and poor investment decisions. In particular, the Report focuses on the critical link between resource abundance, institutional capacity, and governance, as there is a clear relationship between weak or fragile states, non-performing institutions, poor governance, and insufficient transparency. Furthermore, there is strong evidence that resource abundance, especially in the context of poor institutional environment increases the incidence of civil conflicts and wars and also stimulates violence, theft, looting, and fighting between rival groups. However, it is not a linear relationship. Indeed, the root causes of civil wars in Africa are complex and lie in a combination of factors, whether in resource-rich or in resource-poor countries.

Analysis of the management of petroleum and mineral resources in fragile states reveals that it has largely been molded by four interrelated conditions that are defined by the interplay of state power, contest, and conflict over the control of mineral resources. These factors are: public policy failures; state predation or 'shadow state', where rent-seeking substitutes rent creation; rebel-dominated war (shadow) economies; and, vested interests of regional and international actors.

The last decade has seen a rapid increase in trade and investment flows between Africa and Asia, especially with China and India. It is important to note, however, that Africa and Asia have a long history of trade and foreign direct investment. The new stage of competing forces on the African continent has resulted in a plethora of recent analyses dealing mainly, if not exclusively, with the Chinese impact and practices. In general, the analyses are critical of China's presence in Africa, largely seen as another example of predatory capitalism and considered to be non-transparent and supportive of autocratic regimes. However, recent studies and analyses also highlight the positive aspects, underlining how China and India's growing trade with and investment in Africa present excellent opportunities for growth and international integration of Africa into the global economy. Both African and Asian policy makers need to devise appropriate policy responses to further enhance the quality of these relationships, which should encompass "at-the-border, between-the-border and behind-the border reforms". These new South-South economic relations present real opportunities — as well as challenges — to African countries.

In conclusion, the analysis of the so-called resource curse in Africa illustrates that resource-rich African countries have *not* fully exploited the true (potential) benefits of their significant natural resource wealth. Overall, the performance of these resource-rich countries has been disappointing, especially during the 20-year period from 1980 to 2000. In contrast, several countries in Africa have also demonstrated that it is possible to benefit from resource wealth — also in the medium-to-long term. There is thus reason to be cautiously optimistic that more countries have learned the hard lessons from past resource booms and will pursue sound strategies and policies to reap the full benefits of natural resource abundance. The on-going reforms in many of these countries demonstrate the importance of those lessons.

Making Natural Wealth Work for the Poor

In Africa, the **environment** (nature), **economic growth** (wealth), and **governance** (power) are inextricably linked and are the essential elements of poverty reduction. Experience in Africa — and elsewhere — has demonstrated that investments that recognize and integrate these three elements yield positive development outcomes, nowhere more so than in rural areas where the majority of Africans live. Implementing a **nature-wealth-power framework** for development in Africa requires new strategies and instruments. A common feature is acknowledgement that sound natural resource management requires attention not only to environmental and natural resource laws and institutions, but also to the broad range of legislation, organizations, decisions, procedures and actions that influence and otherwise affect the environment. Other key aspects include securing intergenerational benefits, sustained growth, and fiscal allocation that give preference to pro-poor expenditures. Strategies and instruments

must furthermore adjust to changing local circumstances, including changing local perceptions, interests, and priorities.

In most of Africa, **environmental policies** are inadequate and the institutions that implement them are weak and understaffed. While several environmental policy issues demand urgent attention, the two that are critical for sustainable development are strengthening environmental policy and law, and regulating the private sector.

Economic growth is essential for poverty reduction. In recent times, government and donor attention has focused on promoting pro-poor economic growth — creating opportunities that enable the poor to work their way out of poverty. This focuses on opportunities that target the assets of the poor, specifically: labor, land and local natural resources. Pro-poor growth calls for investments that improve the prospects for poor people to share in the opportunities created by economic growth — including building local capacities and providing the infrastructure that the poor need to capitalize on new opportunities. Even with strong economic growth, poverty reduction — especially for the poorest — can be greatly enhanced by investing goods and services targeted at poor people and regions. Yet, inequality is on the rise in many African countries, most noticeably in resource-rich countries

Two types of environmental benefits are particularly important for poverty and inequality reduction as well as sound environmental management: (1) market shares and profit margins of commercially exploited natural resource commodities, and (2) public revenues from the use of ecosystems and extraction of natural resources.

Other economic instruments that have also proven to be effective policy tools for changing behavior and achieving desired outcomes include securing property rights, identifying new markets, and, servicing the unmet needs of the poor. Infrastructure is another essential public good that is a pre-condition for economic growth and equit-able development. The intersection of infrastructure, natural resources and the environment is multi-dimensional.

Good governance is a virtuous relation between active citizens and strong, legit-imate government based on the representa-tion of people's needs and aspirations in policy-making and implementation pro-cesses. The link between good governance and natural resources management is obvious. In an environment of weak institu-tions, exploitation of natural resources may become a key component for competition for power. The best approach to natural resources governance comprises three components: (1) project-based management and public participation, (2) environmental governance, and, (3) good institutional governance.

Sound natural resource management requires paying attention to the range of institutions with roles, responsibilities, and powers over matters that affect natural resources. In Africa, this is underpinned by three fundamental institutional governance-related issues that should be addressed at the central government level: (1) decen-tralization and the distribution of power; (2) responsibilities and roles with power;

and, (3) accountability and the limits of power.

Resource Governance Policy Initiatives

The last decade has seen a growing recognition that improved transparency and accountability for the huge revenues generated by oil, gas and mineral industries is vital to the avoidance of the resource curse and extension of the benefits of natural resource abundance to poverty reduction. Several international policy initiatives, mechanisms, and standards have been launched to address these dilemmas.

The **Extractive Industries Transparency Initiative** (EITI) was launched in 2002 against the backdrop of general failure to transform resource wealth into sustainable development and of associated governance problems in the extractive industries. The EITI aims to intervene in the middle of the value chain — collection of taxes and royalties stage — but neither upstream nor downstream. The EITI has grown into a worldwide initiative and more than 20 countries have committed to its principles and criteria, the majority of them in Africa. However, an assessment of the status of the initiative shows that it is very much focused on the oil and gas sectors, and that its scope and mandate could be expanded, revenue transparency strengthened, and the initiative extended to upstream and downstream issues and to environmental stewardship. The success of the EITI as a concept is increasingly threatened by the lack of clarity about what it means in practice. These problems and issues must be addressed, and EITI is only a first step in the right direction.

The **Kimberley Process Certification Scheme** (KPCS) is the only significant international response to conflict resource issues. KPCS is an international, government-led scheme that was set up to prevent trade in conflict diamonds. It was negotiated by engaging relevant govern-ments, civil-society organizations, and the diamond trade industry and it provides a rare example of co-operation between such stakeholders on a global scale. At present, 15 diamond-producing African countries are Kimberley Process participants. The KPCS has been relatively successful, but it also has its limitations. Nevertheless, this unpre-cedented scheme has imposed tough controls on all gem exports and imports (related to the flow of rough diamonds).

The **African Peer Review Mechanism** (APRM) is an innovative tool aimed at peer review of governance benchmarks and design of action plans for improvement. Participation in the system is voluntary and a panel appointed by the APRM Secretariat oversees implementation throughout Africa. At present, 27 countries have signed up for the APRM and 13 of them have had reviews launched. However, implementation has posed some challenges: for instance, the establishment of an appropriate national structure, the financing of the process, and the organization of a participatory and all-inclusive self-assessment system. Voluntary participation in the APRM assessment has resulted in very high expectations, and it is imperative that the 'dividends' from the APRM be seen in terms of enhanced governance and improved living standards. The APRM is a cornerstone of the African Union's New Partnership for Africa's Development (NEPAD), the first African-initiated and -led instrument to take full ownership of the continent's future by addressing key governance challenges that constitute major constraints to development.

The Way Forward

The continent's natural resource endow-ments have a huge potential to stimulate growth and generate multiplier effects on a massive scale, but management bottlenecks have to be addressed. This hinges on:

- ensuring Africa's ownership of the development process;
- strengthening initiatives to monitor resource revenues;
- achieving a higher level of transparency;
- enhancing governance systems;
- reinforcing institutional capacity;
- investing natural resources wealth in the creation of knowledge for economic innovation;
- negotiating better terms with external partners; and
- integrating the natural resources sector into national development frameworks.

Given the finite nature of non-renewable natural resources and the limitations on sustainable use of renewable resources, it is imperative that the wealth they generate be invested in other forms of capital, particu-larly human capital, social services, and physical capital.

Since streams of natural resource revenues do not last forever and may fluctu-ate considerably, it is a sound practice, for intergenerational benefits, to put aside a share of the export revenues from natural resources into stabilization funds. However, a crucial drawback is that in regimes characterized by weak institutional capacity and low transparency and accountability, such funds may be raided. In applying the concept of stabilization or of future funds, African countries need to consider the lessons learned from both Africa itself and from countries outside Africa that have successfully managed mineral rents for the benefit of future generations.

Implications

The question of how resource windfalls can be successfully harnessed to significantly contribute to Africa's economic growth and development has become a central concern for all stakeholders and major donors in Africa. The analyses presented in the Report reveal unique opportunities for donors and multilateral financial institutions to influence the use of resource wealth to address Africa's development challenges. The following issues are critical in defining donor focus:

- enhancing the development impact of Africa's natural resources;
- policy dialogue and budget support;
- support to fragile states;
- institutional issues and governance
- Africa-Asia trade partnership; and
- environment and climate change.

Overall Conclusion

Experience from Africa reveals that endowment with natural resources, especially with non-renewable resources, comes with opportunities but also with substantial risks. The key challenge for harnessing natural resource opportunities is making the right strategic choices in resource and economic policies, and synchronizing their implemen-

tation in a context that supports fiscal prudence and eliminates macroeconomic distortions. This should be backed by adequate institutional capacity and national and local level participation in natural resource management. Getting the policies wrong, disregarding their sequencing and alignment with the rest of the economy, or ignoring absorptive capacity and good governance issues may transform a natural resource boom into a curse that could effectively stall economic growth, worsen the poverty situation, and become a recipe for social and political instability.

Sound environmental management and, not least, effective governance, have to be high on the agenda to ensure that Africa's natural resource wealth generates more rapid development and poverty reduction. Pro-poor governance, or governance that supports rural development and poverty reduction, should define the focus of development orientation and the needs of the poor should be consistently reflected in development planning and in the use of natural resources. This will build a sound basis for economic growth, social equity, and stability.

This Report identifies the fundamental elements that should underpin the use of natural resource wealth to foster development and economic growth in Africa. Essentially, this involves securing fundamental democratic principles that ensure accountability, public participation, representation and transparency.

Louis Kasekende

Louis Kasekende
Chief Economist
African Development Bank

CHAPTER 1
Introduction

Why Natural Resource Management Matters

The importance of natural resources in Africa's development process cannot be over-emphasized. These resources have become more important than ever before as countries seek additional sources of development financing in order to progress towards the Millennium Development Goals (MDGs). Even so, the fact remains that Africa has failed to tap the potential for its natural resources wealth to serve as a driver for industrialization, economic growth, poverty reduction and sustainable development. Indeed, many African countries are rich in natural resources, but this has not always been a blessing, especially for countries with considerable mineral resources. This has become a persistent challenge for sustainable development and natural resource management in Africa. The continent is endowed with natural resources, which it badly needs for its own development, but which others also want. Furthermore, for most African countries several decades of resource exploitation have not, for the majority of the countries, translated into economic growth or improved the livelihoods and welfare of their growing population.

Africa's record of poor management of its natural resources has been a recurring theme in recent debates on the "natural resource curse" associated with many resource-rich countries. Although natural resource wealth contributes to economic development in some resource-rich African countries — attributable to effective management — the story is different in many other countries on the continent. With a few exceptions, resource exploitation in Africa has worsened socio-economic conditions and, in some cases, ignited protracted conflicts that have taken a heavy toll on national economies. This has led to the emergence of initiatives aimed at promoting transparency in natural resource management. These include the Extractive Industries Transparency Initiative (EITI), the Publish-What-You-Pay initiative and the Open Society Initiative, all aimed at addressing problems limiting the contribution of the natural resources sector to economic growth and poverty reduction.

So why is natural resources management in Africa important, and why is it important at this time? The reasons are several. First, the *volatility of resource revenues*: The huge revenues from Africa's commodity exports are volatile and are subject to large price fluctuations in global markets. These revenues are often temporary and thus require sound fiscal policies to ensure good investment in human capital development and in the development of long-term production capacity. Over the decades, this has proved to be a challenging task. One of the key challenges is how to transform temporary resource revenues into productive capital that will induce and sustain growth over the long-term.

Second, because of their undiversified economies, many resource-rich African countries are prone to real *exchange rate appreciation* induced by rising resource export revenues. This hampers the prospects of non-resource exports in these countries. Indeed, the sheer volume of resource revenues diverts attention from export diversification. This may result in the neglect of labor-intensive manufacturing exports and the import of more goods and services using resource windfalls, at the expense of local production of import substitutes. Furthermore, the recent rise of China and India has created new challenges that make it even more difficult for Africa to carve out a *niche* in labor-intensive manufacturing exports.

Third, natural resource management has re-emerged as critical in Africa because of the challenges of *transparency and accountability*, which remain crucial for harnessing natural resource wealth for economic growth. Against a backdrop of inadequate checks and balances, resource revenues have induced rent seeking and corruption on a massive scale. This undermines the quality of institutions and of governance in resource-rich African countries. Transparency in allocating exploitation rights and in controlling revenues and how they are spent are major concerns. Indeed, policy-makers and development practitioners have been grappling with the fact that natural resource extraction has *not* led to sustainable increases in socio-economic development in a significant number of resource-rich countries, contrary to rational economic expectations. Instead, natural resources are being depleted faster than the rates at which other real assets are being built up.

Fourth, and even more importantly, natural resource management is now crucial

for Africa because there is strong evidence that it can make an important, and sometimes critical, contribution to *economic growth* and *poverty reduction* in the continent. Indeed, natural resource revenues contribute to socio-economic development and poverty reduction in several ways. Most of the linkages are direct and include income generation and growth creation opportunities through lateral or downstream businesses. Indirect linkages concern investments — for instance, improvements in physical infrastructure — which, in turn, enhance social services and have other positive effects. Indeed, natural resources constitute the base for the infrastructure and energy needs of society, the industrial sector, urban development and social wellbeing. However, these contributions are contingent on the fulfillment of critical conditions, chiefly, improving governance and transparency, and eliminating corruption. This is crucial given the evidence that resource mismanagement serves as a recipe for protracted civil conflicts, which do not only debilitate economies, but also lead to state fragility and institutional collapse.

Based on current evidence few countries in Africa have managed their natural resources in ways that have benefited the majority of their populations — with the exception of mainly Botswana, Namibia and South Africa. Over the years, these three countries have implemented solid economic reforms aimed at managing the proceeds and utilizing the resources accruing from the extractive industries. In most of the other countries, however, natural resource wealth seems to end up in the hands of a few, with limited visible benefits for the poor. State stability seems to be a characteristic of countries that have properly managed the use of their resources, while instability and state fragility have emerged as a tendency in countries with poor resource management records — Sierra Leone, Democratic Republic of Congo (DRC) and Angola are examples. Rekindled attention to natural resource management in Africa is an imperative, given the discovery by many African countries of new and extractable resources and the pervasive experience of what is now termed the *natural resource curse.*

This renewed interest in natural resource management clearly focuses attention on one critical question: how can Africa use its resources to foster economic growth and poverty alleviation, given the aforementioned complexities and trade-offs? Although the continent badly needs its resources to sustain and propel its emerging growth, it lacks the technical and financial means to extract the resources. Foreign investment therefore plays a critical role in the exploitation of Africa's resource on a competitive scale, especially with the emerging Asian markets, notably India and China. In this complex scenario, it is reasonable to posit that what Africa gets out of its resources will largely depend on knowing what Africa wants. This proposition leads to another crucial question: where can natural resources take Africa — towards resource dependence, or can the resources serve as a springboard for sustained economic development? The search for answers to this question makes natural resource management a key concern in Africa.

Natural Resources and Sustainable Management

Conceptually, natural resources are stocks of physical assets that are not produced goods and that are valuable to humans. A resource may be considered valuable because of its sheer existence, or because it produces a flow of services or benefits that can be used in production, trade, or consumption. Natural resources are classified as follows:[1] [2] [3]

1) **Raw materials** (renewable, semi-renewable, and non-renewable) are minerals, fossil energy carriers, metal ores, and biomass, which are needed for most human activities. Fossil energy carriers, metal ores, and minerals such as gypsum and china clay are considered non-renewable because their stocks are finite (on a human time scale). In contrast, biomass, which includes quickly renewable resources such as agri-cultural crops and slowly renewable resources such as timber is, in principle, renewable within the human timeframe. However, bio-logical resources that are used as raw materials can be exhausted if they are overexploited. This is an acute threat to commercially fished marine species, for example.

2) **Environmental media** — such as air, water, and soil — sustain life on Earth and produce biological resour-ces. In contrast with raw materials,

---

[1] EEA (2005)
[2] CEC (2003)
[3] Zeeuw (2000)

their declining quality is the main concern: the issue is not how much there is, but what state they are in. For example, the quantities of air and water on earth do not change within human time scales, but their quality is often poor because of pollution. Moreover, the biological diversity of environmental resources is of great importance.

3) Renewable resources may have a permanent character (for example, solar and wind energy) and are then labeled flow resources. **Flow resources** cannot be depleted but they need other inputs or resources to be exploited. For example, energy, materials and space are needed to build wind turbines or solar cells.

4) Physical **space** is needed to produce or sustain all the above-mentioned resources. Land-use, for human settlements, infrastructure, industry, mineral extraction, agriculture and forestry, is an example. Table 1.1 presents a broad classification of natural resources.

Natural resources are further classified according to their rate of **regeneration** as renewable, semi-renewable, or non-renewable. **Renewable resources** are resources that are regenerated on a human time scale and renewed periodically in the context of ecological cycles. Their use can only be increased to a certain extent otherwise overexploitation will occur. However, as long as exploitation is not exhaustive, renewable resources can be used for an infinite period. Therefore, for resource use to be sustainable, the consumption rate should

remain within the capacity of the natural system to regenerate (or renew) in a human relevant period. Examples of renewable resources are water, fisheries, wildlife, and forests. These types of resources are often interconnected within ecological systems; for example, water is needed for forest growth and fisheries. **Semi-renewable** resources are in an intermediate stage of their possibility to renew or to deplete.

Non-renewable resources have a regeneration rate of zero or regenerate over a very long period.[4] Non-renewable resources can be recyclable (for example, minerals, and oils used in plastics) or non-recyclable (for example, oil used as fossil fuel). They are less likely to participate in the circular flows of the ecosystem, and exploitation of one resource usually does not affect the availability of other resources (as long as extraction does not destroy the other resources). The use of these resources to provide material and energy leads to depletion of the Earth's reserves since these resources do not renew in human relevant periods. Table 1.2 presents a summary of resources based on their regeneration rates.[5]

Natural resources may also be classified in terms of their use values based on whether they are **extractive** (natural resource products) or **non-extractive** (natural resource services). Extractive resources are subject to some process of physical removal from their natural surroundings and perhaps physical transformation during their use. Non-extractive resources are resources that yield services without being removed

---

[4] Lujala (2003)
[5] Steiner et al. (2000)

Table 1.1: Broad Classification of Natural Resources

Resource	Type	Description
Renewable Raw Materials	Living	Living resources that can re-stock/renew themselves, e.g. fish, forests
	Non-living	Resources that can renew themselves, but are non-living; include soil and water
Non-Renewable	Metals	Include non-ferrous, base and precious metals
	Non-Metals	Include ferrous, non-ferrous minerals and industrial minerals as well as precious stones and uranium
	Fossil Fuels	Coal, oil and natural gas
Environmental Media	Air	General 'biological' reproducing resources but could be polluted or degraded
	Water	
	Soil	
Space	Land Area	Includes space for human settlement, infrastructure, industry, mineral extraction, agriculture and forestry
Flow Resources	Geothermal	Renewable resources that do not need regeneration
	Wind Energy	
	Tides	
	Solar Energy	

Source: Adapted from EEA (2005)

from their natural setting.[6] Table 1.3 summarizes the use values of natural resources with relevant examples included.

Another strand of the literature defines natural resources according to their geographical concentration and "lootability".[7] In this context, natural resources are defined according to their geographic concentration

when the question relates to whether they are *diffuse* or *point*. In other words, is the availability of the resource restricted to geographically small areas or does it span larger areas? For example, forests cover wide areas and are therefore considered to be diffuse resources. Point resources are highly concentrated and do not cover a significant area on a map. For example, many minerals occur in small areas, and these deposits are represented as points on

---

[6] Field (2000)
[7] Lujala (2003)

Table 1.2: Classification of Natural Resources Based on Regeneration Rate

	Time for Regeneration	Environmental Resources	Energy Resources	Material Resources
Renewable	<1 year, controllable by humans	Agricultural products (non permanent) pollution of water and air	Solar energy, water, ethanol	Salt
Semi-renewable	1–200 years, no human influence	Fish, forests, ground water, (permanent) pollution of water and air	Geothermal energy, water, firewood	Soil
Non-renewable	No economic relevance	Ozone, endangered fauna and flora	Oil, gas, coal, uranium	Minerals

Source: Adapted from Steiner et al. (2000)

a map. Point resources are commonly associated with higher rents than diffuse resources and thus provide incentives for rent seeking. In the literature, abundant point resources are often associated with higher risk of conflict.[8] [9]

Ross (2002)[10] defines natural resources according to their "lootability", "obstructability" and "legality" and forms hypotheses on how these three resource characteristics affect civil war. Ross defines lootability in terms of the ease of resource extraction and transportation. As such, lootable resources include alluvial gemstones, agricultural products, and timber, while deep-shaft minerals and gemstones, oil and natural gas are not. Ross also differentiates between the

ease of transportating the natural resource product and the ease of blocking the available mode of transportation (that is, its obstructability). For example, diamonds or drugs that are flown from a production area are not obstructable, while resources that are transported by trains or trucks are moderately obstructable. Resources transported by pipelines (such as oil and gas) are the most obstructable.

Natural resources are natural capital assets and are not provided by human activity, but their quality and capacity to yield goods and services, and therefore their value as productive inputs, are affected by human activity. In many cases, for example, agricultural land, the relevant input into production, can best be viewed as a combination of natural elements (soil and water) and man-made components (irrigation and transport infrastructure, and

---

[8] Addison et al (2001)
[9] Addison & Murshed (2001)
[10] Ross (2002)

Table 1.3: Classification of Natural Resources Based on Value Uses

	Natural resource products and services	
Natural resource	Extractive	Non-extractive
Minerals	Non-fuel (bauxite) Fuel (coal)	Geological services (weathering)
Meteorological services	Energy resources (geothermal)	Energy resources (solar) Global radiation balances Radio spectrum Natural disasters
Land	Fertility	Space, scenic values
Water	Municipal and industrial supplies, irrigation	Recreation (boating)
Fisheries	Food (saltwater and freshwater fish)	Recreational services (recreational fishing, whale watching)
Terrestrial animals	Food and fiber (farm animals, wild game) Biodiversity products (genetic variability)	Recreational services (bird watching, ecotourism)
Plants	Food and fiber (agricultural crops, wild food crops) Biodiversity products (medicinal plants)	
Forests	Forest products (timber)	Recreation (backpacking) Ecosystem protection (flood control, CO_2 sequestration)

Source: Adapted from Field (2000)

so on). Renewable capital produces a flow of goods and services. Goods produced from renewable natural capital include timber and non-timber forest products and wild caught fish. Goods produced from non-renewable natural resources are mainly oils and minerals. Some of these goods are traded in formal markets and are therefore accounted for in national economic statistics, including timber and fish harvested by formal-sector operators as well as fossil fuels (oil, gas, and coal) and other important minerals. However, many are consumed directly by local inhabitants, including wild fruits, mushrooms or herbs, wild fish caught by small-scale fishermen, "bush meat", palm, timber, and non-timber forest products. Services produced from natural capital include water filtration and purification services provided by wetlands, and regulation of water cycles provided by watersheds. These services are generally not marketed and are invisible in standard economic statistics.

The key challenge concerning renewable resources is how to ensure **sustainable exploitation;** in other words, how to ascertain that extraction rates do not exceed regeneration capacity. In many cases, however, there are multiple sustainable equilibrium rates of extraction. There is often a tradeoff between the objectives of maximizing the economic value of resource extraction, maximizing associated employment opportunities, or maximizing food production.

In light of the above analysis, it is clear that careful use and **management** of resources is the basis for sustainable development. This conclusion has gained international recognition, for example, at the recent World Summit on Sustainable Development (WSSD) in Johannesburg, it was agreed that "protecting and managing the natural resource base of economic and social development are overarching objectives of, and essential requirements for, sustainable development." Natural resources are too often used in unsustainable ways, resulting in production systems that show declining returns to inputs. Land degradation is a case in point: the bulk of Africa's productive land — up to two-thirds — is vulnerable to degradation. Increasing population pressure, technologies applied in unsuitable situations, badly managed or inappropriate access regimes, droughts and the general insecurity associated with access to resources all have a negative effect on agri-

culture, livestock, forestry and fisheries, and may cause wider conflicts. Climate change puts more pressure on natural resource use and increases insecurity among producers. In many parts of Africa, the natural resource base for agricultural production is affected by soil degradation (erosion, soil depletion, and desertification, for example), water scarcity, water quality reduction, siltation, deforestation, over-fishing and overgrazing. Good management of natural resources is therefore important for economic, socio-political, and environmental reasons.

Natural resource management (NRM) is a broad concept that involves integrating efficient resource use and preventing adverse environmental impacts. It also concerns questions about the use and distribution of resources for the sustainable economic development of all levels of government and for the benefit of the citizenry. NRM also involves the management of resource extraction or imports, production and consumption, and the resultant financial resources, wastes and emissions. The key objectives of such NRM include:

- ensuring adequate supply of, and efficient use of, natural resources for the creation of wealth and well-being in industry and society;
- avoiding overloading or destroying nature's capacities for reproduction and regeneration of resources and absorption of residuals;
- securing the co-existence of society and nature;
- minimizing risks related to national and international insecurity and economic turmoil due to dependence on natural resources;

- contributing to economy-wide fair distribution of resource use and adequate burden-sharing;
- minimizing the problem of shifting between environmental media, types of resources, economic sectors, regions, and generations; and
- driving technological and institutional change in a way and towards a direction that provides economic and social benefits to all stakeholders.

The concept of **sustainable development** was first introduced in 1987 in the Brundtland Report as "development that meets the need of the present generation without compromising the ability of future generations to meet their own need". This definition implies two equally important specific concepts: intra-generational equity (the requirement to meet the needs of the present) and inter-generational equity (the requirement not to compromise the satisfaction of the needs of future generations). Ideally, sustainable development should be development that generates optimal economic and social returns without impairing the long-term life-supporting capacities of ecosystems or reducing the chances of future generations to satisfy their own needs.[11] [12]

This definition can be broken down into four conditions for sustainable development: (1) material needs, and other needs, for a better quality of life have to be fulfilled for people of this generation, (2) as equitably as possible, (3) while respecting ecosystem limits, and (4) building the basis on which future generations can meet their own needs. Furthermore, sustainable development has four pillars: the economic, environmental, social, and governance pillars, with the fourth pillar fostering the integration of the first three. Therefore, if the natural resources sector is to contribute positively to sustainable development, it needs to demonstrate continuous improvement of its social, economic, and environmental contribution, with new and evolving governance systems.

Sustainable development also relates to the notion that boosting economic growth, protecting natural resources, and ensuring social justice can be complementary goals. Its key purpose is to help the poor live healthier lives on their own terms. Sustainable development also means development that combines economic growth with poverty reduction and protection of the environment. In other words, it involves achieving "economic growth and social development without degrading the potential of its conditionally renewable natural resources".[13] The role of natural resources in ensuring sustainable development in Africa is critical given that economic growth and social progress depend on the natural resource base. This natural resource base cannot be conserved in light of the pervasive poverty in rural Africa. In addition, Africa is the only continent where the population is growing faster than the economy. Thus, people (especially the rural poor) over-exploit some natural resources in order to survive while many governments mismanage natural resources wealth — this complicates the

---

[11] WCED (1987)
[12] Eurowatch (2002)

[13] Young and Ryan (1995)

issue of sustainable development in Africa. Efficient and effective natural resource management is therefore an imperative that will lay the foundation for sustainable development in Africa by producing maximum sustainable wealth that can generate an investible surplus for economy-wide growth as well as adequate resources to combat poverty and under-development.

Scope and Outline

Given the broad coverage of natural resources, the analysis in this Report focuses on a selection of natural resources — fossil fuels, minerals (metals and non-metals), water, forestry and land use — and on relevant crosscutting issues such as climate change. The rationale for proceeding thus is the need to include a mix of renewable and non-renewable resources, ensure policy relevance and political and economic importance, illustrate the various management approaches adopted hitherto and outline key approaches to be adopted looking forward. Nevertheless, because of the renewed scramble to extract Africa's non-renewable resources, the Report will focus first and foremost on these.

The Report aims to deepen understanding of how to address problems related to natural resource development problems, and to highlight the need for better management at the regional, national and sub-national levels. This has become an imperative for improving the effectiveness of the joint efforts of key stakeholders — concerned governments, companies, donors and non-governmental or civil society organizations — to facilitate the realization of the full natural resource potential and capture resource wealth for the promotion of economic development in Africa.

This Report is partly motivated by the realization that more needs to be done to translate the potential benefits of natural resources into broad-based socio-economic development in Africa. Despite this realization, the necessary policies and concrete actions are not integrated at present, at least not with binding commitments. Therefore, one of the overriding objectives of this Report is to articulate these issues and help identify key stakeholders, particularly governments, donors and private sector organizations to intensify engagements, actions, and dialogue on the role and contributions of natural resource wealth to economic growth and development. In pursuing this objective, the report builds on key lessons from successful and unsuccessful cases of government and other stakeholder engagements and partnerships at the international, national and the community levels.

The objectives of the Report can be grouped under the following four main areas:

1. Define, in operational terms, the contextual meaning of natural resources and how they relate to sustainable development and social outcomes. The Report examines the roles of the different players, along with crucial decision points in natural resource management on the continent. This entails reviewing whether decisions are made transparently and with what level of public accountability in relation to natural resource benefits. The role of good information and public participation in natural resource

issues is also examined, as well as the rights and responsibilities of private and public ownership and of access to natural resources.

2. Examine how close the main stakeholders are to embodying good management practices with respect to Africa's natural resources.

3. Advance the thesis that better natural resource management is one of the most direct routes to reversing Africa's poverty and economic malaise. The report posits that better management must translate into more inclusive processes for making decisions about natural resources, and that institutions must adequately integrate natural resource issues and concerns into their policies and decisions.

4. Propose concrete suggestions on how the various stakeholders involved in natural resource exploitation (at the local, national, and international levels) can help improve public policies and governance in natural resource-endowed countries in Africa. In essence, this involves examining practical steps that can be taken by stakeholders — governments, industry, local communities, donors and others — to build beneficial factors where they are lacking.

The Report is organized into six chapters. Chapters Two and Three discuss Africa's renewable and non-renewable natural resources, respectively. Chapter Four examines Africa's natural resources as a paradox of plenty. Chapter Five presents the ways and means of making natural wealth work for the poor; and Chapter Six presents the main messages and the way forward in the effective and sustainable management and harnessing of Africa's natural resources wealth.

CHAPTER 2
Africa's Renewable Natural Resources

In line with the classification of natural resources presented in Chapter One, this chapter focuses on Africa's *renewable* natural resources, chiefly, water, forestry and land resources. A majority of Africans will remain heavily dependent on these resources for their livelihoods in the foreseeable future. The chapter provides an overview of the stock, production patterns, current status of each resource. This initial presentation is followed by a deeper analysis of the management of the resources and a discussion on adaptation to climate change in Africa. Each resource is presented separately to enhance clarity, but it is worth noting that there are very close linkages between these resources, since poor management and exploitation of one resource is highly likely to affect the others.

Water Resources

Water constitutes a key component of Africa's natural resource endowments, but it is becoming increasingly scarce in the continent. Indeed, one of the current challenges facing Africa is how to comprehensively take stock of its water resources and use them optimally to sustain an acceptable standard of living in the continent. Available statistics reveal that nine African countries already face "water scarcity" on a national scale (less than 1,000 m³ of water per person annually), eight countries face "water stress" (less than 1,700 m³), while at least another six countries are likely to join this list in the coming decades. More than 300 million people in Africa still lack access to safe water and adequate sanitation. The majority of these people are in sub-Saharan Africa, where only 51 percent of the population has access to safe water and 45 percent to sanitation.[1]

By 2025, almost 50 percent of Africans will be living in an area of water scarcity or water stress. Five African countries — Kenya, Morocco, Rwanda, Somalia and South Africa — are expected to face water scarcity within the next 10 years.[2] In South Africa, the demand for water is expected to increase by 50 percent in the next 30 years. This projected demand for water resources is unlikely to be met without considerable investments in the water sector. Because of low rainfall, North Africa is most affected by water scarcity. However, sub-Saharan Africa will also become increasingly affected. There is already considerable national competition for water for agriculture and power generation in Africa's major river basins, particularly in the Nile River Basin.[3]

Water plays a vital role in improving the socioeconomic circumstances of many African countries. Although several economic instruments are being deployed to address the water crisis, the success of these efforts will depend heavily on the availability of sustainable water resources. Meanwhile, successful economic develop-

---

[1] WMO & UNESCO (1988); Bzioui (2005); OECD & AFDB (2007)

[2] WRI (2005)

[3] WRI (2005); Bzioui (2005); DFID (2003)

ment efforts are needed to ensure the sustainable flow of funds for water resources development. This interdependence between water availability and development is exemplified by the link between water and poverty. Because of poverty, access to adequate water and sanitation is low in Africa; in turn, this inadequate access to safe water and sanitation has led to a high incidence of communicable diseases that reduces vitality and economic productivity in the continent. This in turn exacerbates poverty.[4]

Inadequate access to water and sanitation is thus both a cause and a consequence of poverty. Similarly, inadequate water resources can become a constraint to improved agricultural development and food security. It is noteworthy that, even with its current poor performance, agriculture is the largest user of water in Africa, accounting for almost 90 percent of total water use on the continent. However, only 27 percent of cultivable land on the continent is currently cultivated. This ranges from 40 percent of suitable land cultivated in North Africa, the Gulf of Guinea, and the Indian Ocean Islands, to only 19 percent in the Sudano-Sahelian Region. This is believed to be attributable to the relatively low investment in water resource development in Africa. Thus, there is considerable scope for improved agricultural production and food security through investment in agricultural water use.[5]

From this premise, it is clear that water and socioeconomic development are mutually dependent on each other. They can be

nodes in a vicious cycle that puts societies in a downward spiral of poor economic development and poor access to safe and adequate water supply and sanitation. Alternatively, they can be nodes in a virtuous cycle, reinforcing each other in an auto-catalytic way, and leading to an upward spiral in which improved socioeconomic development produces resources needed for improved development of water resources, which in turn buttress and stimulate further socioeconomic development. The cycle that prevails will depend on policy options and political choices, which facilitate or impede the level of investments in domestic water supply and agricultural water use.

Stock of Water Resources in Africa

At first glance, Africa seems to be endowed with abundant water resources given its big rivers, large lakes, vast wetlands, and widespread groundwater. The continent has 17 major rivers with catchment areas that are greater than 100,000 km²; and more than 160 lakes with surface areas exceeding 27 km². Most of the lakes are located around the equatorial region and the sub-humid East African Highlands within the Rift Valley. The water resource potential of the continent is shown in Table 2.1. Box 2.1 illustrates the potential for water transfer.

Irrespective of spatial and temporal climate variability, the overall image at the continental level is that Africa has abundant rainfall and relatively low levels of water withdrawal for the three key sectors, namely agriculture, domestic, and industry. Water resource availability in Africa at the regional level is shown in Table 2.2. Regions are defined as follows:

---

[4] WMO & UNESCO (1988); OECD & AFDB (2007)

[5] FAO AQUASTAT (2005)

Table 2.1: Stock of Water Resources by Country

Country	Average Annual Groundwater Recharge	Groundwater Available per Capita	Surface Water	Overlap *
	(km³)	(m³/yr)	(km³)	(km³)
Algeria	1.7	54	13	1
Angola	72.0	5,591	182	70
Benin	1.8	295	10	2
Botswana	1.7	1,048	2	1
Burkina Faso	9.5	796	8	5
Burundi	2.1	314	4	2
Cameroon	100.0	6,629	268	95
Central African Republic	56.0	15,490	141	56
Chad	11.5	1,503	14	10
Congo	198.0	67,268	222	198
Congo, DRC	421.0	8,150	899	420
Côte d'Ivoire	37.7	2,550	74	35
Egypt	1.3	19	1	0
Equatorial Guinea	10.0	22,092	25	9
Eritrea	No data	No data	No data	No data
Ethiopia	44.0	703	110	40
Gabon	62.0	50,566	162	60
Gambia	0.5	383	3	1
Ghana	26.3	1,301	29	25
Guinea	38.0	5,114	226	38
Guinea-Bissau	14.0	11,541	12	10
Kenya	3.0	100	17	0
Lesotho	0.5	232	5	1
Liberia	60.0	19,023	200	60
Madagascar	55.0	3,450	332	50
Malawi	1.4	128	16	1
Mali	20.0	1,780	50	10
Mauritania	0.3	112	0	0
Morocco	9.0	317	22	3
Mozambique	17.0	864	97	15
Namibia	2.1	1,217	4	0
Niger	2.5	233	1	0
Nigeria	87.0	780	214	80
Rwanda	3.6	466	5	4
Senegal	7.6	802	24	5
Sierra Leone	50.0	10,300	150	40
Somalia	3.3	327	6	3
South Africa	4.8	119	43	3

Table 2.1: (continued)

Country	Average Annual Groundwater Recharge	Groundwater available per Capita	Surface Water	Overlap *
	(km³)	(m³/yr)	(km³)	(km³)
Sudan	7.0	237	28	5
Tanzania	30.0	895	80	28
Togo	5.7	1,231	11	5
Tunisia	4.2	433	3	0
Uganda	29.0	1,332	39	29
Zambia	47.1	5,137	80	47
Zimbabwe	5.0	428	13	4

* The part common for both groundwater and surface water resources.

Source: World Resource Institute (2005), Earth Trends: The Environmental Information Portal

Box 2.1: Water Transfer in Africa

Although irrigation schemes are quite common in Africa and have been practiced for a long period, water transfers as such (from one location to another) are still very rare. Moreover, this practice is mostly done on an intra-country scale, as is the case in Morocco (about 2.7 km³ / year between river basins) and in Libya, where fossil groundwater resources are transferred from south to north through the Great Manmade River Project. The only real example involving countries is the transfer of 2.2 km³ / year from the Malibamatso River in Lesotho to the Vall River in South Africa, within the framework of the Lesotho Highlands Water Project. In return, Lesotho receives assistance, including electricity, for its own consumption.

However, many potential large-scale projects to develop such transfers have been discussed and studied, including in Algeria (from south to north); Kenya (resources from Lake Victoria to the drier zones); Botswana (between the Shashe and Notwane rivers); and, Lake Chad (securing water flows towards the lake from the Niger Basin in Nigeria, or from the Congo Basin).

Source: FAO (2005): AQUASTAT Information System on Water and Agriculture

North Africa — Algeria, Egypt, Libya, Morocco and Tunisia;

Sudano-Sahelian — Burkina Faso, Cape Verde, Chad, Gambia, Djibouti, Eritrea, Mali, Mauritania, Niger, Senegal, Somalia, and Sudan;

Gulf of Guinea — Benin, Cote d'Ivoire, Ghana, Guinea, Guinea Bissau, Liberia, Nigeria, Sierra Leone, and Togo;

Central Africa — Angola, Cameroon, Central African Republic, Congo,

Equatorial Guinea, Gabon, Sao Tome and Democratic Republic of Congo;
Eastern Africa — Burundi, Ethiopia, Kenya, Rwanda, Tanzania, and Uganda;
Islands — Comoros, Madagascar, Mauritius and Seychelles; and
Southern Africa — Botswana, Lesotho, Malawi, Namibia, South Africa, Swaziland, Zambia, and Zimbabwe.

This overview shows that approximately 86 percent of water resources withdrawal is used for agriculture, 10 percent for domestic purposes (municipalities and community water supply), and about 4 percent for industrial use. Average annual rainfall in Africa is about 678 mm per year, albeit with high spatial and temporal variability. First, temporal variability of rainfall is typically 40 percent around the mean — much higher than in temperate zones. Second, the spatial distribution of rainfall is highly varied among humid, sub-humid, semi-arid, and arid zones. The highest rainfall occurs in the Island countries, the central African countries, and the Gulf of Guinea, with an annual average of approximately 1300–1700 mm/year. In contrast, the lowest rainfall occurs in the northern African countries, where the average annual rainfall is only

Table 2.2: Stock of Water Resources by Region

Sub-Region	Regional Rainfall			Internal Renewable Resources (IRR) (2004)			Annual Withdrawals (2004) *			
	1000x km²	km³/yr	mm/yr	km³/yr	% of Africa	Per inhab. m³	km³/yr	% of Africa	m³/ inhab.	% of IRR
North Africa	5753	550	96	49	1	325	93.9	43.7	616	189
Sudano-Sahelian	8591	2671	311	160	4	1418	54.9	25.7	486	35
Gulf of Guinea	2106	2874	1356	952	24	4853	12.4	5.8	63	1.3
Central Africa	5329	7593	1425	1876	48	19845	2	0.9	21	0.1
Eastern Africa	2916	2666	920	281	7	1521	14.2	6.6	77	5
Southern Africa	4739	3110	659	270	7	2518	21.7	10.0	202	8
Islands	591	895	1510	341	9	17042	15.7	7.3	786	4.6
Africa	**30,025**	**20,359**	**678**	**3,930**	**100**	**4527**	**214.8**	**100**	**247**	**5.5**

* Main sectors: Agriculture (86% of Annual Withdrawals); Domestic (10%) and Industry (4%).

Source: FAO, AQUASTAT (2005)

96 mm. More importantly, the rainfall amounts for each of the countries of the continent — also *within* the countries — are as varied as the vegetation and the landscape, giving rise to humid, sub-humid, semi-arid, and arid zones.[6]

The amount of surface and ground water flows generated from rainfall within the sub-regions is low. Annual renewable water resources (ARWR) refers to the sum of all run-off generated within a country, plus any inflows into the country, minus outflows committed to neighbouring countries. Only a certain proportion of the ARWR is actually available for utilization in the country, depending on the practical situation and the economic storage facilities, including reservoirs and aquifers. The low values of the internal renewable resources show that there is considerable room for improvement in the capture and utilization of rainwater. More importantly, this situation is partly responsible for the recurrent droughts in large parts of the continent.

Furthermore, a marked difference has been observed in annual withdrawals between sub-regions and countries (Table 2.3), but in general the withdrawals are low in relation to both the rainfall and the internal renewable resources. A distinct feature is that the annual withdrawals account for 189 percent of internal renewable resources in North Africa (reflecting the use of water originating from outside this sub-region — primarily from the Nile Basin). This is strongly influenced by Egypt, which accounts for 73 percent of withdrawals in North Africa, while Nigeria accounts for 65 percent

in the Gulf of Guinea. For Africa as a whole, the amount of water withdrawn for the three major uses amounts to only 5.5 percent of internal renewable resources. This is less than 6 percent of world withdrawals, reflecting the low level of development and use of water resources on the continent.[7]

Dependence on ground water has also been acknowledged on the continent. This is especially important in the northern African countries — Libya, Tunisia, Algeria and Morocco — and also in southern African countries like Botswana, Namibia, and Zimbabwe. Thus, although groundwater only accounts for about 15 percent of the continent's total renewable water resources and for only 9 percent in southern Africa, its use is relatively significant. As a rule, groundwater resources tend to occur in small sedimentary aquifers along major rivers and in coastal deltas and plains. Limited groundwater resources, generally sufficient for local water supply, can also be found in the widely occurring crystalline (basement) rocks.[8]

While some areas have abundant water supply, others suffer from water scarcity. For example, northern Africa and southern Africa receive (only) about 9 percent and 12 percent, respectively, of the continent's rainfall. In contrast, the Congo River watershed in the central humid zone, home to 10 percent of Africa's population, receives over 35 percent of the annual total. In southern Africa, the Lake Malawi basin, southern Tanzania, and northern Madagascar have become wetter in the last 30 years. This is in

---

[6] FAO AQUASTAT (2005); FAO (1995)

[7] Ibid.

[8] Bzioui (2005); DFID (2003)

Table 2.3: Water Withdrawal by Country

Country	Actual Resources per capita	Total Water Withdrawal	Water Withdrawal per Capita	Sectoral Withdrawals (%)		
	(m³ per person)	(million m³)	(m³ per person)	Agriculture	Industry	Domestic
Algeria	443	6,074	201	65	13	22
Angola	13,070	343	28	61	16	22
Benin	3,585	250	40	74	11	15
Botswana	8,022	140	81	43	19	38
Burkina Faso	933	780	66	88	0	11
Burundi	509	234	37	82	1	17
Cameroon	17,520	985	65	74	8	18
Central African Republic	36,912	22	6	4	19	77
Chad	4,857	234	30	80	1	19
Congo	217,915	39	11	10	30	59
Congo, Democratic Republic	No data	356	7	31	16	52
Côte d'Ivoire	4,794	931	59	65	12	23
Egypt	794	68,653	1,013	78	14	8
Equatorial Guinea	51,282	106	232	1	16	83
Eritrea	1,466	304	82	95	1	4
Ethiopia	1,519	2,648	40	93	6	1
Gabon	121,392	128	102	40	11	48
Gambia	5,472	32	24	67	11	22
Ghana	2,489	520	27	48	15	37
Guinea	26,218	1,517	187	90	2	8
Guinea-Bissau	20,156	110	81	91	1	9
Kenya	932	1,576	52	64	6	30
Lesotho	1,678	54	30	19	41	40
Liberia	66,533	107	36	56	15	28
Libya	106	4,800	919	89	3	8
Madagascar	18,862	14,970	937	96	2	3
Malawi	1,401	1,005	88	81	5	15
Mali	7,458	6,930	582	99	0	1
Mauritania	3,826	1,698	642	88	3	9
Morocco	934	12,758	438	90	2	8
Mozambique	11,266	635	36	87	2	11
Namibia	8,921	268	142	63	5	33
Niger	2,710	2,187	204	95	1	4
Nigeria	2,252	8,004	70	69	10	21
Rwanda	613	76	10	39	14	48
Senegal	3,811	1,591	169	90	4	6

Table 2.3: (continued)

Sierra Leone	30,960	380	86	93	2	5
Somalia	1,309	3,298	378	100	0	0
South Africa	1,106	15,306	348	73	10	17
Sudan	1,879	37,314	1,187	97	1	3
Tanzania, United Republic	2,416	1,996	57	93	1	6
Togo	2,930	166	36	47	8	45
Tunisia	459	2,726	285	82	2	16
Uganda	2,472	295	13	39	15	45
Zambia	9,630	1,737	167	76	8	16
Zimbabwe	1,547	2,612	207	86	5	10

Source: World Resource Institute (2005), Earth Trends: The Environmental Information Portal

contrast with the situation in Mozambique, southeast Angola, and western Zambia, which have become significantly drier over the same period. The extremes in variability have been greater in Tunisia, Algeria, the Nile Basin, and in the extreme south of the continent. Finally, variability of rainfall is also experienced in the Sahel as testified by recurrent floods and droughts.[9]

It is evident in many ways that the African continent has an exceptional disadvantage with regard to water resources. A comparison of annual average precipitation in Africa with the rest of the world shows that Africa's level is comparable with that of Europe and North America. However, the higher evaporation losses in the African continent result in a substantially lower percentage of precipitation contributing to renewable water resources, thus setting Africa apart from other continents. Africa's total runoff, reflected in its useable and renewable water resources, is thus very low. In addition to the limiting nature of water resources, the temporal and spatial variability of precipitation — owing to the strong influence of the Inter-Tropical Convergence Zone (ITCZ) on the climate in Africa — has strong implications for management strategies (discussed later in the chapter). This variability is exacerbated by unpredictability and considerable yearly variations. The unavoidable expression of this is endemic drought and occasional severe floods.

In terms of overall water availability per capita of renewable water resources, the countries with the least available freshwater per person (see Table 2.3) are Burundi (538.3 m³) and Kenya (947 m³). Conversely, the most water-abundant areas per capita are, not unexpectedly, the equatorial high rainfall areas of the Democratic Republic of Congo (259,547 m³), Gabon (126,789 m³) and

---

[9] DFID (2003)

Liberia (70,348 m³). These trends indicate that only a few African countries — mainly in Northern Africa — are currently *physically water scarce*, that is, countries that have developed all their water reserves. The majority of the countries experience *economic water scarcity*, which means that they have abundant or at least sufficient water resources, but lack the resources and means to develop them.[10] By 2025 it is projected that more than 25 countries in Africa will experience water scarcity or water stress. Thus, the need for more investments in water resource development remains as critical as ever. This involves investing in reservoirs and storage structures to capture more runoff, building diversion structures, improving water quality and strengthening dialogue to increase cooperation in water resource management, both at the local and international levels.

Forestry

Forest ecosystems play multiple roles at global as well as local levels, and provide a range of important economic, social, and environmental goods and services. This in turn affects the wellbeing of poor rural communities, local and national economies, as well as global environmental health.[11] The literature is replete with overwhelming evidence of the significance of forests for human existence. In fact, forests (Box 2.2) can be regarded as nature's bountiful and versatile renewable resource. They are an integral part of the environment in which we live, and have been direct providers of

---

[10] Kamara & Hilmy (2004)

[11] Sengupta and Maginnis (2005)

Box 2.2: Definition of the Forestry Sector

There is no commonly agreed definition of the forestry sector. Ideally, the definition of the sector should encompass all economic activities relating to the production of goods and services from forests. These include commercial activities that are dependent on the production of wood fibre (that is, production of industrial roundwood, wood fuel and charcoal; sawnwood and wood based panels; pulp and paper; and wooden furniture). They also include activities such as the commercial production and processing of non-wood forest products and the subsistence use of forest products.

Source: FAO (2007), Forest Finance

shelter and food for people and their livestock, and of water, medicinal plants, building materials and fuel. Forests can help reduce food insecurity, alleviate poverty, improve the sustainability of agricultural production and enhance the environment in which many impoverished rural people in the developing world live.

Forests and woodlands also regulate the environment indirectly by slowing soil erosion, fertilizing soils, controlling and storing run-off water, and regulating its release into rivers and lakes. Globally and locally, forests help regulate the climate and protect coastlines. Furthermore, forests and woodlands sustain many cultural, spiritual and religious values and also play an important role in the socio-economic development of industrial countries.

Expectations of benefits from the world's forest resources are high, but forests are affected by human activities, in particular by processes such as slash-and-burn cultivation, air pollution, pests and agricultural and urban expansion. With the recent emphasis on sustainable development, the use of forests and woodlands has come under greater scrutiny with a view to preserving a healthy resource base and sustaining social and economic benefits. The acknowledgment of competing interests in reaping the benefits of forest and woodland resources has, among other aspects, led to more holistic thinking and approaches towards achieving sustainable forest management.

Forestry Production and Stock in Africa

Forests cover about 30 percent of the world's surface (approximately 3.87 billion hectares), of which 95 percent is natural forest and 5 percent, planted forests. Tropical and subtropical forests (and woodlands) comprise about 56 percent, while the remaining 44 percent is temperate and boreal forest. Over time, global forest cover is estimated to have been reduced by at least 20 percent, and perhaps by as much as 50 percent.[12]

Total forest cover in Africa in 2000 was estimated to be close to 650 million hectares, representing 17 percent of global forest cover, and about 22 percent of Africa's land area. At the same time, about 43 percent of Africa's land mass was estimated to be extreme desert and only 21 percent estimated to be suitable for cultivation. African forests can be broadly classified into the following nine categories: (i) tropical rain forests; (ii) moist forests; (iii) tropical dry forests; (iv) tropical shrubs (including mangroves); (v) tropical mountain forests;

(vi) subtropical humid forests; (vii) subtropical dry forests; (viii) subtropical mountain forests; and (ix) plantations.[13]

It is difficult to provide accurate estimates of these different forest covers, as country data is either fragmented or unreliable.[14] The special category, mangroves, is particularly important because mangroves provide coastal stabilization in deltas and along coastlines. It is estimated that mangrove forests (black, white, and red) alone cover 3,390,107 ha in Africa.[15] The following sub-sections present a more detailed analysis of the forest cover in various sub-regions.

In *North Africa*, because of the prevailing arid and semi arid conditions, forests and woodlands are not a regular occurrence, except along the western Mediterranean coast. Some mangrove forest patches can also be found along the Red Sea coastline. The total forest and woodland area in this sub-region is estimated at 68 million hectares, and constitutes 8 percent of the total land area and about 10 percent of Africa's forests. In addition, wood patches are commonly found in mountain range areas, and trees are also cultivated as windbreaks or hedgerows around farms, and along roads and canals, constituting additional forest-like resources in the region. All wooded areas, although not included in the forest area figures, are important for forest products, grazing, and control of desertification through soil stabilization and regulation of hydrological systems. With respect to revenue generation,

---

[12] World Bank (2000)

[13] FAO (2001a); UNEP (1999)
[14] UNEP (2007)
[15] Ibid.

there is no significant commercial timber production — practiced or planned — in the sub-region, although small forest plantations do exist. According to existing studies, local people use over two-thirds of forest plants for food, medicinal purposes, construction, energy, and livestock rearing, while about 35 percent of plants are known to have multipurpose uses.[16]

The climatic conditions in the *East Africa* sub-region, contrary to the North Africa sub-region, support a wide variety of forests and woodlands. These range from dense tropical forests in the humid and mountainous regions of Uganda, Burundi, and Rwanda, to the dry savannas of the horn of Africa. This sub-region is also home to abundant mangrove and coastal forests that are of particular importance to the livelihood of people. Because of the isolated locations and the high density, the mangroves and the Mountain Forest of East Africa harbour large numbers of animals and plants and have been identified as one of the 25 internationally recognized hotspots of biodiversity. The Mountain Forests in Tanzania, for instance, harbour at least 30 percent to 40 percent of Tanzania's plant species. Approximately 13 percent of the total land area of eastern Africa is covered by forests and woodlands, which constitute about 5 percent of the total African forest cover. However, the percentage of forests and woodlands ranges from 30 percent in Kenya to less than 1 percent in Djibouti. Fuelwood and charcoal supply the majority of the sub-region's energy — meeting 96 percent of energy needs in Uganda and 75 percent in Kenya.[17]

Non-wood forest products are also used extensively in eastern Africa. The potential of medicinal plants in eastern Africa has been widely acknowledged, and the plants grown in forests are used by the Maasai, Kipsigis, Turkana, and many other tribes. The Maasai, for example, have a well-established pharmacopoeia for treating livestock diseases. The use of more than 60 species or subspecies of plants for ethno-veterinary purposes has also been documented among the Olkonerei Maasai.[18] Despite the fact that commercial timber exploitation is limited in the sub-region, the forests and woodlands are important because of the natural resources they provide to local communities.

The total forest and woodland area in *southern Africa* amounts to about 32.7 percent of the sub-regions total area and constitutes 34 percent of all of Africa's forests.[19] Angola has the highest forest cover with 56 percent of the land area under forests, whereas Lesotho has the lowest with less than 1 percent. Forest products provide a ready source of revenue throughout the sub-region, and the communities living in forest or woodland areas depend heavily on forest products to meet their everyday food and energy needs. Forests and woodlands are important to local communities, mainly as a source of domestic fuel — either wood or charcoal. For example, about 80 percent of Mozambique's population live in rural areas and depend on wood for cooking,

---

[16] AOAD (1998); Hegazy (1999); FAO (1999)

[17] FAO (2001b); Wass (1995)
[18] FAO (2001b)
[19] FAO (2001b)

space heating, heating water for domestic use, and drying foodstuffs.[20]

The charcoal industry generates about USD30 million annually and is the sole source of income for about 60,000 people.[21] Important non-wood forest products include honey, beeswax, bamboo, reeds, mushrooms, caterpillars, fodder, wild edible plants and fruits, leaves and bark for weaving, and resins. The medicinal plant trade is extensive and profitable in southern Africa, with about 3,000 species (10 percent) of southern African plants used medicinally and around 350 species commonly and widely used. Other species harvested from the wild contribute as much as 40 percent to household incomes or typically between USD 200 to USD 1000 per household year.[22]

Central Africa's high and reliable rainfall supports extensive forest cover throughout the sub-region, with the exception of the northern parts of Cameroon, Chad, and the Central African Republic. Forests and woodlands cover about 45 percent of the land area of this sub-region and constitute 37 percent of Africa's total forest cover. Most countries in this sub-region are therefore well endowed with forests. Gabon has the greatest cover (85 percent) and Cameroon, the Democratic Republic of Congo (DRC), and Equatorial Guinea all have over 50 percent. The only exception is Chad, which, because of its northerly location and arid environment, has only 10 percent forest cover. This total forest network is the second largest contiguous area of tropical forest in the world and thus plays a very important role in atmospheric carbon sequestration and mitigation of potential climate change. In fact, DRC alone accounts for 134 million ha of forest area, and qualifies as the country in the world with the 7th largest forest area; behind only the Russian Federation, Brazil, Canada, United States, China and Australia; and ahead of such countries as Indonesia and India.[23]

Other benefits of the forests include extremely high levels of biodiversity, which have enormous untapped potential for agricultural, pharmaceutical, and nutritional applications. Commercial logging is important to the economy of most of the countries in this region because it secures substantial amounts of foreign exchange. Cameroon, for example, is among Africa's leading producers and exporters of sawn timber and tropical logs, and ranks fifth in the world. In 2001, Equatorial Guinea exported USD 62 million of wood-based panels, representing 14 percent of its GDP. The forest ecosystems in this sub-region furthermore provide habitat to several communities that depend on the forest for their livelihoods and offer great opportunities for tourism.[24]

The *West Africa* sub-region is characterized by a marked gradation of climate, reflected in the zones of vegetation cover. There are about 72 million hectares of forests, representing 12 percent of the sub-region's land area and 11 percent of Africa's total forest cover. Commercial timber production is an extensive and lucrative

---

[20] UNEP (2007)
[21] Kalumiana (1998)
[22] Cavendish (1999); Shackleton, Shackleton and Cousins (2000)

[23] FAO (2006); FAO (2001b)
[24] FAO (2001b); World Bank (2001)

occupation, which contributes significant proportions of income and foreign exchange to the economies in the sub-region. Forest and woodland products are also extremely important to local communities, which depend on forest and savannah resources for their energy needs, most of which are met by wood. In 2000, over 175 million m³ of wood were used in West Africa for fuelwood and charcoal production. Other forest resources heavily used by local communities include wildlife (bushmeat), medicinal plants, wood and rattan for construction, furniture and crafts, honey, nuts and fruits, and animal fodder, gums, dyes, teas, spices, and aromatics.[25]

Overall, 21 percent to 22 percent of the African continent is covered with forests, ranging from open savannahs to closed tropical rainforests. Forests provide many goods and services that benefit local communities and national economies; and they also provide international biological and environmental benefits. Commercial forest products include timber for the construction and paper industries, but more importantly, forest resources provide local communities with food, construction materials, grazing areas for livestock, cultural and medicinal products, sites for religious practices and leisure activities, and fuel for cooking, heating, and lighting. Forests also protect and stabilize the soil, recycle nutrients to maintain soil quality and regulate water quality and flow. They are vast sinks for atmospheric carbon dioxide and thus play a critical role in mitigating global climate change, the impacts of which are predicted to be most severe for African countries and other developing nations. By protecting soils and regulating temperatures, rainfall, and hydrological systems, forests provide basic support systems for agriculture and industry, and, consequently, for the economies of African nations.

Long-Term Trends in Forestry Pattern in Africa

Tracking long-term trends in forest cover involves compiling and analyzing large quantities of data that are not always consistent or comparable. The task is further complicated by different definitions of what constitutes "forest" (see Box 2.1). Forests may be defined in terms of administrative categories, land use, or land cover. The nature, extent (dimension), and bio-ecological characteristics of forest areas also change, because of both human and natural causes.[26] A simplified overview of key forest change dynamics is presented below in Figure 2.1.

The model has only two classes: forests and all other land. A *reduction* in forest area may occur through one of two processes: Deforestation, by far the most important, implies that forests are cleared by people — who convert the land to other uses such as agriculture or infrastructure — or is destroyed by natural disasters. Forest resources degenerate when they are not capable of regenerating naturally and no efforts are made to replant trees. In contrast, an *increase* in forest area may occur through afforestation (planting of trees on degraded forest land), or through natural expansion of forests through bush fallow.

---

[25] FAO (2001a); FAO (2001b)

[26] FAO (2007)

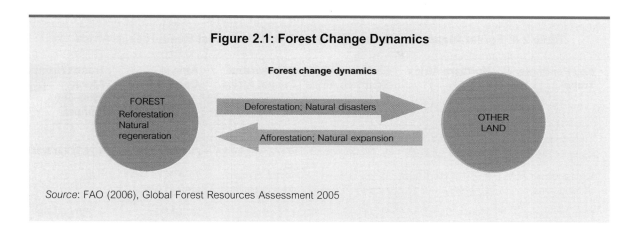

Figure 2.1: Forest Change Dynamics

Source: FAO (2006), Global Forest Resources Assessment 2005

The Food and Agriculture Organization of the United Nations (FAO), in collaboration with the United Nations Environment Programme (UNEP) and the United Nations Economic Commission for Europe (UNECE), produces an assessment of the world's forests every 5–10 years. Table 2.4 presents the results of such an assessment. The data is broadly categorized into northern Africa, eastern and southern Africa, and western and central Africa based on recent assessments.

Based on the figures and assessments, the FAO (2006) concludes that the situation at the global level has remained relatively stable over the last 10–15 years. However, as outlined in Table 2.4, the trend in Africa is of particular concern, as there appears to have been very limited progress towards sustainable forest management, as measured (indirectly) through the selected key parameters. There are some indications that the net loss of forest areas has slowed down and that areas designated for conservation of biological diversity have increased slightly. Nevertheless, the continued rapid loss of total forest

area (4 million ha annually) is disconcerting.

Deforestation, forest degradation, and the associated loss of forest products and environmental services are serious challenges facing African countries. The size of natural forests and woodlands in Africa has been drastically reduced over the last century, especially since independence, as countries have struggled to improve their economies through the exploitation of natural resources. The most intensive pressures stem from deforestation for commercial timber sales; clearance for agricultural and urban developments; and over-harvesting of wood for fuel, medicinal products, and construction materials. Large patches in the remaining forests have also been degraded as a result of clear felling, fires, selective harvesting and encroachment — factors that are not always evident when estimating total forest areas as a round number.

A study of forest cover and quality in Ethiopia showed that, between 1971 and 1997, up to 70 percent of forest cover was cleared or severely degraded by human

Table 2.4: Forest Areas, Key Parameters and Trends in Forest Resources in Africa

Key Parameter / Trend	Northern Africa	Eastern and Southern Africa	Western and Central Africa	African Continent	Trends for Africa 1990–2005 (annual)
Total forest area, by sub-region	131,048 ha (3.3% of global)	226,534 ha (5.7% of global)	277,829 ha (7.0% of global)	635,412 ha (16 % of global)	– 4,263,000 ha
Forest cover in % of land area	8.6% of land area in region	27.8% of land area in region	44.1% of land area in region	21.4 % of land area in Africa	n.a.
Primary forest area 2005 (native species dominant)	13,919 ha (11.9 % of total forest)	12,241 ha (5.7%)	11,510 ha (11.6 %)	37,669 ha (8.7% of global forest area)	– 270,000 ha
Area reserved for conservation	13,036 ha (9.5% of region's forest)	20,158 ha (10.4%)	41,390 ha (35%)	74,585 ha (16.4 % of forest area)	182,000 ha (+)
Threatened tree species	5 in average per country in region	21 in average per country	34 in average per country	21 in aver. per country in Africa	n.a.
Annual average area of forest affected by fire	6176 ha (29.3% of forest area in region)	483 ha (0.8% of forest area in region)	519 ha (1.1% of forest area in region)	7177 ha (5.5% of forest area in Africa)	n.a.
Area reserved for production	44,185 ha (35% of region forest)	44,051 ha (19%)	52,796 ha (45%)	138,032 ha (30% of forest area)	– 911,000 ha
Productive plantations (area)	6,033 ha (5.1% of region's forest)	2,792 ha (1.3%)	1,939 ha (1.9%)	10,764 ha (2.5% of forest area)	42,000 ha (+)
Wood removals	Ind. roundwood 8 km3; fuelwood 173 km^3 (96%)	Ind. roundwood 34km^3;fuelwood 151 km^3 (82%)	Ind. roundwood 36km^3;fuelwood 267 km^3 (88%)	Total remow.: 670 km^3 (22% of global)*	10,767,000 m^3
Value of wood				4594 m. US $	n.a.
Value of non wood forest products				897 million USD	n.a.
Number of people employed (2000)				870,000 (+25% since 1990)	12,000 (+)
Public ownership to forest area	98.2%	95.1%	99.7%	97.6% (global aver. is 84.4%)	n.a.

* For industrial roundwood, 4% of global removals, but for fuelwood 49%

Source: FAO (2006), Global Forest Resources Assessment 2005

activity.[27] The impact of degradation also includes loss of biodiversity, radically increased rates of soil erosion, reduction in water quality, increased risk of flooding in surrounding areas, and loss of livelihoods for local communities. Other analyses also describe similar situations of forest degradation in Nigeria, where the country lost about 55.7 percent of its primary forest between 2000 and 2005. Logging, subsistence agriculture, and collection of fuelwood are cited as leading causes of forest clearing in this West African country.[28]

The major forestry issue in East Africa is the conversion of natural forest to alternative land-use, predominantly cultivation and grazing, although urban encroachment is also a contributing factor.[29] Between 1990 and 2000, East Africa lost 9 percent of its total forest and woodland cover. The highest rates of deforestation observed were in Burundi (9 percent per year), Rwanda (4 percent per year), and Uganda (2 percent per year).[30] Clearance of forest and woodlands for agricultural use — to feed the growing population — is perhaps the single most important cause of deforestation in this area.

Southern Africa has one of the fastest growing populations in the world and faces the challenge of having to increase its food supply by about 3 percent per year. This has invariably led to increased agricultural intensity in the sub-region. Fuelwood harvesting and tree cutting for charcoal production are other main sources of pressure

that have led to significant deforestation in this sub region.[31]

The main problem in Central Africa is large-scale deforestation. Indeed, the greatest threat to forests in the sub-region is commercial logging and the unsustainable harvesting practices of many companies. The highest annual rates of deforestation recorded are in Cameroon (0.9 percent), Chad and Equatorial Guinea (0.6 percent each), while insignificant rates are recorded in Gabon and Sao Tome & Principe.[32]

With the ever-increasing population of most African countries, there is rising demand for forest resource products, especially firewood, charcoal, and roundwood. This has led to a drastic reduction in forest cover in the continent. For example, firewood and charcoal production and consumption rose from 250 to 502 million m^3 (annually) during the 1970–1994 period.[33]

Land

Land is one of the most critical resources in Africa and the basis of survival for a majority of its population. Land resources are generally referred to as terrestrial features that exist above mean sea level. They include landforms such as plains, valleys, plateaus, mountains, deltas and peninsulas, islands and basins; soils; and plants and animals. In terms of value, land resources also include mineral and fossil fuel deposits, natural and farmed timber, crops, animals and fish.[34] Land cover is the physical,

---

[27] EIS News (1999)
[28] FAO (2001b)
[29] According to the FAO (2001b)
[30] Ibid.

[31] Chenje (2000)
[32] FAO (2001b)
[33] FAO (1997)
[34] Hamblin (1998)

chemical, ecological or biological categorization of the terrestrial surface, for example, grassland, forest, or concrete. Land use pertains to the arrangements, activities and inputs people undertake in a certain land cover type to produce, change, or maintain it, for example, raising cattle, recreation, or urban living. Land use concerns the products and/or benefits obtained from the use of land as well as the land management actions (activities) carried out by humans to produce these products and benefits.[35] It is important to note that a specific land use often corresponds to a single land cover, for example, pastoralism to unimproved grassland. However, a given land cover class may support several distinct land uses for example, a forest may be used simultaneously for hunting, timbering, shifting cultivation, fuelwood collection, recreation, wildlife preservation, and watershed and soil protection. In contrast, various land uses (for example. as carried out within a given farm system) may involve the maintenance of several distinct covers, such as cultivated land (fields), woodlots, grassland, and built-up areas. A significant change in land use (such as a land use "conversion") is likely to cause a change in land cover, but land cover may change even if the land use remains unaltered.[36]

With a total land area of more than 3,025.8 million hectares (ha), Africa is the second largest continent in the world, after Asia, and its landmass is more than three times that of the United States of America. Sudan is the largest of Africa's 53 countries, covering 250.39 million hectares. Seychelles is the smallest, covering only 45,600 hectares. The African continent stretches nearly 8,100 km from north to south and about 7,600 km from east to west. The African landscape is a rich and dynamic mosaic of resources, which include forests and woodlands, arable land, mountains, deserts, coastal lands, and freshwater systems.[37] Figure 2.2 shows Africa's eco-regions while Figure 2.3 presents the continent's climatic zones.

Wetlands cover about one percent of the continent's total surface area and are found in virtually all countries. Some of the more prominent wetlands include the Congo Swamps, the Chad Basin, the Okavango Delta, the Bangweulu swamps, the floodplains and deltas of the Niger and Zambezi Rivers, and the Greater St. Lucia Park wetlands in South Africa. Wetlands are critical in terms of biodiversity, but they also support many communities, providing a diversity of livelihood activities. For example, in Tanzania's Rufiji Delta, a study covering 720,000 ha found that crop production has a gross market value of USD 3.8 million per year, and natural resources have an economic direct use value of USD10.3 million per year.[38]

A significant amount of the precipitation in Africa originates from the mountain ranges that thus function as the headwaters of most of the large African rivers and also deliver the resources for drinking water, hydroelectricity and irrigation of crops for the population.

---

[35] WRI (2002–2004); FAO (2000); UNEP (2006)
[36] Ibid.

[37] UNEP (2006)
[38] Ibid.

Figure 2.2: Africa's Eco-Regions

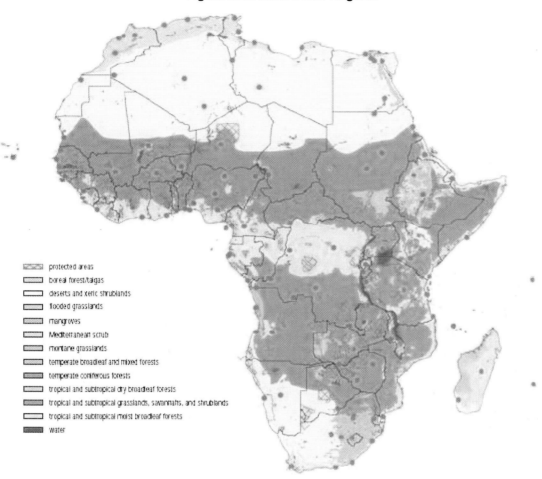

protected areas
boreal forest/taigas
deserts and xeric shrublands
flooded grasslands
mangroves
Mediterranean scrub
montane grasslands
temperate broadleaf and mixed forests
temperate coniferous forests
tropical and subtropical dry broadleaf forests
tropical and subtropical grasslands, savannahs, and shrublands
tropical and subtropical moist broadleaf forests
water

Source: UNEP (2006), Forests and woodlands in Africa (Encyclopedia of Earth)

A total of 1,274 million hectares in Africa are extreme deserts, the Sahara Desert in northern Africa — the largest desert in the world — covers 906.5 million hectares. The Kgalagadi Desert in southern Africa, which covers about 26 million hectares, is about the size of France, and together with Namibia's Skeleton Coast, is the world's largest body of sand. These desert ecosystems support distinctive plants and animals that have adapted to the harsh environment.[39]

Africa has priceless land resources, which provide environmental goods and services from local to global levels. Land is a

[39] Ibid.

Figure 2.3: Africa's Climatic Zones

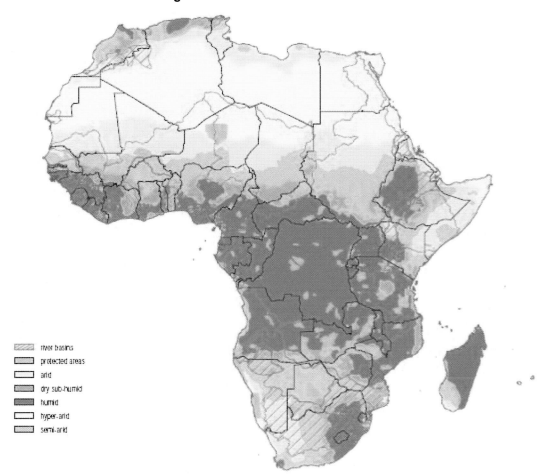

Legend:
- river basins
- protected areas
- arid
- dry sub-humid
- humid
- hyper-arid
- semi-arid

Source: UNEP (2006), Forests and woodlands in Africa (Encyclopedia of Earth)

critical factor in natural and human-managed production systems, and influences the level of natural capital, and social and economic development. Access to land and to the resources it offers is at the core of enhancing opportunities and choices, particularly for people whose livelihood depends directly on it. In Uganda, for example, land constitutes about 50 to 60 percent of the asset endowment of the poorest households.[40] Land and its value are closely related to the environment, with the sustainability of one being a product of the other. However, the value of land resources

---

[40] World Bank (2003)

cannot only be measured in monetary or eco-biological terms; it also includes values related to culture, aesthetics, heritage and bequest.

In summary, land in Africa is used for many activities, including agriculture and forestry; mining and oil extraction; tourism and recreation; urban expansion and infrastructure development (such as transportation). It also acts as a sink for domestic and industrial waste. It is critical in the cradle-to-grave cycle of both living and non-living things, providing habitats and other ecological goods and services, and sustaining investment and human livelihoods. There are many aspects to consider and challenges to be overcome, but Africa's significant land resources are crucial for sustainable development, and hence for the achievement of all the targets under the eight MDGs. For example, increasing agricultural production — the dominant economic activity in most parts of the continent — is the key to addressing extreme poverty and hunger.

Sub-Regional Characteristics

There are three main land use categories in northern Africa: cultivated land, forests, and rangelands. Agricultural land constitutes about 28.8 percent (or 233,590 hectares) of total land. It is estimated that about 18.7 percent of arable land is currently cultivated, although the extent of cultivated areas ranges from 2.6 percent in Egypt to 77.4 percent in Morocco. Rangelands currently occupy about 13.5 percent of total land area (mostly in Algeria and Sudan) although, over the past 50 years, half of these have been reclaimed for cultivation. However, more

than 57 percent of the total northern African land is threatened by desertification.[41]

Eastern Africa is characterized by intensive farming practices and a large rural population practicing subsistence-oriented agriculture, more than 70 percent by some estimates.[42] The total area of eastern Africa is 2,665,000 square kilometres, with 78.090 million hectares (or 29.3 percent of total area) of potential arable land. However, actual arable land is 26.221 million hectares (or 33.6 percent of potential arable land). Uganda has the highest proportion of potentially arable land (14.169 million hectares), whereas in Rwanda, all arable land is in use and the increasing population and need for food crops is pushing farmers to cultivate marginal areas — to such an extent that actual arable land stands at 156.8 percent of potential arable land. More than 30 percent of the East African land area is covered by permanent pasture, hence the dominant land use is livestock grazing. As well, about 73 percent of the total area is characterized by desert and dryland conditions, significant proportions of which are in Somalia, Djibouti, and Eritrea.[43]

The total land area in southern Africa is 693,000 million hectares, of which about 20 percent is arable land. Arable land and domesticated land is used for agriculture, forestry, wetlands and wildlife conservation, and human settlements. Crop production is the dominant land use, contributing to about 34 percent of GDP. Livestock farming is

---

[41] FAO AQUASTAT (2005); UNEP (2006); AOAD (1998)
[42] WHO/UNICEF (2000)
[43] UNEP (2006)

another common form of land use, but it has been constrained in periods due to drought and diseases such as foot-and-mouth disease, cattle-lung disease, and anthrax. The proportion of the population of southern Africa employed in agriculture was estimated at 71 percent in 1970, 64 percent in 1980, and 60 percent in 1990. Proportions by country varied from 87 percent in Malawi to 14 percent in South Africa. Agriculture in southern Africa is also characterized by the employment of a migrant labour force, which engages in seasonal subsistence farming. Major threats to land use in the sub-region relate to land tenure arrangements (weak individual property rights) and associated equity issues. In addition, soil erosion (about 15 percent of land is considered degraded) is a significant threat to agricultural productivity.[44]

In Central Africa, land resources and land use is sensitive to climatic and vegetation characteristics, with forestry and plantation agriculture largely found in the humid zones. The region's total area stands at 536.6 million hectares. DRC has the largest total land cover at 234.5 million hectares, while Sao Tome and Principe has the smallest land area at 96,000 hectares. Large-scale agricultural development has been limited by national market failures and international trade barriers. Shifting cultivation has been the traditional means of coping with variability, but this practice has been on the downtrend and is no longer sustainable in large areas because there are much larger populations that now require land. Land degradation (including erosion and soil compaction) is a major threat to the sustainable use of land resources in the sub-region. Armed conflict is also a threat to the sustainable management and use of land resources in Central Africa.[45]

The total land area in western Africa is 605.54 million hectares, of which 72.789 million hectares is arable land and 183.46 million, permanent pasture. However, about 70 percent of the sub-region (covering mainly the Sahel zone) is semi-arid to desert. Land cover and land use in the sub-region are largely determined by climate and a dramatic gradation is seen from south to north in rainfall and vegetation cover. Cultivation is thus limited and the dominant agricultural activity is livestock rearing. For example, cultivation accounts for just 4 percent of the land area in Mali and Niger, and for less than 1 percent in Mauritania. In contrast, permanent pasture accounts for 25 percent of the land area in Mali and nearly 40 percent in Mauritania. Togo and Nigeria have the largest percentage of land under cultivation (42 percent and 33 percent, respectively), followed by Côte D'Ivoire and Ghana (23 percent each). Climate variability is greatest in the Sahel (Mali, Mauritania, Niger, and northern Senegal) where drought is common and often severe.[46]

The four island countries of the western Indian Ocean, with a coastline of 11,646 kilometres, have a total land area of 59.2 million hectares, 99 percent of which is Madagascar, the fourth largest island country in the world. The percentage of land used

---

[44] UNEP (2006); Chenje (2000)

[45] UNEP (2006)

[46] Ibid.

for agriculture in these island countries is 53 percent, with Madagascar and the Seychelles dominating.[47]

Characteristics of African Agricultural Land Use

The economies of most African countries largely depend on land-based activities such as agriculture, mining, and tourism. Agriculture is perhaps one of the most challenging factors that influence the pattern of land use dynamics in Africa. It contributes about 40 percent of regional GDP and employs more than 60 percent of the labour force. In many countries, these percentages are considerably higher, generally in eastern, western and central Africa. The official estimates of the contribution of agriculture to the formal economy and to employment in many African countries, although substantial, does not even fully take into account the significant contribution of small-scale cultivation and livestock production to livelihoods. This is especially relevant for areas where pastoralism is practiced (most commonly in the more arid areas of northern, eastern and southern Africa).[48]

Agriculture in Africa can be classified as bimodal — divided into smallholder and large-scale/estate agriculture. The underdeveloped nature of smallholder agriculture has largely been shaped by economic policies (economies of scale factor), which are disadvantageous to small-holders but promote larger farmers, who stand a better chance of securing credit

facilities to support their agricultural practices. Agriculture in Africa is predomin-antly rain-fed (except in northern African countries and the western Indian Ocean Island states, where irrigation potential has been well developed). Furthermore, most of the countries experience large inter-annual and intra-annual variations in rainfall, with frequent extremes of flooding or drought. This translates into vulnerability for crop failure and economic insecurity.[49]

Ownership and Land Access in Africa

Over the last decade, land reform policies around the world have, with a few exceptions, such as in Zimbabwe, revolved around variations of market based land reform. This trend fits with broader shifts in global economic policies, following the end of the Cold War, that have seen a reduced role for the state, liberalization of markets, and privatization of state enterprises and assets.[50]

Access to land, the ability to exchange it with others and to use it effectively is very important for poverty reduction, economic growth, and private sector investment. Such access also empowers the poor and ensures good governance. Access to land varies widely across different parts of the African continent, owing to differences in colonial ties, customary laws, rule of law, and countries' historical antecedents. Typically in Africa, land can either be purchased or inherited, and this, to a great extent, determines patterns of land accessibility and ownership. Land tenure is profoundly

---

[47] Ibid.
[48] UNEP (2006); ECA (2004)

[49] ECA (2004); (UNEP (2002); UNEP (2006)
[50] ILRI (2007); Moyo (2000); ECA (2004)

political, and it continues to be a critical factor in the development of African politics and economies. Land tenure, in particular ownership and access rights, has been widely recognized to have important bearings on effective, efficient, and sustainable management and production regimes.[51] The typology of land tenure thus varies from country to country, but, overall, includes freehold tenure, state leasehold, and community-based tenure (legally recognized indigenous tenure and community-based), often in combination, as seen in Kenya, Uganda, and Rwanda. Regardless of the type of tenure that is prevalent, there are a number of challenges: In countries such as Uganda, Somalia, Kenya, and Rwanda, compulsory and systematic tenure conversion to individual ownership has not brought significant benefits to smallholder farmers. In Ethiopia, tenure insecurity is described as one of the major problems associated with the existing land system (see Box 2.3). In Kenya, where formal titles to land are held by many farmers, the lack of any significant relationship between land title and crop yield is perhaps explained by the limited use of land titles in obtaining formal credits.[52]

One of the key issues related to land tenure in Africa is the degree to which the tenure arrangement encourages or discourages sustainable farm practices and investment in land. It is generally believed that a more secure tenure system provides the necessary incentives for farmers to better manage their land and invest in land improvement. Analysis of data on farmers'

opinions on the current land tenure system and perceptions of tenure security shows some relationship with engagement in long-term land improvement practices. Various informal methods employed by farmers in land transfers include mortgage, renting, sharecropping, sales, gift, contracts, exchange of plots, and inheritance. The dominant practices are sharecropping of land (44 percent), sale of land (31 percent), and renting of land (16 percent).[53] From these assessments, one can conclude that although the existing rural land policy in much of Africa has limited the development of formal rural land markets, farmers continue to be involved in informal land transactions mainly for economic reasons.

The major features of the existing land tenure system, such as declining farm size, tenure insecurity, and subsistence farming practices, have been identified as some of the causes of the often poor performance of the agricultural sector. The land tenure system is also cited by many as the major impediment to the adoption of sustainable and long-term land improvement and management practices. As a result, the land tenure issue has attracted widespread attention and debate among policymakers, government and non-government actors, the private sector, the donor community, researchers, and the public at large. The land tenure problem remains a challenge that needs to be addressed through comprehensive and thorough research and analysis.[54]

High population densities and grazing rights have led to frequent conflicts over

---

[51] ILRI (2007)
[52] ECA (2004); ILRI (2007)

[53] Ibid.
[54] EEA/EEPRI (2002)

Box 2.3: Land Issues in Ethiopia

In Ethiopia, lack of adequate access to, and control over, land by peasants is said to be among the principal factors exacerbating rural poverty and food insecurity and conflicts. The history of forced land redistributions over the last thirty years remains a major cause of perceived tenure insecurity in the Ethiopian highlands. Various land policies in the country have also marginalized pastoralists in the semi-arid lowland areas. However, there is an increasing clamour for reduction in state control over land use and for transferring more land rights to land users in the regional states. There have been modest policy and legal reforms at both regional and federal levels. Efforts have been made to increase farmers' confidence that they will reap the fruit of their labour and investment (IRLI, 2007).

Furthermore, Howard and Smith (2006) noted that women are disadvantaged by unequal gender relations in land allocation in Ethiopia. Their work indicate that in rural Ethiopia, as elsewhere, in addition to the formal, de jure, land access mechanisms prescribed by the state, informal means of access to land abound. These include intra-family transfers and land transactions, land access through community membership, and resettlement and squatter settlement.

land and land-based resources in most Africa countries. Examples of outright land and land resource-related wars include the conflicts in Rwanda and the Democratic Republic of Congo. International organizations such as the United Nations Commission on Human Rights (UNCHR) continue to support local civil society efforts to mediate in land disputes. Several local and international organizations have also

published case studies on land problems. Despite these activities, civil society groups have seldom formed formal networks on land issues, and hence the impact on government thinking, including development of land laws, has not been maximized.[55]

Good political, economic, and corporate governance is of primary importance to ensure that Africa's land resource wealth serves as an engine for sustainable socio-economic development rather than a source of inter and intra-state conflict and under-development.

Management of Renewable Natural Resources

The preceding chapters presented water, forestry and land as some of Africa's basic natural resources. Each of these resources is fundamental to Africa's commercial and subsistence related activities. Yet, the analysis clearly reveals that the resources are fragile and susceptible to degradation. Consequently, proper management of the resources and of the wealth they generate is crucial for the future development of Africa. Basic natural resource management concepts (Chapter 1) stipulate that an integrated effort is required to ensure efficient resource use and prevent adverse environmental impacts. In other words, a holistic approach is needed because of the multiple inter-linkages between natural resources. A multidisciplinary integrated approach is also called for, as recognized by the AfDB and by other stakeholders (Box. 2.4).

---

[55] ILRI (2007)

Box 2.4: AfDB Sector Policies and Guidelines for Renewable Natural Resources

Since its inception, the AfDB has developed a number of sector policies and guidelines, which have guided its investments in natural resource sub-sectors. The mainstreaming of sustainable natural resource management has been closely linked to the Bank's environmental and social sustainability concerns, which date as far back as the late 1980s. The Bank's natural resource management concerns are largely reflected in its environmental policies and operations guidelines, and there is no single policy that encompasses all natural resources, but the guidelines on fisheries, forestry, and land management are nevertheless closely linked to the Bank's agricultural sector strategy, under which operations related to these sub-sectors are undertaken.

The Bank's NRM activities — especially those related to water resources, extractive industries, and environmental management — have increased significantly in recent years. As a result, the Bank has revised and updated its policies and strategies to accommodate emerging initiatives and partnerships; and increased activity levels, investments, new initiatives, and engagements in partnerships with other donors and stakeholders. Bank Group operations in the renewable resources area currently face three key challenges: (i) how to sustain the productivity of the natural resource base; (ii) how to halt practices that "mine" the resource base beyond its regenerative capacity; and (iii) how to support interventions that increase productivity per unit of resource used. Concerns about sustaining the productivity of the natural resource base have led the Bank to focus on land use and land management issues and on the use of common pool resources. In this context, the Bank promotes rigorous analyses at all stages of the project cycle to detect potential and actual ecological effects of investments and determine how best to avoid or minimize degradation or depletion.

Sources: AfDB Annual Report (2005); (2006)

Management of Africa's Water Resources

As mentioned in previous sections, a considerable number of countries in Africa experience water scarcity or water stress. This is attributable to a number of factors, ranging from basic natural and climatic conditions to absence of proper water resources utilization and administration (at the local, national, and regional levels). The demand for water, which, in many cases, exceeds supply, has already led to unsustainable practices and increasing competition for water resources between sectors, communities, and nations. Africa's progress towards sustainable development and the achievement of the MDGs crucially depends on amending unsustainable practices and prioritizing the management of water resources for industrial, domestic, and agricultural uses. Some of the Initiatives implemented to date are presented below.

Basin Level Initiatives: In conformity with the global approach to water resources management, Africa manages its scarce water resources through various partnership arrangements among riparian countries in the continent's major river basins, and among local communities within the basins and catchments. Eight of the continents nine largest international basins have basin authorities that have been ratified by the states sharing the river basin. The Congo River basin, which is also the largest, occupying about 12.5 percent of the continent's area, is the only basin that does not have a basin organization.[56] The continent's major river basin organizations and the areas of the continent they occupy are:

- The Nile Basin Initiative (10.3 percent), created in 1999 (Box 2.5);
- the Lake Chad Basin Commission (7.8 percent), created in 1964;
- the Niger Basin Authority (7.5 percent), created in 1980;
- the Zambezi Watercourse Commission (4.5 percent), created in 2004;
- the Orange Commission — Sengu River (3.0 percent), created in 2000;
- the Organization for the Development of Senegal River (1.6 percent), created in 1972;
- Limpopo Basin Commission (1.3 percent), created in 2002; and
- the Volta River Basin (1.3 percent), created in 2004.

In spite of the formal steps taken to create these organizations, most of them have been beset by bureaucratic inefficiencies and financial and capacity constraints. As such, the majority of them have not been able to operate as envisaged and results have fallen short of expectations. In addition, the organizations have not been able to keep up with emerging science-based water management innovations and thus lack key techniques for water allocation, development, and distribution. According to the Fourth World Water Forum[57], the various initiatives aimed at establishing and strengthening water basin organizations (WBOs) face a considerable shortage of human and financial resources with respect to the various initiatives aimed at establishing and strengthening water basin organizations (WBOs). In essence, only the South African and the Senegal River Development Organizations (OMVS) have a resource base that will allow them to perform their duties. This notwithstanding, the collective approach to water resources management could, if further supported and developed, reduce waste and ensure efficiency in water resources allocation and utilization in Africa. Furthermore, despite the fact that numerous water resources in Africa are shared among countries, issues relating to water rights and to ownership of international waters remain largely unresolved, resulting in national interests prevailing over shared interests.[58]

Integrated Water Resource Management (IWRM): The IWRM framework for planning and managing water resources has also been embraced in Africa and in various management initiatives for river basins. IWRM promotes the coordinated development and management of water, land, and related resources, in order to maximize economic and social welfare in an equitable manner without compromising the sustainability of vital ecosystems. It is generally agreed that IWRM principles are prerequisites for enhanced water resource development in Africa. In principle, all African countries have

---

[56] FAO (2005); WWC/CONAGUA (2006)

[57] WWC/CONAGUA (2006)
[58] Ibid.

Box 2.5: The Nile River Basin Initiative

The Nile Basin Initiative, created in 1999 at the initiative of the African Council of Ministers on Water (AMCOW) for the countries riparian to the Nile Basin (Nile COM), furthers a first agreement in 1959 between Egypt and Sudan on Nile River water usage, and also on commitments for the environmental protection of the Nile Basin. Ten countries located in the Nile Basin (Burundi, DRC, Egypt, Eritrea, Ethiopia, Kenya, Rwanda, Sudan, Uganda, Tanzania and Eritrea as a 'prospective member') are participants. The initiative aims to achieve sustainable socio-economic development through the use of, and equitable sharing of benefits from, water resources in the Nile Basin. Its main objectives are to: (i) develop the Nile River water resources in an equitable and sustainable manner in order to ensure prosperity, security, and peace for the inhabitants; (ii) guarantee effective water management and optimal resource use; (iii) promote cooperation and combined action between member countries; and, (iv) combat poverty and promote economic integration.

Source: FAO, AQUASTAT (2005)

---

agreed to engage in watershed management and in IWRM — in other words, manage water resources at the basin level rather than at the politically defined boundary level (see Boxes 2.5 and 2.6 as well as examples below). Thus, the planning and management of water-related activities is seen as an all-encompassing activity involving relevant actors and stakeholders.[59]

Ethiopia and Kenya provide good examples of IWRM. In 2001, Ethiopia engaged stakeholders to provide input for the development of a sectoral strategic action plan aimed at achieving its national water policy objectives. The resulting General Water Resource Development Program (2002–2016) was established to address water quality management as part of an IWRM plan for key river basins. Under this program, institutional bodies and facilities would be strengthened and new ones established for effective management and monitoring of water quality. These include laboratories at

national and regional levels, river basin commissions, authorities and a national water resource council.[60] Similarly, in the East Africa sub-region, Kenya has made considerable progress in reforming the water sector, especially in relation to water supply and sanitation. As stated in its 2002 Water Act, the objectives include enhancing the provision, conservation, control, apportionment, and use of water. As a result of these reforms, Kenya established a Water Resource Management Authority, and drafted its first National Water Resource Management Strategy in 2004 to provide a clear road map for managing and developing water resources in a sustainable manner through community participation, capacity-building, and a demand-driven approach.[61]

Water resource management at the true IWRM (visionary) level is still in its infancy in Africa. A national-level assessment of 34 countries on the continent, conducted by the

---

[59] WWC/CONAGUA (2006); UNEP (2006)

[60] UNEP (2006); Bzioui (2005)
[61] UNEP (2006)

Box 2.6: The African Water Facility (AWF)

The AWF, an instrument of the African Ministers Council on Water (AMCOW), is hosted by the AFDB Bank Group at the request of the AMCOW. Its mission is to improve the enabling policy and institutional environment and to strengthen water resource management in Africa in order to attract the significant investments needed to achieve national and regional water objectives. Specifically, the AMCOW mobilizes resources to finance water infrastructure and water investment facilitating activities in Africa. Interventions under the AWF focus on achieving the following three main outcomes:

1. *Improved Integrated Water Resources Management*: RMCs have strengthened their capacities to manage their water resources effectively, based on IWRM principles that create an environment that is conducive to coherent and sustainable investments;
2. *Improved Transboundary Water Resources Management* (TWRM): Regional organizations manage transboundary water resources under a cooperative framework that fosters investments with shared benefits; and
3. *Increased Water Sector Investments*: RMCs and regional organizations benefit from projects and programs through increased investments resulting from a sound investment climate, better preparation, and available funding.

By facilitating the very considerable water investments that are needed to provide water security and improve water resources management in Africa, the AWF offers African countries a great opportunity to address the critical problems that they face in water supply. The AWF also identifies information, knowledge management, and monitoring and evaluation as key crosscutting components designed to provide broad support for IWRM and TWRM activities. During the 2005–2009 period, the AWF plans to mobilize EUR 500 million from bilateral and multilateral donors for these activities. Resources committed to date amount to approximately EUR 60 million from seven donors: the European Union (EU), Canada, Norway, Sweden, Denmark, Austria, and France.

Source: African Development Bank, Water and Sanitation Department

AfDB in 2005, revealed that only 14 countries had water resources management policies and strategies, and that only 16 countries prioritized water in their Poverty Reduction Strategy Policies (PRSPs).[62]

Public Private Partnerships in water resources management and water supply programs have been gaining popularity in

some African countries. These partnerships are being used to ensure sustained development of infrastructure and water supply. Several of such partnerships have recorded successes in providing services to large urban centres, districts, as well as rural communities.[63] At the national level, responses to increased competition over freshwater resources include revision of water resource development policies and greater involvement of stakeholders —

---

[62] Assessment conducted by AfDB; presented at Fourth World Water Forum, Mexico (WWC/ CONAGUA, 2006).

[63] UNEP (2002)

Box 2.7: Meeting the MDG Drinking Water and Sanitation Targets (Goal 7, Target 11)

Water is an essential resource for human beings. Safe drinking water, sanitation and good hygiene are fundamental to health, survival, growth and development. The Millennium Development Goals (MDGs) have set a common course aimed at pushing back poverty, inequality, hunger, and illness. All eight MDGs are, in one way or another, related to water resources. Indeed, the world has pledged, to reduce by half the proportion of people without sustainable access to safe drinking water and basic sanitation before 2015. This is reinforced with goals and initiatives for the "International decade for Action, Water for Life, 2005–2015".

Although the world has achieved considerable results, sub-Saharan Africa (SSA) remains an area of great concern: Even though the percentage of people with access to clean water rose from 49 percent to 56 percent over the 1990–2004 period, the absolute number of people without access to drinking water actually increased by 23 percent (taking into account the population growth factor). With slow progress, low coverage, and a huge disparity between urban and rural coverage, SSA is unlikely to attain the MDG target (for this specific region: 75 percent coverage by 2015).

Source: WHO/UNICEF (2006), Meeting the MDG Drinking Water and Sanitation Target.

---

especially local communities and the private sector — in water resource management and in water supply. However, many countries face implementation challenges. For example, Ethiopia's Water Resource Policy (1999) focuses on providing a clean and safe water supply, but there are no appropriate directives and regulatory instruments to enforce the legislation.[64]

Some of the areas where vigorous emphasis is being placed in order to achieve the MDG targets (see Box 2.7) include water resources management, watershed management, adequate water accessibility and quantity, water quality, adequate institutional capacity, and international water rights. Measures implemented so far include, the *Rural Water Supply and Sanitation Initiative* (RWSSI), a major water initiative launched by

the AfDB in collaboration with its RMCs and other donors in 2003. The objective of the RWSSI is to mobilize African governments and the international donor community to accelerate Africans' access to sustainable drinking water and basic sanitation, so as to meet critical MDGs (Box 2.8).

Major international programs for water resource management include the Lake Victoria Environmental Management Program (LVEMP) and the Nile Equatorial Lakes Subsidiary Action Program (NELSAP). The LVEMP was established in 1995 by Kenya, Uganda, and Tanzania to improve sustainable use of the basin's natural resources. It focused primarily on fisheries management, pollution control, invasive alien species control, and land use management.[65] The international community

---

[64] UNEP (2006); Bzioui (2005)

[65] UNEP (2006)

Box 2.8: The Rural Water Supply and Sanitation Initiative (RWSSI)

The RWSSI strategy focuses on the following key elements:
- Raising awareness about the rural water supply and sanitation situation in Africa;
- Mobilizing more funds from donors, RMCs, NGOs, and other stakeholders;
- Adopting fast track mechanisms for national RWSS programs;
- Adopting a demand-driven programmatic approach, as opposed to a multi-project approach;
- Prioritizing sanitation, focusing on hygiene, and on public health education;
- Strengthening the capacity of decentralized government institutions, communities, the private sector, and artisans;
- Ensuring beneficiary participation, in the design phase as well (in an IWRM context);
- Enhancing sustainability by promoting technology, water innovation, and indigenous knowledge, based on beneficiary consensus, ease of implementation, cost-recovery schemes, and local knowledge for operations and maintenance

Until 2002, over 80 percent of Bank Group AfDB financing for water supply and sanitation focused on urban areas, as did most other donor support. Since over 65 percent of Africans live in rural areas, the Bank Group made a strategic decision in 2003 to shift its water supply and sanitation financing to rural areas, which have the lowest access to basic services and the highest poverty levels. The target of the RWSSI is to increase safe water and basic sanitation coverage to about 80 percent of the rural population by 2015. If fully successful, the achievement of the RWSSI targets will expand access to potable water supply to 277 million people, and sanitation services to 295 million people by 2015.

While this challenge holds the significant promise of improving sustainable livelihoods as well as rural water and sanitation services in Africa, its achievement over the 2000–15 period has huge investment implications. The cumulative investment for achieving the targeted 80 percent coverage by 2015 is estimated at USD 14.2 billion over the 15-year period. The Bank is committed to financing 30 percent of the total costs from its African Development Fund (ADF) and African Development Bank (ADB) windows. It has called on multilateral and bilateral donors to provide 50 percent of the financing, and on RMC governments and beneficiary communities to contribute 15 and 5 percent, respectively. Since the launching of the RWSSI in 2003, the Bank has approved 13 RWSSI programs and projects for a total of USD 536 million in financing.

Source: African Development Bank, Water and Sanitation Department

---

has supported these and other efforts in Africa to cope with the problematic water situation. Several international agreements and protocols have been established, especially in responses to escalating conflicts over shared watercourses. Examples of such internationally motivated initiatives include the Regional Program for the Sustainable Development of the Nubian Sandstone Aquifer (NSA), the Southern African Development Community (SADC) Protocol on Shared Water Courses, and the Nile Basin Initiative, described in Box 2.5.

Forestry Management in Africa

Several African governments are currently shifting emphasis from passive to active involvement in the forestry sector (for

---

Box 2.9: Trade-Off Between Poverty and Deforestation — Win-Win Approaches?

There is a potential dilemma of trade-offs between poverty reduction and environmental protection: deforestation causes environmental damage, but it also increases the supply of farmland and generates rural income and employment (sometimes sustainable, sometimes not). However, recent comprehensive studies suggest that poverty reduction and environmental protection are not inherently in opposition (at 'loggerheads'), nor are they automatically aligned. Outcomes depend on the policies adopted and on specific conditions on the ground. In other words, there are ample options for 'win-win' approaches, especially when labor demand can be boosted outside agriculture. Key approaches include:

- Tenure, zoning, and land-use regulation – for example, revisiting the ownership and management of government lands, regulating exploitation of private lands and promoting participatory land management;
- Making forest management more attractive to agriculture – for example, by funding markets for environmental services and removing barriers to sustainable management of forests for timber and other products; and
- Coordinating regional development interventions – such as road networks and agricultural policies to achieve synergies where possible.

Source: Chomitz (2006)

---

example, Nigeria is conducting a comprehensive inventory and valuation of its forests and woodlands). Governments are also introducing mechanisms that will encourage sustainable utilization of forest and woodland resources, including the issuance of concessions on standing volumes rather than on harvested volumes. Specifically, governments are putting in place stronger policies and allocating additional resources to enforce them. This is based on the recognition that conservation and the sustainable use and management of Africa's forests and woodlands are the necessary foundation for the promotion, development, and growth of other sectors. In its 2006 report, "Forests and Woodlands in Africa" the UNEP[66] recommends that countries develop and implement national biodiversity strategic action plans, nature reserves, and protected area systems. Setting actual targets on biological diversity and continuously monitoring progress are particularly important for the well-being and livelihood needs of Africans. A recent work under the World Bank umbrella[67] focuses on the interrelationships between agricultural land expansion and deforestation processes as evidenced in Africa, for instance, and presents an appealing approach, where a number of tools — often in combination — can be applied to achieve 'win-win' situations (Box 2.9).

Many issues have to be taken into consideration in managing forest resources in Africa. The first and most fundamental is determining which areas can and should be maintained as protected areas, and which should be allowed to be developed for production (cropping, forestry, livestock, and

---

[66] Ibid.

[67] Chomitz (2006)

Box 2.10: Integrated Forestry Conservation and Development

Effective resource conservation and management must involve strong local participation. This is fully integrated in the concept of integrated conservation and development, which involves the following key aspects:

- Local people retain the rights to continue traditional use of resources inside state-owned protected areas (to the extent that this is not detrimental to the ecosystem) and are, of course, allowed to continue such activities on all land returned outright to them.
- Local communities are allowed to generate income from protected areas through environmentally compatible activities such as tourism, hunting with traditional weapons, and gathering of non-timber forest products. All of these activities are directly dependent on the protected area. Local communities given exclusive rights to carry out these activities will have an incentive to conserve the forest or wilderness area.
- Commercial logging of protected areas is entirely excluded. Logging can be allowed and carefully managed only in those areas specifically identified for logging, but even then, only with techniques and management practices that ensure long-term sustainability.
- Buffer zones are established around core protected areas, and ownership of the land and associated resources in them is returned to the local people. Buffer zones are meant to provide the local people with sufficient forest and agricultural products to prevent overexploitation of the protected areas. They also serve to keep potentially destructive wildlife away from villages, crops, and domestic livestock.
- Agriculture and social development activities can be provided outside protected areas to attract local people away from (the forest areas) and as an incentive to avoid encroachment.

Source: Cleaver and Schreiber (1994), Reversing the Spiral (World Bank)

fisheries); i.e. broader land use planning. In this context, the criteria for selecting natural ecosystems for preservation and protection include the following: biological importance; productive potential; provision of "environmental services" (prevention of soil erosion and flooding, recharge of aquifers, maintenance of river flow); importance of the survival of indigenous peoples and their livelihood systems; productive potential; current status (whether or not the ecosystem is already degraded); and, likelihood of successful preservation.

Reducing pressure on forests at the local level can be achieved by limiting access to them in the first place. This has been done using local forest guards in countries like Nigeria and Ghana to protect the forest from unlawful exploitation by local people. Reduced access to forest products however, has a number of serious implications including increasing shortage of fuelwood and negative impacts on the income and nutrition status of dependent local people. In such circumstances, government action is needed to address key concerns. Such actions would include actively engaging the private sector and civil society in forestry and woodland resources management, and reviewing the legal and institutional capacities of the public sector institutions responsible for forestry resources. Private investor participation can be enhanced by carrying out up-to-date forest inventories. One of the challenges in this regard is that existing information on forests and woodlands is

---

Box 2.11: AfDB Forestry Strategies and Initiatives

The African Development Bank's engagement in the forestry sector started as far back as 1978. In 1994, the Bank adopted a specific *Forestry Policy*, under its agricultural operations, to guide its lending to the sub-sector. The policy emphasizes the need for sustainable management of Africa's forest resources to ensure a critical balance between ensuring the sustainable supply of wood and non-wood products and maintaining the healthy regeneration capacity of the continent's forests.

Regional cooperation plays a significant role in the conservation of important forest areas. In light of this, the Bank Group continues to work closely with African regional and sub-regional organizations, as well as with technical institutions to establish protected and classified forest areas; promote intra-African trade in wood and non-wood products; create regional and sub-regional forestry projects; harmonize forest policies; set up linkages between forestry sub-regional institutes and forestry faculties of universities; and establish policy and operational networks for exchange of information.

In 1999, the Bank reviewed its forestry portfolio as well as the policies of other donors. Following this review, the Bank shifted the focus of its financing from industrial forestry plantations to social, rural development, and environmentally focused forestry projects. The bulk of the Bank's current forestry portfolio comprises broad-based projects that incorporate an integrated approach to natural resources management. Since 1978, the Bank has financed 31 forestry projects in 21 countries, for a total commitment value of UA 458.47 million. However, a downward trend in the demand for forestry projects has been noted. The projects are designed as integrated programs with components from other sectors such as agriculture and water resources. Most of the interventions have diversified the income sources of rural people and increased employment opportunities. Furthermore, the projects are multi-sector based, collaborative and participatory in nature, and designed within the context of sustainable natural resource management and integrated forestry development. Women, who are sometimes marginalized in decision making in Africa, are key stakeholders in the design (and implementation) of most Bank-financed forestry projects.

Source: African Development Bank, Agriculture and Agro-Industry Department

---

often outdated and incomplete. This is partly because most of it is obtained from secondary sources.[68]

Reflecting the recognition that effective resource conservation and management must involve strong local participation, the concept of "integrated forestry conservation and development" has been gaining traction in forestry development in Africa and elsewhere (Box 2.10). Experience with the implementation of this concept is still limited in Africa. A number of pilot efforts have been initiated — by the African Development Bank (Box 2.11) — but these are still in the very early stages. A potential danger to watch for is the risk of the "magnet syndrome": priority provision of infrastructure and social services around areas to be protected may, in fact, *attract* people to the area if social and infrastructure development farther away is significantly lagging behind that around the area to be protected.[69]

---

[68] UNEP (2006)

[69] Ibid.

Land Reforms in Africa

Arguments for land reform programs in Africa typically revolve around issues of equity, poverty reduction, economic development, and political stability — but land reforms are also considered important contributors to human freedoms, civil liberties, and sustainable democracies. Access to land remains critical for people's survival in most developing countries where "land is the primary means for generating a livelihood". During the 20th century, many governments developed land reform policies aimed at meeting these objectives and at dealing in a controlled way with the demands and tensions around land.[70]

In some African countries, there has been continuity from colonial to post-colonial land reforms. For example, in Kenya, land reforms started by British rulers in the 1950s were pursued with even greater vigour by the first post-independence government. The reasons for this — often problematic — continuity included the weak nature of many post-colonial states, constitutions that preserved existing institutions and laws, the extent and influence of foreign investments, and the need to earn foreign exchange.[71] In other African countries, independent governments implemented their own radical and redistributive land reforms (also see Boxes 2.3 and 2.12). In the 1970s, for example, the Marxist regime in Ethiopia abolished the feudal system of landholding, nationalized all land, and distributed it to those willing to work it. In

> **Box 2.12: Land Reform in Botswana**
>
> The commitment of African governments to land reforms can be described by the Botswana land policy paper which is aimed at the "review of all land related laws and policies" and sets out "a comprehensive policy which will promote equitable land distribution and address land use conflicts, land pricing and land rights, as well as strengthen land management. The new policy will establish a favourable environment for both domestic and foreign direct investment, thus contributing to economic diversification and global competitiveness. In addition, a number of land-related Acts will be reviewed, including: the Town and Country Planning Act, the Deeds Registry Act, the Tribal Land Act, the State Land Act and the Land Survey Act. These Acts will be aligned with the Land Policy and other relevant pieces of legislation".
>
> *Source*: Botswana Minister of Finance, Budget Speech to Parliament, 5 February 2007

Mozambique, the abandonment of farms by the Portuguese at independence made the nationalization of land relatively easy. The land was divided into state farms, cooperative farms, and the distribution of land to individuals was organized through a registered license process that left the state with an overriding power.[72] Land was also nationalized through legislation in many other countries, including: Tanzania, Guinea, Sudan, Mali, Nigeria, Burkina Faso, Zaire, Uganda, Somalia, and Zambia.[73]

Advocates of reforms in land rights and land markets frequently posit two important

---

[70] DLA (1997); Prosterman & Riedinger (1987); World Bank (2003)

[71] Okoth-Ogendo (1993)

[72] Ibid.

[73] Bruce (1993)

hypotheses: (i) African countries should grant land titles to their citizens because titles increase land tenure security and facilitate access to input, land, and financial markets; and, (ii) land markets constitute the most efficient mechanism for allocating resources and improving access to productive resources by the poor, especially women and other marginalized groups. Land titling, however, is not a panacea for reforming land tenure systems in Africa. Owing to differences in environmental risks, the level of demand for agricultural land, the performance of existing tenure systems, the legacy of colonial and postcolonial reforms, and other socioeconomic factors, the need for, and impact of, titling will also differ. These diverse conditions have led land rights to evolve along different pathways and thus to require different reform options. Because land is an immovable resource, all transactions really refer to the bundles of rights associated with a specific piece of land. Land rights set boundaries for opportunities and constraints regarding the control, management, and use of land, whereas land markets are mechanisms by which right holders and non–right holders can transfer, rent, and acquire different bundles of rights to land.[74]

In addition, the importance of customary land tenure systems varies from country to country. In Botswana, Malawi, Mali, Morocco, Niger, and Zambia, customary land rights are the dominant tenure systems. Under these systems, land values are generally equal to the discounted net present value of current and future productivity per hectare. As such, land productivity is used to determine the terms of land contracts. These land rights are generally viewed as an impediment to agricultural growth because they entail limited access to formal credit and input markets. Nonetheless, such rights offer many opportunities to poor households because: (1) they are easily acquired through group membership and social networking; (2) land contracts are based on risk-sharing strategies, whereby landowners and tenants share input costs and output; and (3) right holders have informal mechanisms for acquiring credit and avoiding loss of their lands.[75]

In Botswana, Swaziland, and Zambia, distorted land policies have favoured the emergence of landowning elites and private agribusinesses at the expense of small producers. In Tunisia, however, titling is widespread because the government has reduced titling fees and promoted irrigation and production of high value crops (olive and nut trees). Registered customary private land rights are the dominant land rights in North Africa and in a few countries in sub-Saharan Africa (such as the Central African Republic, Kenya, Mali, and Niger). Registration facilitates the recording of all transactions at the local level, reduces the incidence of conflict, and, transforms the value of land. Registration therefore enlarges the possibilities for right holders to make land transactions in both formal and informal land markets, and gives them easier access to credit in state-managed credit schemes.[76]

---

[74] Tidiane (2004)

[75] Ibid.
[76] Ibid.

Many countries in Africa are clearly struggling to implement the laws and policies that they have formulated in recent years. These difficulties stem from over-ambition, lack of capacity, scarcity of financial resources, and the assumption that customary law can be swept away with the stroke of a pen, or women's land rights protected by another. Social reality at the local level is generally very different from what is imagined in the capital city. Land issues are in fact not new in Africa.[77] The land tenure situation has been evolving in response to demographic and technological changes, wars, conquests, and changes in governance. Moreover, from colonial times to the present, land has been an object of policy intervention and every spot of land in Africa has a history of changing land policies and different forms of land politics. Any new policy must therefore take previous policies and their effects into account in addition to the socio-economic conditions of land tenure they aim to alter.

In conclusion, concerning land relations and policies designed to benefit the poor, there are two competing models of governance and development on offer in and for Africa:[78] The first model involves adopting the agenda of the international community and its international financial institutions and donors by making land available for international investment and development through free and open land markets and homogenized national land laws, thus reaping the benefits of globalization. Such an agenda downplays issues of

security of tenure for the poor, decentralized land management, and women's rights to land. The second model involves developing national agendas to ensure that national considerations are at the forefront of land management. This is not meant to repel globalization, as that would be impractical, but to give primacy of place to the land concerns of the poor, both women and men, who now constitute the majority of land holders in all countries in Africa and are likely to be for considerable time to come.

Climate Change, Risk Management and Adaptation in Africa

Climate Change is emerging as perhaps the most important international development challenge of the 21st Century. The economic and social welfare of societies and, indeed, their long-term sustainability is highly vulnerable to climate change. The recently published report[79] of the Intergovernmental Panel on Climate Change (IPCC) unequivocally concludes that there is "very high confidence" that increased emissions of Green House Gases (GHG) like carbon dioxide (CO_2) is the cause of significant climate changes. Developing countries are the most vulnerable and bear the highest risks on their natural resources as climate change and climate variability critically jeopardize their economic development and ability to reduce poverty. In the developing world, the direct and indirect impacts of climate change threaten to reverse decades of development efforts, particularly in Africa.

---

[77] Lund et al. (2006)
[78] IRLI (2007)

[79] IPCC (2007a)

Climate change is thus a major threat to sustainable growth and development in Africa, and to the achievement of the Millennium Development Goals. Africa is particularly vulnerable to climate change because of its overdependence on rain-fed agriculture, compounded by factors such as widespread poverty and weak capacity. Climate change is already having profound and irreversible impacts on the African continent. Noticeable impacts, among others, include:

(i)   increased frequency of natural disasters, droughts, floods and other weather extremes that lead to loss of life, economic disruption, social unrest and forced migration as well as major environmental problems;

(ii) sea level rise and flooding that threaten agriculture, human health, infrastructure, particularly in coastal cities and islands;

(iii) prolonged drought periods that cause stress on water resources and reduced food security due to diminished agricultural productivity;

(iv) increase in outbreaks of vector-borne diseases and other health impacts; and

(v)   various threats to forestry, water resources, biodiversity, and other natural resources.

Key sectors such as agriculture, fisheries, forestry, industry, energy and transport are very sensitive to climate change. Natural disasters destroy strategic national investments in infrastructure, while there is no requisite insurance to cover the losses. Small Island developing countries in Africa are particularly vulnerable. Climate change also negatively affect ecosystems, more specifically coral reefs.

The impacts of climate change are inequitably distributed: poor countries are hardest and earliest hit, while rich countries are responsible for three quarters of GHG emissions that cause climate change. Even if greenhouse gases emissions were curbed immediately, further warming would still be expected with its associated negative impacts. To address these risks, climate change issues and response strategies need to be integrated into the overall development agenda. It is therefore important to build in climate risk management and adaptation into current and future development efforts.

Recognizing the importance of incorporating climate information in the continent's development agenda, the Heads of State and the African Union in 2004 reaffirmed their commitments to establishing and strengthening centers of excellence and networks dedicated to agricultural and environmental issues, and to creating and enhancing regional early warning systems to combat natural disasters.

Impacts of Climate Change on Africa's Natural Resources

As stated in the previous section, Africa is highly vulnerable to climate change, in particular because of factors such as widespread poverty, recurrent droughts, inequitable land distribution, and overdependence on rain-fed agriculture. Although adaptation options, including traditional coping strategies, theoretically are available, in practice the human, infrastructural and economic response capacity to carry out timely response actions are well beyond the regions economic means. With respect to natural resources, areas of particular concern include health, forestry, agriculture, water resources, coastal zones, and ecosystems and biodiversity, the hypothesized longer-term impacts include changing rainfall patterns affecting agriculture and reducing food security; worsening water security; shifting temperature affecting vector diseases; reduced economic growth prospects; and more challenging hurdles in reaching the MDGs. According to the recent IPCC report, the cost of adaptation in Africa could be as high as 5 to 10 percent of the continent's GDP. The adverse impact of climate change on the region's natural resources is examined in detail in the following section.

Ecosystems: As elaborated in earlier sections water resources, forests, and land areas are under threat from population pressures and poor land use practices. The apparent effects of these threats include loss of biodiversity, rapid deterioration in land cover, and depletion of water availability through destruction of catchments and aquifers. Changes in climate will interact with these underlying changes in the environment, adding further stress to a deteriorating situation.

Water Resources — Half of Africa will face water stress: Three-quarters of African countries are in zones where small reductions in rainfall could cause large declines in river water. Some climate models show that 600,000 square kilometers classified as moderately water constrained will become severely water limited. By 2020, between

75 and 250 million people are projected to be exposed to increased water stress due to climate change.[80] Changing climatic conditions are responsible for the melting of glaciers on the mountains of Kilimanjaro and Kenya. This is likely to result in a decline in the water level of some rivers leading to serious water shortages in Lake Victoria. This in turn may affect the flow of River Nile, and may lead to major conflicts in the countries traversed by the river. The same scenario is likely to apply to the Zambezi, Niger and all other major rivers in Africa, since the rivers' sources are in the high rainfall potential areas in the tropical highlands of Africa, which are likely to suffer adverse impacts of climate variability and change.

Hydrology: A drop in water level in dams and rivers may adversely affect the quality of water by increasing the concentrations of pollutants in the water, thereby increasing the potential for the outbreak of diseases and reducing the quality and quantity of fresh water available for domestic use. It may also affect the habitats of some species (birds, fish and other aquatic species), which depend on lakes and rivers as a habitat.

Agriculture, Livestock and Food Security: Agriculture is the economic mainstay and the lead sector in employment, and farming in large areas depends entirely on the "perform-ance" of the rainy season — a situation that makes the region particularly vulnerable to climate change. Agricultural production, including access to food, is thus projected to

---

[80] IPCC (2007b)

be severely compromised by climate variability and change. This would further adversely affect food security and exacerbate malnutrition in the continent.[81]

Diseases will likely spread: Climate change is also associated with the occurrence and spread of pest and diseases affecting plants and livestock.

Marine Environment Zones, Mangroves and Coastal Ecosystems: Africa's coastal zone would be adversely affected by sea-level rise associated with climate change. Sea-level rise and climatic variation may reduce the buffer effect of coral reefs and mangrove systems along the coast, increasing the potential for erosion. A sizable proportion of the coastline would be lost through a combination of inundation and erosion, with consequent loss of agricultural land and urban areas. This may have severe and grave effects on many coastal cities. Furthermore, local food supplies are projected to be negatively affected by decreasing fisheries resources in large lakes and in the oceans due to rising water temperatures, which may be exacerbated by continued over-fishing.

Mainstreaming Climate Risk Management and Adaptation in Development

Adaptation measures to address adverse climate change impacts usually transcend different areas of activities and are often site-specific, rather than sector-specific. Common implementation challenges for adaptation measures include the following:

- Adaptation technologies most often address site-specific issues, and therefore have to be designed and implemented with local considerations in mind. This may hamper replication on a large-scale and retard the implementation of large-scale programmatic interventions.
- Adaptation technologies primarily aim at preventing or reducing climate impacts on different sectors; as such, adaptation is often not considered a development priority.
- There are difficulties in ascertaining necessary timeframes for adaptation and for overcoming institutional barriers.
- Adaptation issues are (despite the sector focus often applied) usually cross-sectoral and must be dealt with by different ministries in a synergetic manner through powerful integrated strategies. The lack of awareness and recognition of climate threats by policy makers often impede the placement of adaptation and long-term climate risk planning in the economic development agenda.
- Adaptation constraints are compounded by the lack of local institutional capacity and resources to support community resilience building; and the lack of local financial resources in poor communities.

Africa has the lowest GHG emissions, yet it is likely to be hardest hit by climate

---

[81] Ibid.

change. Adaptation to the unavoidable impacts of climate change will need strong support from the international community and involve all stakeholders, including the private sector. Adaptation to climate change should be understood as a continuous process which addresses current climate variability and extremes and future climate risks. Actions by local communities that are most directly affected play a very important role. Linking climate change adaptation and disaster risk management thus becomes a logical first step (see Box 2.13). However, there is an urgent need for African governments to recognize that future climatic conditions may be much different from present ones — thus the need to anticipate rapid change through improved forecasts and planning and to develop new coping strategies. Furthermore, climate change adaptation is complex, often requires site-specific measures, and will seriously challenge the low institutional and technological capacity in Africa.

Many African economies are highly dependent on natural resources. Appropriate adaptation, therefore, must safeguard natural resources and ecosystems, value the goods and services that they provide, and ensure their environmentally sound and sustainable exploitation. Adaptation approaches based on better management of natural resources, such as "no regrets" options — that is, those measures that are expected to generate benefits even without long-term climate change — are an important avenue to pursue. In addition, following a sustainable development path provides a basis for economic diversification, increased levels of social and environmental resilience and

flexibility and human capital formation, which are all crucial components of adaptation. Indeed, much adaptation is an extension of good development practice and should therefore be integrated into environmentally sound development policy and planning at every level.

Funding is critical but the implementation of adaptation by developing countries will need other types of support from external partners and sub-regional initiatives. The second African regional workshop on adaptation[82], which took place in Accra in September 2006, highlighted the importance of capacity support (for example, in using general circulation models at national levels to project possible future climate change), and the transfer of low-carbon technologies to Africa where very limited engagement by the private sector and continuing concerns about intellectual property rights, have severely restricted technology transfer. The promotion of regional co-operation efforts was generally recognized as highly desirable in the areas of surveillance and early warning systems, sharing of experiences, and the development of transboundary adaptation projects involving water sharing in Africa's 50 river basins.[83]

African Governments need to respond decisively to the impacts of climate change by diversifying supply, building a low-carbon energy mix, and opening up markets to private sector innovation and investment. Governments need to ensure a transparent and level playing field to create a market for

---

[82] UNFCCC (2006); (2007)
[83] Ibid.

Box 2.13: The African Development Bank and Climate Change Adaptation

To AfDB is engaged in a number of activities aimed at achieving substantive progress in the area of adaptation. Its lending and non-lending operations in this regard include the following:

(i)   Promoting vulnerability assessments, use of risk assessment tools, and of climate adaptation strategies that address different dimensions and root causes of poverty, including gender inequality;

(ii)   Promoting the mainstreaming of climate issues into key national, sub-national, local and sectoral development planning and decision-making processes, such as PRSPs or national and local strategies for sustainable development;

(iii)   Ensuring that development programmes and projects are designed to minimize climate change and variability risks;

(iv)   Increasing access to good quality information about the risks and impacts of climate change and variability. Early warning and information distribution systems are essential in this regard;

(v)   Empowering communities to participate in climate change vulnerability assessments and feed in their knowledge to provide useful climate-poverty information;

(vi)   Promoting traditional risk-sharing mechanisms, such as asset pooling and kinship, potentially complemented by climate specific insurance schemes, such as, weather index insurance and micro-insurance approaches;

(vii)   Improving infrastructure design and investment, both related to the private and public sector, to take into account the potential impacts of long-term climate change and increased climate variability.

(viii) Helping RMCs Regional Member Countries (RMCs) improve governance, including an active civil society and open, transparent, and accountable policy and decision-making processes;

(ix)   Helping RMCs integrate climate issues into economic planning and management at both the national and regional levels, including high-level inter-ministerial co-ordination at national levels and increased role for regional economic communities.

The impact of climate change is already being felt in Africa and is posited to continue to be a serious challenge in the future. It is therefore vital for African governments to build resiliency into their infrastructure, agriculture, health and education sector developments, to be able to adapt to and combat climate change impacts. The AfDB is seeking ways to collaborate with its partners to assist RMCs build climate resiliency building by developing and mainstreaming climate risk assessment and climate information tools at macro and micro levels to influence development plans, policies and project designs.

low-carbon energy. This is crucial to ensure the long-term security of energy systems and continued economic growth in a world affected by climate change. The Bank's future action in climate change will focus on promoting a broader shift towards low-carbon economies by promoting energy efficiency and renewable energy; supporting the dissemination of carbon reduction technologies, namely improved and modern biomass technologies; small hydropower and solar and wind; widening access to cleaner second and third generation fossil fuels; and supporting wider use of efficient and clean technologies to avoid high-carbon technology lock-in.

These responses must take into account not only Africa's acute vulnerability but also its legitimate development needs, and the broader principles of equity and fairness in a global framework aimed at reducing global greenhouse gas emissions. Action is needed at a number of different levels. Faster progress is needed on reducing global emissions. Africa faces massive challenges in adapting to the impact of climate change and in managing the increased levels of climate risk — increased support and financing for this is essential. Africa's need to develop its energy must be recognized. Current carbon finance mechanisms are not delivering the resources which Africa needs and should be re-examined. African governments themselves need to fully integrate their response to climate change into economic planning and management at both the national and regional levels.

Summary

Africa is endowed with abundant natural resources — about 9 percent of global freshwater resources or 3,930 km³ /year of internal renewable resources. Average annual rainfall on the continent is about 678 mm per year, but remains highly variable, both spatially and temporarily, with Central Africa and the Indian Ocean Islands receiving more rainfall than North Africa and parts of the Sudano-Sahelian Regions. Most African countries (except some in northern Africa) are not currently threatened by *physical water scarcity*. However, the majority experience *economic water scarcity*, implying that they lack the resources and means to develop their water resources.

It is projected that 25 African countries will experience water scarcity by 2025. This underscores the relatively low levels of development and exploitation of Africa's water resources, precisely at a time when the continent is lagging behind in terms of the basic water-related indicators of the MDGs. The increasing need for water resource development also raises the potential for conflicts among riparian states, and among competing uses (domestic, industry, and agriculture). Thus, there is a crucial need for cooperation at all levels — local, regional and international — to efficiently manage Africa's water resources. In particular, there is a need to invest in water resource development, which includes the capture, storage, diversion and distribution of water, and to strengthen dialogue with a view to increasing cooperation in water resource management both at the local and international levels. An estimated 300 million people in Africa lack access to adequate water supply and even more lack adequate sanitation. This underscores the crucial role that the state must play in developing policies and strategies, and in undertaking and facilitating investments in the water sector.

Africa has a significant share of the world's forests (30 percent), which support the livelihood of numerous people on the continent, especially in rural areas. Although forest distribution varies among sub-regions, with the bulk of it occurring in Central Africa, the role of the forestry sub-sector in Africa's overall economy remains significant. This role has even broadened in recent times, with recognition of the forests' importance for environmental functions. However, the demand for land and for forest products is also increasing and there is growing concern about the loss of Africa's forest cover; likewise, for new management initiatives to address the challenges. The Report has highlighted some key aspects of these initiatives.

African economies are still dependent on land-based activities such as agriculture, mining, and tourism. Nevertheless, access to land and the ability to trade land rights remains a challenge, although it is recognised as a crucial factor for poverty reduction, economic growth, and private sector investment, as well as for empowering the poor. Access to land issues vary widely across different parts of the African continent, largely because of differing cultural practices and colonial histories. A common element in all the variants is that land issues in Africa remain largely political and the challenge of addressing land access is largely embedded in the challenge of ensuring good governance.

Finally, climate change has emerged as a significant threat to the management of Africa's natural resources especially in the agriculture sector, where it has very severe food security implications. Therefore, natural resource management policies and strategies need to adequately incorporate climate change issues, particularly the need for adaptation to minimize the continent's vulnerability to the impact of climate change.

CHAPTER 3
Africa's Non-Renewable Natural Resources

Introduction

This chapter focuses on Africa's non-renewable natural resources — fossil fuels (coal, gas, and oil) and minerals — in line with the classification of natural resources presented in Chapter One of this Report. These natural resources are examined in terms of their stock (reserve), production (extraction), consumption patterns in Africa, trade characteristics and outlook for the future. The first part of the chapter thus provides a detailed analysis for each main resource. This is followed by a review of AfDB support to the extractive industries, and finally, an overview of key management principles and practices implemented in Africa.

Metals and mineral exports contribute significantly to the economies of resource-rich African countries. In fact, all of Africa's top five exports are mineral-related — as illustrated in Table 3.1.

Although Africa ranks high in terms of resources, its share of world base metal and mineral fuel *consumption* is very modest, a consequence of the continent's low level of industrialization, economic status, and per capita consumption patterns. For instance, Africa's share of world steel consumption is only about 2 percent.

Fossil Fuels

Coal

The majority of Africa's coal resources are located in southern and western Africa. The major deposits are found in Botswana, the Democratic Republic of Congo (DRC),

Table 3.1: Top Five African Exports by Value (2005)

Product	Value in 2005 in USD Thousand	Share in World Exports, %
Petroleum oils and oils obtained from bituminous minerals, crude oil	133,534,293	17
Petroleum oils and oils obtained from bituminous minerals (other than *crude oil*)	19,283,817	5
Natural gas, liquefied	7,968,296	18
Diamonds, non-industrial un-worked or simply sawn, cleaved or bruted	7,497,806	22
Bituminous coal, pulverized or not, but not agglomerated	3,180,845	8

Source: Trademap (2007), International Trade Database Online: http://www.trademap.org

Mozambique, Nigeria, South Africa, and Zimbabwe; while minor deposits are found in Senegal, Benin, Niger, Somalia, Ethiopia, Tanzania, Zambia, Malawi, Madagascar, Egypt, and Morocco (see map in Figure 3.1). By a large margin, the majority of the continent's estimated recoverable coal reserves are located in South Africa — 34 billion tons as estimated in 2005 — making South Africa the sixth-largest holder of coal reserves in the world.

Coal is the world's fastest growing fossil fuel with an annual production increase of 6.4 percent since 2004. African coal production rose 1.9 percent in 2005, compared with 2004 levels, accounting for about 5 percent of total world anthracite and bituminous coal production[1]. Most of the increase in African coal production was attributable to South Africa, which alone accounted for 98 percent of the regional coal output (Zimbabwe accounted for about 1 percent and others even less). More than 99 percent of South Africa's coal production was bituminous. South Africa produced 244.7 million tons of saleable coal in 2006, making the country the fifth-largest coal producer in the world, after China, the United States, India and Australia[2]. Output also increased in Botswana and Zambia, but fell in Zimbabwe, owing to resource depletion in a key mine.

In 2005, Africa accounted for 3.4 percent of world coal consumption, up 12.3 percent from 2001 levels[3]. Within the region, South

Africa accounted for 91.6 percent of total African coal consumption. Some 177.1 million tons of production was sold locally in South Africa in 2006, for about R16.2 billion (approx. USD 2.5 billion). Of the local sales, demand was primarily from the energy sector, which uses coal to meet more than 77 percent of primary energy needs and 90 percent of electricity production needs.[4]

The overwhelming majority of African coal is exported through the port of Richards Bay in South Africa. Total exports in 2006 stood at 66.4 million tons, valued at USD 3 billion. Coal export infrastructure constraints were the reason for the decrease in exports compared with the previous year (Table 3.2).

As Table 3.2 shows, the value (USD) of South African coal has risen considerably, mainly attributable to increased demand — primarily in Europe — and the resulting better prices. This increased demand stems from the lack of availability of coal from

Table 3.2: South African Exports of Bituminous Coal

Year	Value	Quantity (Kg)
2002	USD 1,766,650,752	67,703,353,344
2003	USD 1,715,920,512	67,723,550,720
2004	USD 2,349,846,532	65,066,798,084
2005	USD 3,178,112,786	72,462,039,856
2006	USD 3,046,010,963	66,436,604,280

Source: UN Comtrade (2007), United Nations Commodity Trade Database Online

---

[1] British Petroleum (2006)

[2] South African Department of Minerals and Energy (DME) (2007): http://www.dme.gov.za

[3] British Petroleum (2006)

[4] DME (2007): The South African Department of Minerals and Energy: http://www.dme.gov.za

Figure 3.1: Oil, Gas and Coal Resources of Africa

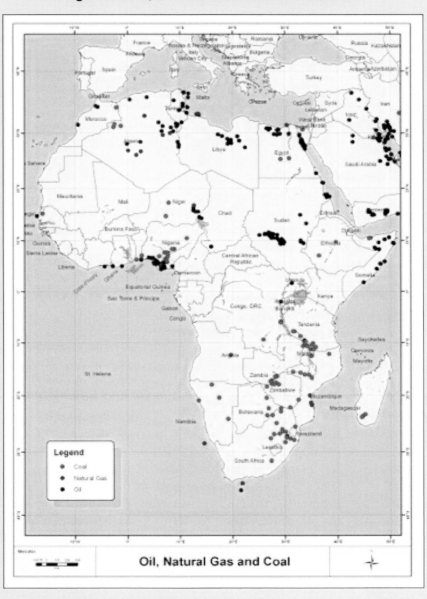

Oil, Natural Gas and Coal

Source: Council for Geoscience and Mintek (2007)

Table 3.3: World Coal Production by Region, 2004–2030 (Quadrillion Btu)							
Country	2004	2010	2015	2020	2025	2030	Average Annual % Change, 2004–2030
Africa	5.9	7.1	7.7	8.0	8.6	8.9	1.6%
China	43.0	55.4	64.6	74.3	83.4	93.4	3.0%
Total World	113.4	136.6	152.1	167.7	183.8	199.9	2.2%

Source: Energy Information Administration (EIA) (2007)

European producers, depleting stockpiles, and an unstable and unreliable supply from Russia. Exports to Asia, which have been eroded somewhat in recent years, may return to former levels with a potential rise in demand for South African export coal, especially from India.[5]

The outlook for African coal production is relatively bright, with an expected average increase of 2 percent per year up to 2011:

- South Africa is likely to be responsible for the majority of the increase, as its production could increase to 266 million tons by 2009.
- Mozambique is expected to become the second-ranked coal producer in Africa, with the development of the Moatize Project in 2009.
- The National Development Corporation of Tanzania has plans to start production at Mchuchuma in 2008.
- Zimbabwe's output could rise because of the opening of the 3 Main Mine.
- In Botswana, production is expected to rise at the Morupule Colliery

because of domestic power plant expansion.
- Production is also expected to rise in Malawi and Nigeria.

In the longer term, world coal production is forecasted to increase at an annual rate of 2.2 percent up to 2030 (Table 3.3), whereas African production is expected to rise at a below-average rate of 1.6 percent over the same period (and Chinese production at around 3 percent per annum).

Crude Oil and Petroleum

Africa's major *known* deposits of crude oil are located towards the north of the continent, in Algeria, Chad, Egypt, Libya, Morocco, and Tunisia; and in Nigeria and Angola in the south. Table 3.4 presents an overview of the most important oilfields.

In 2005, Africa produced 9.8 million barrels of oil per day, bringing its share of world crude petroleum production to 11.6 percent. Nigeria accounted for more than a quarter of the continent's production (see Table 3.5). The rise in Nigeria's output resulted from investments and an increased production quota authorized by the

[5] Creamer Media (2006)

Table 3.4: Major African Oilfields

State	Deposit Name	Size of Resource (Barrels)	Status
Algeria	Hassi Messaoud North & South	> 300 million	Continuously producing
Algeria	Rhourde El Baguel; Hassi Berkine South; ZarzanTine; and Edj'leh	All 4 Resources: 160–300million	Continuously producing (all)
Angola	29 offshore and onshore blocks	Several resources >160 million within blocks	Some producing
Chad	Doba	160–300million	Deposit never exploited
Egypt	El Morgan ; and July Oilfield	160–300million	Continuously producing
Gabon	Emeraude; Loango	> 300 million	
Libya	Zelten	160–300million	Derelict mine
Libya	Waha; Amal; Serir; Gialo; and Dahra	All Resources: 160–300million	Continuously producing (all)
Morocco	Meskalia	160–300million	Continuously producing
Nigeria	Usan; Ukot; Aparo; Agabami; and Bonga Sw	All Resources: 160 million	Continuously producing (all)
Nigeria	Jones Creek	160–300million	Continuously producing
Tunisia	El Borma	160–300million	Continuously Producing

Source: Council for Geoscience and Mintek (2007)

Organization of Petroleum Exporting Countries (OPEC). Increases in production were also recorded in Libya, Chad, Sudan, Angola, Algeria, and Equatorial Guinea, mostly attributable to production start-up in new fields.

African consumption of petroleum products increased to 1.01 billion barrels in 2005 from 0.97 billion barrels in 2003 and 0.89 billion barrels in 1999. However, this represented only 3.2 percent of consumption of world petroleum products (Figure 3.2). Middle distillate products accounted for 42 percent of demand; light distillates, 23 percent; and fuel oils and others, around 17 percent each. Egypt accounted for 22 percent of African consumption of petroleum products; South Africa, 19 percent; Algeria, 9 percent; while other African countries made up the remaining 50 percent.[6]

In 2005, Africa exported 37 percent of its petroleum to Europe; 36 percent to the United States; 9 percent to China; 2 percent to Japan; and 14 percent to other countries in the Asia–Pacific region. The following special characteristics are worth noting:[7]

---

[6] British Petroleum (2006)

[7] TradeMap (2007): International Trade Database Online: http://www.trademap.org

Table 3.5: Major African Producers of Crude Petroleum (million tons)

Country	2001	2002	2003	2004	2005
Nigeria	99.5	88.8	106.9	123.6	127.26
Libya	63.7	61.6	69.0	75.8	82.0
Algeria	57.1	61.4	68.5	71.8	74.6
Angola	36.4	44.6	43.6	49.0	61.0
Egypt	32.6	34.9	35.0	33.2	31.9
Sudan	10.4	11.5	12.6	14.9	18.6
Equatorial Guinea	9.0	11.7	12.3	17.4	17.8
Gabon	15.0	14.7	12.0	11.8	11.6
Congo	12.1	11.5	10.8	10.6	11.3
DRC	13.1	12.5	11.6	11.1	11.0
Chad			1.3	8.8	9.3
Tunisia	3.3	3.5	3.1	3.3	3.4
Cameroon	4.1	3.7	3.5	3.2	2.9

Source: British Geological Survey (BGS) (2006)

- Countries forming part of the Economic Community of West African States (ECOWAS) sent 56 percent of their exports to the United States and 20 percent to Europe.
- North African countries sent 78 percent of their exports to Europe and 22 percent to the United States.
- Intraregional exports to African countries accounted for only 2 percent of total African petroleum exports.

African crude petroleum production is expected to increase from 2007 to 2011, dependant on continued growth in demand, discovery of new oilfields as well as the potential detrimental effect of civil conflicts and war. Production rose nearly 18 percent from 2004 to 2007:[8]

- In Nigeria, annual output is likely to increase to 1.2 billion barrels in 2007, and the share of African crude petroleum production is expected to rise by about 31 percent in 2011 — although the recent civil conflict in the Niger Delta makes estimates somewhat uncertain.
- Sudan's output more than doubled, from 2004 to 2007, and the level is expected to remain steady.
- In Libya, an increase in production is likely, partially attributable to higher output from Elephant Field onshore Block NC-174 in the Murzuq Basin.
- Higher production is expected from Block 15 in Angola.
- Output is also likely to increase in Algeria.

Natural Gas

Africa's largest deposits of natural gas are located in Algeria and Mozambique, with other significant occurrences in Libya, Niger, Morocco, Nigeria, Rwanda, Ghana, Egypt, Tunisia, and off the coasts of South Africa, Tanzania and Namibia.

African production of dry natural gas amounted to 163 billion cubic meters in 2005, an increase of 13 percent from 2004. Libya accounted for most of the increase in output (up 79.5 percent), with higher production attributable to the start-up of the Wafa Field. The initialization of the North Tano, Songo Songo, and Temane projects

---

[8] USGS (2005)

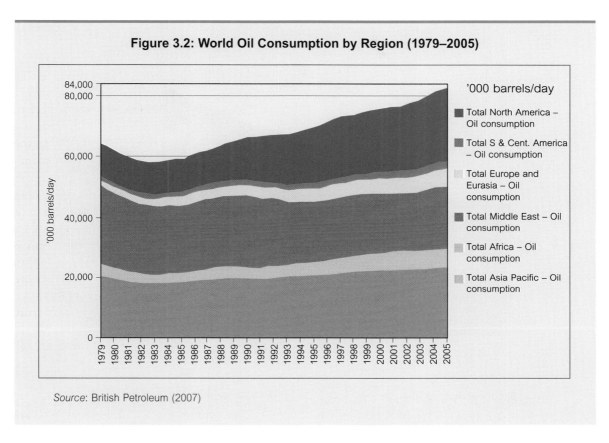

Figure 3.2: World Oil Consumption by Region (1979–2005)

'000 barrels/day

- Total North America – Oil consumption
- Total S & Cent. America – Oil consumption
- Total Europe and Eurasia – Oil consumption
- Total Middle East – Oil consumption
- Total Africa – Oil consumption
- Total Asia Pacific – Oil consumption

Source: British Petroleum (2007)

in Ghana, Tanzania, and Mozambique, respectively, also helped boost production. Nevertheless, Algeria is by far the biggest producer, accounting for 54 percent of Africa's dry natural gas output in 2005. Nigeria contributed 13 percent, up from only 5 percent in 1999. Table 3.6 shows natural gas production by country between 2001 and 2005.

The African continent consumed nearly 3 percent of the world's natural gas in 2005 (Figure 3.3). This is equivalent to 71.2 billion cubic meters, compared with 68.6 billion cubic meters consumed in 2004 and 50.9 billion cubic meters in 1999. Egypt

Table 3.6: Natural Gas — Major African Producers (billion cubic meters)

Country	2001	2002	2003	2004	2005
Algeria	78.2	80.3	82.8	82.0	87.8
Egypt	18.3	19.6	17.6	14.0	34.4
Nigeria	15.6	15.1	19.2	22.3	21.8
Libya	6.2	6.2	6.4	7.0	11.7
Other	2.2	3.7	4.3	4.8	6.3

Source: BP Statistical Review (2006); BGS (2006)

Figure 3.3: Natural Gas Consumption per Region (1979–2005)

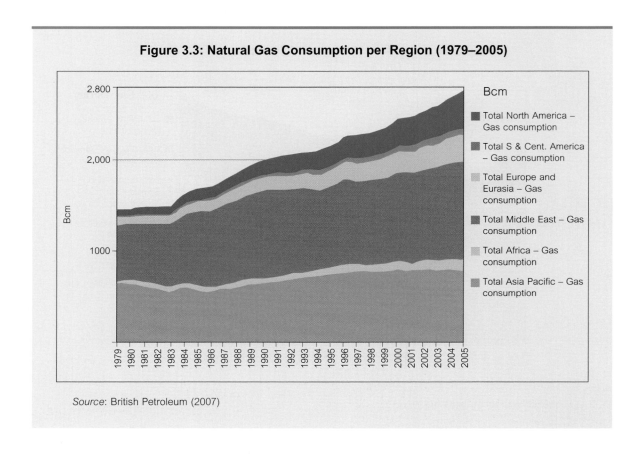

Source: British Petroleum (2007)

accounted for 36 percent of Africa's dry natural gas consumption; Algeria, 34 percent; and others, 30 percent.[9]

In 2005, Africa exported 37 million tons of natural gas, worth more than USD 10 billion. Liquified natural gas (LNG) accounted for 79 percent of exports, giving Africa an 18 percent share in world LNG trade. A significant share of African natural gas exports were to Europe, with Spain as the primary importer. Algeria is by far the

largest exporter, exporting to the value of almost USD 9 billion in 2005.[10]

African production of dry natural gas is expected to rise an additional 5 percent from 2007 to 2011, having already gone up nearly 28 percent from 2004 to 2007:[11]

- Algeria's output of natural gas is likely to increase because of new

---

[9] British Petroleum (2006)

[10] DTI (2005): Department of Trade and Industry (DTI) (SA) Economic Database: http://www.dti.gov.za/econdb/

[11] USGS (2005)

production from the Gassi Touil Field in 2007.

- In Libya, production is likely to increase considerably to 8 billion cubic meters in 2011.
- The increase in Nigeria's production is partially attributable to the West African Gas Pipeline, and the planned elimination of natural gas flaring.
- Production could also increase at Temane in Mozambique and Songo Songo in Tanzania.
- However, Egypt's production is likely to start declining by 2009.

Minerals (Metals and Non-Metals)

The African continent is endowed with a diverse mix of minerals[12], including precious, ferrous, non-ferrous, and industrial minerals. Table 3.7 illustrates Africa's domination of some of the world's mineral resources supply. For example, it is the top producer of platinum and gold and has very large shares of world reserves. One country, South Africa, stands out in Africa. It is the world's leading producer of chromite and ferrochromium, gold, palladium, platinum, and vanadium and the world's second ranked producer of manganese and ferromanganese, rutile, and zircon. Nevertheless, considering the reserves, the production of several minerals

Table 3.7: African Mineral Resources (2005)

Mineral	African % of World Production	Rank	African % of World Reserves	Rank
Platinum	54	1	60	1
Gold	21	1	42	1
Chrome	40	1	44	1
Manganese	28	2	82	1
Vanadium	51	1	95	1
Cobalt	60	1	55	1
Diamonds*	78	1	88	1

* Mine production
Source: United States Geological Survey (USGS) (2005); BGS (2006)

is comparatively small in Africa and, for some minerals, the production trend has been declining. For instance, mine production of bauxite, copper, and lead decreased in the period from 1990–2005.[13]

The following sections further outline production trends and other key aspects of the most important mineral resources found in Africa.

Energy Minerals

Uranium: Africa's largest deposits of uranium are located in Namibia and Niger, with further above-than-average occurrences in Algeria, the Central African Republic, Gabon, and South Africa. However, several large African uranium deposits are still unexploited; for instance some considerable deposits in Namibia and South Africa.[14]

---

[12] A mineral is a naturally occurring substance formed through geological processes; it has a characteristic chemical composition, a highly ordered atomic structure, and specific physical properties. A rock, by comparison, is an aggregate of minerals and need not have a specific chemical composition. Minerals range in composition from pure elements and simple salts to very complex silicates with thousands of known forms.

---

[13] USGS (2005); BGS (2006)
[14] Council for Geoscience and Mintek (2007)

African uranium production dropped slightly by 2.2 percent in 2005, following a sizeable increase of 19 percent in 2004. The continent contributed 16.6 percent to global production. Niger overtook Namibia as the continent's primary producer, accounting for 46 percent of African uranium production, while Namibia accounted for 45 percent, and South Africa, 9 percent. Comparatively, in 1990, Niger's and South Africa's shares of continental production were 30 percent and 27 percent, respectively. Total African production was 6,914 tons, with the majority being exported to France[15]. Needless to say, uranium is a very important export commodity for Niger and Namibia.

In 2005, Africa accounted for only 0.47 percent of the global supply of electricity generated by nuclear power. South Africa was the only regional consumer of uranium, with 2.9 million tons of oil equivalent used. This situation is not expected to change in the foreseeable future.[16]

Continental uranium mine production is expected to rise by more than 4 percent per year from 2004 to 2011, and Africa's total share of world uranium mine production is expected to remain at about 16 percent in 2011. A number of important developments are expected:[17]

- In South Africa, the Dominion mine is scheduled to open this year (2007) and to produce more than 1,500 tons per year of uranium by 2010.
- Paladin Resources Ltd. of Australia is developing the Kayelekera Project in

Malawi, which could produce about 850 tons annually of uranium, starting in 2008 or 2009.

Precious Metals and Minerals

Gold: Africa's largest deposits of gold are located in South Africa, Ghana, and Tanzania, with further sizeable occurrences in Mozambique, Zimbabwe, the DRC, Algeria, Mali, Sierra Leone, Senegal, the Ivory Coast, Guinea, Burkina Faso, Niger, and Ethiopia (see Table 3.8 and Figure 3.4).

The mine production of gold in Africa was 552 tons in 2006, a 14 percent decline compared with production in 1995. This is due mainly to a long-term decline in South African production. Correspondingly, Africa's share of world gold mine production fell from 32 percent to about 21 percent from 1990 to 2006. Despite the significant fall in production, South Africa remains the world's top gold-producing country, producing 294 tons in 2005 (Table 3.9) and 270 tons in 2006, although closely followed by the United States and Australia with approximately 260 tons each (in 2006).[18]

In 2006, South Africa accounted for 54 percent of African gold production; Ghana, 12 percent; Tanzania, 11 percent; and Mali 10 percent. South Africa's share of continental gold production has fallen steadily, from 89 percent in 1990 to 81 percent in 1995, because of rising production costs associated with deeper underground operations (lower production) and increased production in Ghana, Guinea, Mali, and Tanzania (Table 3.9).

[15] DME (2007)
[16] British Petroleum (2006)
[17] USGS, (2005); Mining Review Africa (2005)

[18] Creamer Media (2007)

Figure 3.4: Precious Minerals and Metals in Africa

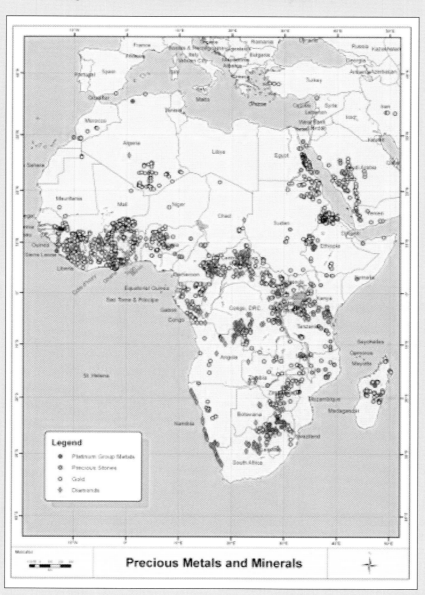

Source: Council for Geoscience and Mintek (2007)

Table 3.8: Gold - Major African Deposits

State	Deposit Name	Size	Status *
Ghana	Prestea	25t–50t	Intermittently producing
Ghana	Obuasi (Ashanti Gold Mine)	25t–50t	Continuously producing
S. Africa	West Rand	50t–100t	Continuously producing
S. Africa	East Rand	50t–100t	Continuously producing
S. Africa	Far West Rand	50t–100t	Continuously producing
S. Africa	West Wits Line	50t–100t	Continuously producing
S. Africa	Evander	50t–100t	Continuously producing
S. Africa	Klerksdorp	50t–100t	Continuously producing
S. Africa	Free State Gold Field	50t–100t	Continuously producing
S. Africa	New Consort	25t–50t	Continuously producing
Tanzania	Bulyanhulu	25t–50t	Continuously producing

* Excludes abandoned mines.

Source: Council for Geoscience (CGS) and Mintek (2007)

Table 3.9: Major African Producers of Gold (tons, metal content)

Country	2001	2002	2003	2004	2005
South Africa	394.7	398.2	372.7	337.2	294.8
Ghana	70.0	69.5	70.7	63.1	66.5
Tanzania	30.0	43.2	48.0	48.1	45.4
Mali	41.2	56.0	45.5	37.9	44.1

Source: BGS (2006)

In a global context, Africa's consumption of gold is insignificant. Indeed, although the continent produces 21 percent of world gold, it only accounts for 4 percent of total global consumption.[19]

Africa accounts for approximately 3 percent of total trade in unwrought forms and 6 percent in non-monetary gold powder. The major importers of African gold in unwrought forms were Switzerland, Canada, the United Kingdom and South Africa, for smelting purposes. The major importers of African non-monetary powder gold are Israel, the United States of America, Belgium, South Africa, and Germany. There is also significant intra-regional trade for gold. South Africa imports about 150,000 kg annually, mostly from West African countries, to supply its gold refineries. The majority of African gold mine production is thus refined in South Africa prior to export to other regions.[20]

Gold mine production in Africa is expected to rise slightly until 2009 and then to decline by about 4 percent in 2011. Expected decreases in output in Mali, South Africa, and Tanzania could more than offset

[19] UNCTAD (2006)

[20] TradeMap (2007), International Trade Database Online: http://www.trademap.org

increased production in other countries. The long-term decline for the main producing country, South Africa, is likely to be reversed temporarily in 2009 because of the completion of several important mine projects; but the long-term trend is expected to prevail with the abandoning of mines and reduced production. The situation is basically the same in Mali and Tanzania with some important projects coming 'online', while others are being shut down or are in decline. In Ghana, however, the outlook calls for a modest increase in output owing to higher production from the Wassa Mine. Botswana's output could increase sharply because of higher production from the Mupane Mine.[21]

Several African countries that were involved only in artisanal gold production in 2004 are likely to open large-scale gold mines in the near future. In Mauritania, the Tasiast Gold Mine is expected to start production this year (2007). The recently opened Taparko Mine is expected to increase Burkina Faso's output. Plans are underway to mine gold-rich zones in Bisha, Eritrea from 2008 to 2010. In the DRC, the Kilo Moto Mine could open in 2009. Furthermore, by 2008, World Bank-sponsored projects in Madagascar and Uganda could lead to significant increases in reported artisanal gold production.[22]

Platinum Group Metals: Virtually all of the continent's platinum group metals (PGMs) resources are located in South Africa's Bushveld Igneous Complex (BIC), with smaller deposits in Zimbabwe. The BIC,

located in the northern reaches of South Africa, was formed about two-billion years ago and has a series of distinct layers, three of which have economic concentrations of PGMs. Platinum and palladium production from the BIC represents 72 percent and 34 percent, respectively, of annual global production. Estimates of the platinum and palladium resources of the BIC of proven and probable reserves of platinum and palladium stand at 203.3 and 116.1 million oz., respectively. Inferred resources were estimated at 939 million ounces of platinum and 711 million oz. of palladium. These figures stand to increase if other PGM-bearing reefs in the BIC are mined, or if mining extends to depths below two kilometers.[23]

Zimbabwe's platinum deposits are located in a geological sequence known as the Great Dyke — an igneous intrusion that is 30 km wide and 550 km in length and spans almost the length of Zimbabwe in a north-to-south direction. Within the dyke there is horizontal layering, with distinctive zones of certain rock types evident. PGM-bearing ore is found between the surface and 500 m in depth.[24]

In 2005, Africa's production of platinum increased by 3 percent. South Africa, which is the continent's largest producer of PGMs, accounted for 97 percent and 96 percent of the production of platinum and palladium, respectively. Indeed, it produced 5.11 million oz. of platinum, which represented 77 percent of global platinum production in 2005. This rise in production was

---

[21] USGS (2007)
[22] Ibid.

[23] Johnson (2007)
[24] Ibid.

Table 3.10: South African Platinum Exports by Destination

Importers	Exported Value 2005 (in Thousands of USD)	Share of SA's Unwought Platinum Exports,%	Export Growth in Value 2004–2005 (%, P.A.)	Total Import Growth in Value of Partner Countries 2001–2005,%, P.A.
World	2,003,326	100	79	17
USA	672,376	34	25	15
Germany	405,127	20	21	26
Japan	343,286	17	309	24
UK	287,719	14	311	42
Switzerland	229,857	11	273	9

Source: Trademap (2007), International Trade Database Online: http://www.trademap.org

attributable to higher output from the Kroondal, the Impala, the Modikwa, and the Rustenburg Mines. Zimbabwe also recorded a higher output in 2005, with 156,000 oz. of platinum produced, and production is expected to increase in the coming years — to around 3 percent of global production.[25]

Africa does not consume significant amounts of platinum — the vast majority of the platinum is exported to major automotive and jewelry manufacturers in the United States and Asia. Total global demand for platinum in 2005 stood at 6.775 million oz., up on the previous year's demand of 6.695 million oz. and above the total supply of 6.650 million oz. for the year. Demand in 2007 is forecast to reach a record 7.02 million oz. while supply is expected to be slightly less — in other words, in all likelihood leading to continued high prices.[26]

The majority of African platinum is exported either in unwrought or semi-manufactured forms to Europe, Asia, or the United States. Table 3.10 further illustrates the value and destination of South African platinum. Europe remained the top export destination for unwrought platinum in 2006, having overtaken the United States in 2005. Asia (especially Japan) maintains its position of primary importer of semi-manufactured platinum products, mainly for use in the jewelry sector.

African mine production of palladium is expected to increase by a further average of 3 percent per year to 2011, and platinum, by between 2 percent and 3 percent per year.

Diamonds: Africa is the richest and by far the most important continent for diamond-mining, accounting for more than half of world production. The main African sources are in the south, with lower concentrations in the west and central parts of the continent.

World mine production of diamonds in 2005 is estimated at 170 million carats (Mct), a 10-percent increase compared with the revised total for 2004 (154 Mct). It is estimated that the value of mine production increased 16 percent, from USD 10.6 billion

---

[25] Johnson (2007); BGS (2007)
[26] Johnson (2007)

the year before to USD 12.4 billion in 2005. In 2005, Africa's share of world diamond production by volume stood at 52 percent. The increase in worldwide production (volume) resulted from significant increases in production in Australia, Russia and, not least, South Africa. The DeBeers Group, which has mines in Botswana, South Africa, Namibia, and Tanzania, contributed 49 Mct carats, or 29 percent, to world production by mass and an estimated USD 5.1 billion (41 percent) by value.[27]

Botswana retained its rank as the top producer in Africa by value in 2005 (Table 3.11). Most of Botswana's output was produced by the three larger Kimberlite Mines: Jwaneng (15.6Mct), Orapa (14.8Mct), and Letlhakane (1.1Mct). However, production in the Democratic Republic of Congo (DRC) has increased in recent years owing to operations by small operators and artisanal miners.

Table 3.11: Major African Producers of Diamonds (Mct)

Country	2001	2002	2003	2004	2005
Botswana	26.2	28.3	30.4	31.1	31.8
DRC	19.6	22.0	29.0	29.0	27.0
South Africa	11.1	10.8	12.6	14.3	15.8
Angola	5.1	5.7	6.3	7.5	10.0
Namibia	1.5	1.4	1.5	2.0	1.9

Source: BGS (2006)

Diamond production continues to be an important industry for specific countries in West Africa, although the sub-region only accounts for about 2.5 percent of Africa's total production (see Figure 3.5). Nevertheless, diamond resources — and other natural resource-related and geo-political issues — have been key factors in several civil wars and regional conflicts in the area. This is described in further detail in Chapter 4.

The United States continues to be the major global market for gem-quality stones. In 2006, the U.S. market for unset gem-quality diamonds was estimated to have exceeded USD 16.2 billion, accounting for more than an estimated 35 percent of world demand[28]. The major diamond trading centers of Belgium, Israel, and India continue to be the main importers of polished diamonds from Africa.[29]

Although Africa produces more than half of the world's gem-quality diamonds, the majority of its rough diamonds are exported without any value addition — owing to the lack of beneficiation facilities (Table 3.12). The majority of beneficiation takes place in the major diamond trading hubs of Belgium, Israel, and India.

With regard to the influence of the Kimberley Process Certification Scheme (KPCS) on illegal diamond trade (described in detail in Chapter 5), available data suggests that a considerable percentage of the international trade in rough diamonds is now carried out within the framework. Today, over 99 percent of all diamonds are

---

[27] DME (2007)

[28] USGS (2007)
[29] TradeMap (2007): International Trade Database Online: http://www.trademap.org

Figure 3.5: Diamond Operations in West Africa

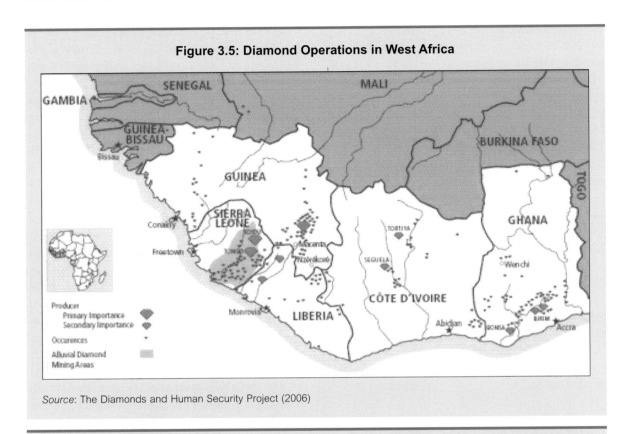

Source: The Diamonds and Human Security Project (2006)

Table 3.12: African Diamond Exports

HS Code	Product Label	Africa's Exports to World	
		Value 2005 (in Thousands of USD)	Annual Growth in Value 2001–2005, (%)
710210	Diamonds, unsorted, worked or not	48,975	−73
710221	Diamonds, industrial, unworked or simply sawn, cleaved, or bruted	169,052	123
710231	Diamonds, non-industrial, unworked or simply sawn, cleaved, or bruted	7,497,806	60
710239	Diamonds non-industrial not specified elsewhere, excluding mounted or set diamonds	851,999	12

Source: Trademap (2007), International Trade Database Online: http://www.trademap.org

certified, through the Kimberley Process, to be from conflict-free sources.

African production of rough diamonds is expected to rise by an average of 3 percent per year to 2011:[30]

- In Angola, the Fucauma, the Kamachia-Kamajiku, the Luarica, and the Rio Lapi Garimpo Mines are expected to contribute to higher output, Angola's share of African diamond production could rise to 11 percent in 2011.
- Production could also rise in Congo (Kinshasa), with the expansion of established schemes.
- Mining exploitation is being pursued in Lesotho, with promising opportunities.
- Zimbabwe's production could increase because of higher production in Murowa.
- Output is also expected to rise in Botswana, Namibia, and South Africa because of higher production at mines operated by the DeBeers Group.

Ferrous Metals

World consumption of ferrous minerals has surged in recent years, due mainly to an acceleration in worldwide growth, especially the continuing double-digit growth of the Chinese economy and the demand for crude steel supply. In 2005, world steel production rose to a new record of 1,128.9 million tons, 6.6 percent higher than the previous record of 1,058.5 million tons attained in 2004. In China, output increased 26.3 percent to 349.0 million tons, account-ing for a 31 percent share of world production; Chinese imports of iron ore rose 32 percent in 2005. World crude steel production continued to increase during 2006 and was 6 percent higher in the first half of 2007, compared with the same period in 2006. Apart from China, the main growth occurred in India and in other Asian countries (China and India alone increased their output by 18 and 17 percent, respectively[31]).

Metal prices have generally trended higher, along with worldwide economic growth. However, the realization by steelmakers and other stakeholders that considerable price hikes in 2004 were unsustainable led to subsequent attempts to contain or even reverse the increases in metal prices. The results have been very mixed: the prices of manganese ore and alloys dropped considerably in 2005, while those of chrome ore, silicon metal and vanadium increased significantly. Nevertheless, all indications are that the trend of rising metal prices will continue as long as worldwide growth continues — especially in parallel with the growth in Asia.[32]

The major *known* deposits of ferrous metals in Africa are presented in Figure 3.6.

Chrome: Africa's major chromite deposits are located towards the south of the continent, in South Africa, Madagascar, and Zimbabwe (several mines with 1–10 million

---

[30] USGS (2005)

[31] IISI (2007): International Iron and Steel Institute (IISI): http://www.worlsteel.org

[32] DME (2007)

Figure 3.6: Main Deposits of Ferrous Metals in Africa

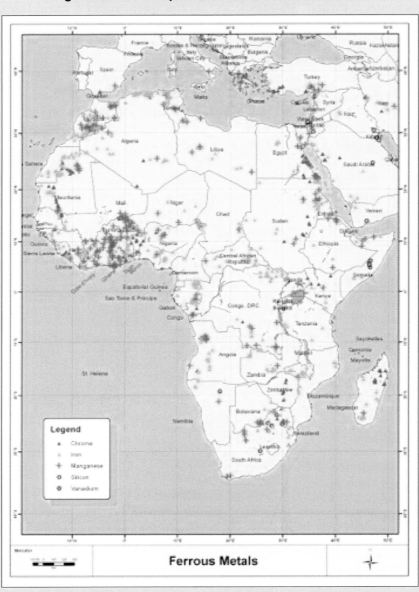

Source: Council for Geoscience and Mintek (2007)

Table 3.13: Major African Producers of Chromite Ores and Concentrates, (000 t)

Country	2001	2002	2003	2004	2005
Madagascar	60.7	10.7	45.0	77.3	140.8
South Africa	5502.0	6435.2	7405.6	7676.3	7502.8
Zimbabwe	780.1	725.8	572.6	668.3	614.2

Source: BGS (2006)

tons; and even up to 100 million tons in South Africa). Other significant deposits, larger than 100,000 tons, are located in Egypt, Sierra Leone, and Sudan. Together, South Africa and Zimbabwe hold more than 84 percent of the world's chromite reserve base — with South Africa contributing 72 percent of this reserve.[33]

In 2005, world chromite production rose to 19.3 million tons, a 12 percent increase over 2004 production levels, in response to a shortage of stainless steel scrap and strong ferrochrome prices. Africa contributed no less than 8.0 million tons to the global figure. South Africa was the world's largest producer of chromite, with 7.5 million tons — accounting for nearly 40 percent of total global production, with Zimbabwe adding 0.61 million tons (Table 3.13).

A total of 93 percent of world chromite ore output was converted into ferrochrome for metallurgical applications (in 2005). Of the remaining 7 percent, the refractory industry accounted for 1 percent, while foundries and chemical industries utilized 3 percent each. African exports of chromite ores and concentrates amounted to 1.5 million tons in 2005. This translates into more than 80 percent of chromite produced being beneficiated (consumed) locally instead of being exported (as a raw material) — in principle a good sign for local industry. However, the majority of the produced ferrochrome in Africa is exported to the world's major steel-producing countries. South Africa thus exported 87 percent of its 2.8 million tons of ferrochrome production, while Zimbabwe exported 90 percent of its 0.26 million tons. Stainless steel production accounts for more than 90 percent of ferrochrome consumption and is the primary influence on world chrome demand.[34]

The strongest growth in stainless steel demand continues to come from China, which saw a 68 percent increase from 2005 to 2006 (partially based on new capacity coming on-stream during 2006). Total world steel demand grew 7.3 percent to 1,087 million tons in 2006. Moreover, confirming trends established in recent years, forecasts point to an increase in steel use, in line with general economic growth. The predicted growth is 5.8 percent — to 1,150 million tons in 2007. This would require an increase in ferrochrome production approaching 286 million tons, and in ore output approaching

[33] DME (2007)

[34] BGS (2006); DME (2007)

Table 3.14: Major African Producers of Iron Ore (million tons)

Country	2001	2002	2003	2004	2005
Algeria	1.2	1.1	1.4	1.7	1.8
Egypt	1.8	2.7	2.9	2.2	2.5
Mauritania	10.3	9.6	10.1	10.7	10.7
Nigeria	—	0.0078	0.0086	0.0084	0.008
South Africa	34.7	36.4	38.1	39.3	39.5
Tunisia	0.2	0.18	0.16	0.26	0.2
Zimbabwe	0.36	0.27	0.41	0.23	0.22

Source: BGS (2006)

788 million tons. Ferrochrome production capacity in South Africa, in particular, is indeed expected to increase through new projects.[35]

Iron Ore: Africa's iron ore deposits are well spread out over the continent, with resources larger than 100 million tons in Algeria, Guinea, Mauritania, South Africa, and the Ivory Coast. Other significant deposits, larger than 10 million tons, are located in 21 other African states (Table 3.14). However, most of the known reserve base is in South Africa.

In 2005, iron ore produced in Africa amounted to 55.9 million tons (pure iron content). South Africa was the leading producer in Africa, accounting for 73 percent of continental output, followed by Mauritania, 20 percent; and Egypt, 6 percent.[36]

In a global context, Africa consumes insignificant amounts of iron ore. China has been the world's largest iron ore-consuming nation since 1992 and has further strength-ened its position in recent years. Between 1998 and 2006, China accounted for 84 percent of total market expansion. About two-thirds of African iron ore is exported. Not surprisingly, a high proportion of iron ore from Africa was exported to China and the Pacific Rim countries, accounting for close to 65 percent of export volumes in 2005. Overall export sales shrank 4 percent to 26.6 million tons, but the revenue from export sales rose 81.6 percent from 2003 to 2005, owing to higher iron ore prices.[37]

Demand for, and production capacity of, iron ore are expected to increase over the coming years. Iron ore producers thus appear confident that the current boom will continue and absorb any additional capacity planned ahead. Chinese demand for iron ore is likely to be the key determinant of the outlook for the global industry in the short to medium terms; hitherto, growth has continued to be impressive. South Africa's iron ore industry is generally well geared for future demands and has initiated various

---

[35] DME (2007)
[36] BGS (2007)

[37] USGS (2005); Harmse and Finca (2007)

infrastructure developments, including the provision of more rolling stocks as well as expansion of 107 export facilities at the ports, thus raising South Africa's capacity to meet the surging demand for its iron ore.[38]

Manganese: Africa's manganese deposits are well spread out over the continent, with resources larger than 10 million tons found in Burkina Faso, Gabon, Ghana, Namibia, South Africa, and Togo. Other significant deposits (larger than 1 million tons) are located in 17 other African states. However, like chrome and iron ore, the majority of the known reserve base is in South Africa.

The 3 major African producers are South Africa, Gabon, and Ghana. Significantly higher outputs have been noted in recent years, especially in Gabon and in South Africa (Table 3.15).

African exports of manganese ore and concentrates amounted to 6.67 million tons — worth an estimated USD 723 million (2005). From 2001 to 2005, manganese ore exports experienced an impressive annual growth rate of 26 percent. The majority of exports were from South Africa; however,

Table 3.15: Major African Producers of Manganese (million tons)

Country	2001	2002	2003	2004	2005
Gabon	1.8	1.9	2.0	2.4	2.9
Ghana	1.0	1.1	1.5	1.6	1.7
South Africa	3.2	3.3	3.5	4.3	5.0

Source: BGS (2006)

although South Africa holds 80 percent of world manganese resources, it only accounts for about 20 percent of the manganese ore world export market.[39]

The outlook is clearly that growth in world crude steel output, the major driver of demand for manganese, will continue to secure a strong demand for African manganese resources. It is estimated that world steel production will reach 1245 billion metric tons by 2010, further stimulating manganese demand and production.[40]

Industrial Minerals

Phosphate: Africa's phosphate rock deposits are well spread out over the continent. The larger resources (> 10 million tons) are located to the south and north of the continent, while other significant deposits (larger than 1 million ton) are found in 20 other African states. Morocco contains the largest phosphate rock reserve in the world, with total resources currently estimated at 85.5 billion m^3.[41]

African production of phosphate rock amounted to about 33.8 million tons in 2004. While output has generally increased in Morocco and Egypt has been on a rising trend in recent years, it has been stable or even down-trending in other countries. Morocco, the leading producer, accounted for 61 percent of continental phosphate rock output in 2004; Tunisia, 17 percent; and South Africa 8 percent.[42]

---

[39] TradeMap (2007): International Trade Database Online: http://www.trademap.org

[40] IISI (2007)

[41] IFA (2007): International Fertilizer Industry Association (IFA): http://www.fertilizer.org

[42] BGS (2006)

---

[38] DME (2007)

Table 3.16: African Crude Fertilizer Exports

Country	Exports (in Thousands of USD)				
	2001	**2002**	**2003**	**2004**	**2005**
Algeria	16,765	16,677	10,865	18,285	N/A
Egypt	413	7,054	9,180	13,449	N/A
Morocco	373,287	364,032	362,863	420,969	513,017
Senegal	16,440	19,051	9,193	8,453	1,374
South Africa	1,494	949	3,914	1,403	3,583
Togo	43,687	41,448	34,960	48,164	34,866
Tunisia	33,725	32,190	25,706	19,745	26,581

Source: TradeMap (2007), International Trade Database Online: http://www.trademap.org

Phosphate rock is mainly used in fertilizer production. It is thus noteworthy that, although Africa has considerable phosphate resources and has around 12 percent of the world's population, it currently accounts for only 2 percent of world fertilizer consumption[43].

In 2005, the value of African exports of phosphate fertilizer amounted to more than USD 560 million. Around 95 percent of export earnings came from superphosphates. Morocco was the primary African exporter, accounting for 90 percent of total export value (Table 3.16).

The general outlook for the world phosphate market is that demand will outpace supply in the forthcoming years, with demand for phosphate fertilizers growing at an average of 2.3 percent per year. African phosphate rock production is expected to increase to 14.8 million tons (P_2O_5 content) in 2009:[44]

- In Morocco, planned expansions should increase Morocco's production to 9 million tons from 2007 and onwards.
- In Senegal, production is expected to rise because of higher capacity (Tobene Mine).
- Production is also expected to rise in Tunisia in the short term, although the long-term export trend seems to be downward.

Fluorspar: World fluorspar[45] production in 2005 is estimated at 4.98 million tons, up from 4.87 million tons in 2004; 4.48 million tons in 2003; and 4.18 million tons in 2002. The market in 2005 continued to be dominated by China, with an estimated

---

[43] IFA (2007)
[44] Ibid.

[45] Fluorspar is used mainly in steelmaking and in the production of hydrofluoric acid and aluminium fluoride. Hydrofluoric acid is a key ingredient for the production of all organic and non-organic chemicals that contain the element fluorine. Aluminium fluoride is used in the production of aluminium (Mineral Information Institute (MII), 2007.

output of 2.4 million tons (48.2 percent of the world total), of which only 730,000 tons was reportedly exported, indicating a considerable inland use and continued reduction in material being made available for world markets. The other major producers were Mexico, 873,000 tons (17.5 percent); Mongolia, 358,000 tons (7.2 percent); South Africa, 275,000 tons (5.2 percent); and Russia, 210,000 tons, (4.2 percent). Namibia, Kenya and Morocco also have a considerable production (Table 3.17.[46]

African fluorspar consumption accounted for only 1.5 percent of global consumption in 2005 — down from 2.3 percent in 2002. The bulk of the produce is thus exported, amounting to over 550,000 tons in 2005 (with an estimated value of USD 83 million). Furthermore, while low-grade fluorspar exports (less than 97 percent calcium fluoride) dropped by 1 percent per year, from 2001 to 2005, high grade fluorspar exports increased by 25 percent per year over the same period.

Table 3.17: Major African Producers of Fluorspar (in Thousands of Tons)

Country	2001	2002	2003	2004	2005
Kenya	118	85	80	107	109
Morocco	96	94	81	81	85
Namibia	81	81	79	104	114
South Africa	286	227	235	275	275

Source: BGS (2006)

Worldwide demand for fluorspar is expected to increase. However, the immediate outlook for the next year is a relatively stable development, with the increase in demand met by further production increases, most likely in Mexico, Mongolia/CIS and possibly also Africa. The tight market has stimulated interest in various projects, including the establishment of an aluminium fluoride plant in Richards Bay, South Africa. Price levels are also likely to remain at the current high levels, but may have peaked and could ease slightly in the medium term.[47]

Other Industrial Minerals: Africa possesses significant amounts of several "other industrial minerals", including clay and limestone. The largest of these known deposits are listed in Table 3.18. It is worth noting that Africa's four largest clay deposits, located in Burkina Faso and Nigeria, have not been exploited to date.

Non-ferrous Metals and Minerals

Aluminum: The majority of Africa's aluminum resources are located in the west of the continent, with major deposits in Burkina Faso, Cameroon, Ghana, Guinea, Ivory Coast, and Sierra Leone. Other significant deposits (larger than 1 million tons) are located in 11 other African states. The map in Figure 3.7 presents an overview of the main non-ferrous metal and mineral deposits in Africa.

International Aluminum Institute figures show that African production of primary aluminum totaled 1.75 million tons in 2005, up 2.4 percent from the 1.71 million tons

---

[46] Mining Journal (2006); BGS (2007)

[47] DME (2007)

Figure 3.7: Major African Deposits of Non-Ferrous Metals and Minerals

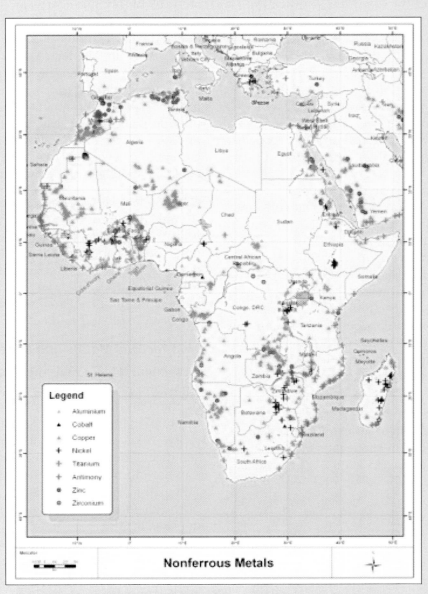

Source: Council for Geoscience and Mintek (2007)

Table 3.18: Major African Deposits of Other Industrial Minerals (> 1 million tons)

State	Deposit Name	Comm1	Status
Burkina Faso	Doumtenga	Clay	Deposit never exploited
Burkina Faso	Bani	Clay	Deposit never exploited
Malawi	Changalumi	Limestone	Continuously producing
Mozambique	Salamanga	Limestone	Intermittently producing
Nigeria	Biseni	Clay	Deposit never exploited
Nigeria	Enugu	Clay	Deposit never exploited

Source: Council for Geoscience (CGS) and Mintek (2007)

produced in 2004. This rather modest increase largely reflects the ongoing expansion in Egypt and is in marked contrast to the 19.8 percent jump recorded from 2003 to 2004. However, overall, African production has increased noticeably since 2001, recording a 28.8 percent increase over this period. The expansion is attributable to capacity improvements in South Africa and Mozambique, where production increased by 27 percent and 108 percent, respectively (Table 3.19).

Meanwhile, Africa's production of bauxite, which is mined to produce alumina and primary aluminum, remained nearly unchanged in 2004 at 15.5 million tons. From 1990 to 2005, Africa's share of world bauxite production actually fell from 16 percent to less than 11 percent. Guinea accounted for about 97 percent of African bauxite production, with Ghana accounting for most of the remainder.

In 2005, African refined aluminium consumption rose 3.4 percent, while world refined aluminum consumption rose 5.7 percent to 31.6 million tons. Not

Table 3.19: Major African Producers of Primary Aluminum (in Thousands of Tons)

Country	2001	2002	2003	2004	2005
Cameroon	80	67	77	85	90
Egypt	190	195	194	216	243
Ghana	161	131	15		13
Mozambique	266	273	407	547	553
South Africa	662	706	732	866	846

Source: BGS (2006)

surprisingly, Asia showed the biggest increase with a 9.4-percent increase (consuming 14.11 million tons).

In 2005 16.5 million tons of aluminum ores and concentrates were exported from Africa, worth about USD 650 million (up 31 percent from 2004), accounting for a sizeable 49 percent of global aluminum trade. The increase was largely driven by a 160-percent rise in demand from the Ukraine. Intra-regional trade accounted for only 0.16 percent of exports. The major importers of African aluminum are Spain,

Ukraine, Ireland, the United States, Germany, and France.[48]

Global aluminum demand is anticipated to continue outstripping production in 2007 and onwards. World industrial growth is being driven by China and the United States. Chinese aluminum consumption is expected to rise 14 percent to 8.1 million tons owing to rising demand from the automobile industry, construction, and infrastructure development for the Beijing Olympics scheduled for 2008.[49]

Copper: Major African copper resources are located towards southern Africa and in the Copperbelt of central Africa, with major deposits in Botswana, Burkina Faso, the DRC, Namibia, South Africa, and Zambia. Other significant deposits (larger than 50,000 tons) are located in 17 other African states.

The Copperbelt, a curved zone measuring 600 km in length by 50 km in width, contains one of the world's greatest concentrations of copper and cobalt deposits. The arc of the deposits extend from Ndola, Zambia, in the east (including the well-known Zambian mines), stretches across the border into the DRC, back into the northwest portion of Zambia, and west into Angola. The Copperbelt deposits are truly exceptional on a world scale, with most having original resources measuring hundreds of millions of tons of ore with grades greater than 2 percent copper. For example, Nchanga in Zambia contains 450 million tons at 4 percent copper, while the cobalt-rich Kolwezi district in the DRC totals over 600 million tons at a grade of 7 percent copper equivalent. The Copperbelt remains largely unexplored using modern exploration practices and new ore bodies similar to the present deposits await discovery.[50]

In 2005, Africa's total copper mine output was 669,000 tons, an 8.9 percent increase compared with 2004, with Zambia and South Africa leading (Table 3.20). Africa's refined copper production rose nearly 6 percent from 2003 to 2004; increased production in Zambia more than offset lower South African production. In comparison, world refined copper production rose by 800,000 tons (4.9 percent) to 17.3 million tons in 2006. This rise was in-line with global GDP growth projections of 4.9 percent.[51]

In 2006, world refined copper consumption increased from 16.6 million tons to 17.0 million tons. However, African consumption of refined copper accounted for only 1 percent of global consumption

Table 3.20: Major African Copper Producers (Mine Production, in Thousands of tons)

Country	2002	2003	2004	2005
Zambia	307	346	412	435
DRC	28	56	69	98
Namibia	18	16	11	10
South Africa	90	89	85	103

Source: BGS (2006)

---

[48] TradeMap (2007): International Trade Database Online: http://www.trademap.org
[49] DME (2007)

[50] Creamer Media (2005)
[51] BGS (2006)

Table 3.21: Copper Production and Consumption (in %, 2005)

	Developed Countries	Africa	L. America and the Caribbean	Developing Asia	SE Europe and CIS	All Regions
Copper production	43	9	21	6	21	100
Copper refined production	34	4	22	27	13	100
Copper consumption	46	1	6	42	5	100

Source: UNCTAD (2006)

(Table 3.21). South Africa alone accounted for more than 80 percent of Africa's refined copper consumption.[52]

Most of Africa's copper production is exported in refined form. Copper exports contribute heavily to the export earnings of Botswana, the DRC, and Zambia. The outlook for African copper mine production is very promising, and the output could nearly double as early as 2009:[53]

- Output is likely to rise sharply in Zambia (owing to ramping up of production, expansion, and opening of new mines from 2005 and onwards).
- Production in Congo could more than triple by 2009 (development of new mines).
- In Mauritania, the Guelb Moghrein Mine has started production.
- Mining from a copper-rich zone at Bisha is likely to start in Eritrea in 2010.
- However, Congolese production is likely to decline by 2011 (shutdown of mines).

Nickel: African nickel resources are well spread out throughout the continent, with major deposits (larger than 100,000 tons) in Botswana, Burundi, Ivory Coast, and Madagascar. Other significant deposits (larger than 50,000 tons) are located in 11 other African states.

In 2005, African nickel mine production increased by over 5 percent; output increased in both Botswana and South Africa, but decreased in Zimbabwe (Table 3.22). The majority of South Africa's nickel output was a co-product of platinum mining.[54]

Table 3.22: Major African Nickel Producers (Mine Production, in Thousands of Tons)

Country	2001	2002	2003	2004	2005
Botswana	22.4	23.8	27.4	22.2	28.2
South Africa	36.4	38.4	40.6	39.8	42.4
Zimbabwe	8.0	7.8	6.6	9.7	7.7

Source: BGS (2007)

---

[52] DME (2007)
[53] USGS (2007)

[54] BGS (2006)

Africa accounted for only 3 percent of global nickel consumption in 2005. South Africa was the primary African consumer, with the stainless steel industry accounting for most of the demand.[55]

African exports of nickel have increased dramatically in recent years, with an annual growth rate of 221 percent from 2001 to 2005. Global exports of nickel ores and concentrates were valued at USD 298 million in 2005. However, by volume, African exports represented 1.5 percent of global nickel ore traded. Intra-regional trade accounted for a large portion of African nickel exports, with 74 percent going to South Africa. China recorded the biggest year-on-year export growth in 2005, with an increase of 343 percent from 2004.[56]

The outlook for expanding nickel production in Africa is bright, with several countries investigating promising opportunities — including Botswana, South Africa, Tanzania, Zambia, and Zimbabwe. Of these countries, Botswana and South Africa already produce nickel and are most likely to see new or expanded capacity in the near future. Some expected country by country developments are as follows:[57]

- The startup of the Ambatovy nickel and cobalt mine in 2008 in Madagascar is a significant development and will account for the majority of the increase in African production in coming years. Madagascar, which did not mine nickel until 2005, could have a 40 percent share of African nickel mine production by 2011.
- By 2009, South Africa's output is expected to rise by about one-third, most of which would be attributable to increased capacity at the Nkomati Mine.
- In Zimbabwe, the Shangani Mine is expected to close by 2008, and the Hunter Road Mine to open by 2011.
- Botswana's production is likely to fall because of the shutdown of the Selebi-Phikwe Mine in 2011.

Zinc: Africa produces 4 percent of global zinc. The majority of its zinc deposits are located towards the north, west, and south east of the continent. Deposits are found in Algeria, Burkina Faso, DRC, Kenya, Namibia, South Africa, Tunisia and Zambia (Table 3.23) In 2005, South Africa was ranked 8th in terms of worldwide zinc reserves.[58]

Table 3.23: Major African Zinc Producers (Mine Production, in Thousands of Tons)

Country	2001	2002	2003	2004	2005
Namibia	37.6	41.0	108.0	202.0	246.0
South Africa	61.2	64.2	41.2	32.0	32.1
Tunisia	40.0	35.7	38.0	29.0	15.7
Algeria	5.7	4.5	1.5	0.1	2.2
Morocco	89.6	90.5	85.2	87.0	128.0

Source: BGS (2006)

---

[55] DME (2007)
[56] DME (2007); USGS (2005)
[57] USGS (2005)

[58] DME (2007); Council for Geoscience (CGS) and Mintek (2007)

Although Africa produces 4 percent of global zinc, it consumes only 2 percent of it. Since 1995, there has been a significant shift in the global distribution of zinc usage. The largest consumer region ten years ago was Europe, which held a third of the market — followed by the USA (16 percent), and China and Japan (10 percent each). By 2005, China had become the most important user of refined zinc metal, with a 28 percent share of the market, Europe's share was 25 percent; while that of the USA and Japan had fallen to 10 percent and 6 percent, respectively.[59]

In 2005, Africa exported 282,911 tons of zinc (2 percent of the global market) at a value of USD 83.8 million. Spain and France were the two major importers of African zinc, importing 21 percent and 20 percent, respectively. Spanish imports grew 32 percent between 2001 and 2005. The clear outlook is that African zinc mine production is likely to increase:[60]

- The majority of expected increases in 2007 are attributable to higher production from the Hajar Mine in Morocco.
- In South Africa, the expansion of the Black Mountain Mine is expected to increase production substantially.
- Output is also likely to increase in Algeria.
- In Congo (Kinshasa), the proposed reopening of the Kipushi Mine and other activities may lead to further increases in production.

---

[59] ILZSG (2007): International Lead Zinc Study Group (ILZSG): http://www.ilzsg.org/
[60] USGS (2005)

- Higher production from the Skorpion smelter in Namibia alone could increase regional production of zinc metal by 12 percent in 2007. Namibia could thus account for 54 percent of Africa's zinc metal output in 2007.

The African Development Bank's Engagement in Africa's Extractive Industries

The overarching objective of the AfDB's engagement in extractive industry (EI) issues in Africa is to help its regional member countries (RMCs) use natural resources to achieve sustainable development, reduce poverty, and improve standards of living on the continent. Africa's *non-renewable* natural resources are considerable and the extractive industries have a very high potential to contribute to economic growth and poverty alleviation in resource-rich countries. Engaging in EI activities is therefore consistent with the core mission of the Bank.

In the early 1990s, the focus of RMCs' development strategies shifted from public to private sector-led growth. Consequently, the Bank also shifted its interventions in the EI sector from assisting the rehabilitation or expansion of large-scale public sector companies to

- promoting initiatives (institutional capacity building and policy reforms) that encourage private investment in the sector; and
- direct investments in private sector operations.

In addition, recent reforms supported by Bank Group programs have sought to address public financial management in resource-rich countries and stressed pro-poor public expenditures and job creation for vulnerable groups — in particular, those living in the zones where the extractive industries are located.

With respect to capacity building, the Bank Group has supported the efforts of several resource-rich RMCs to strengthen the capacity of institutions dealing with or involved in the management of the EI. In this regard, the Bank has supported activities such as (i) modernizing mining cadastre and geological surveys, to make them useful information tools for potential investors; (ii) strengthening the environmental management capacity of EI sector institutions; and, (iii) training stakeholders, government staff and others involved in the management of the sector. Bank Group EI sector activities are underpinned by several supportive policies (Industrial Sector Policy for Public Sector Operations, Private Sector Operations Policies, Enclave Projects Policy, Environmental and Social Policies and Guidelines).

The Bank's EI activities prioritize transparency, governance, and corruption. In line with its commitment to transparency and accountability and with its policy on good governance, the AfDB formally endorsed the Extractive Industries Transparency Initiative (EITI) at the Third Plenary EITI Conference held in Oslo in October 2006. The AfDB, as well as the World Bank and the International Monetary Fund, now holds an observer seat on the new EITI Board.

Several studies and other support activities have been, or are being under-taken as part of the AfBD's activities in the EI sector. These include the following:

- A survey of donor-funded technical assistance for building capacity in EI governance in Africa, with the objective of identifying gaps and overlaps. (This survey was initiated in collaboration with the World Bank and NORAD);

- A study on EI governance in Africa, focusing on the scope of the African "resource boom", the risks that it brings in light of past experience, and how EI revenues can be translated into sustainable development;

- Global advocacy for improving EI sector governance in Africa and creating political will and institutional capacity among RMCs to endorse and implement the EITI; and

- Exchange of knowledge among oil, gas, and mining specialists from the World Bank, NORAD, and the AfDB. An experience-sharing meeting between the AfDB and World Bank oil, gas, and mining specialists took place in Tunis in February 2007, during which agreements were made to increase collaboration in EITI imple-mentation, create a legal rapid response advisory facility for resource-rich RMCs, develop small-scale mining, and support the creation of a geo-logical database for RMCs.

The Bank Group's Legal Service Department is working on the establishment of an African Legal Support Facility under the Bank's "Law for Development Strategy". The Facility will ensure that RMCs have access to the requisite legal support services needed to further their development objectives. The specific EI–related services to be provided by the Facility include

- the provision of technical support for the preparation of appropriate EI laws and regulations in RMCs;
- a review of existing legislation to ensure that budget, revenue, taxation and related laws allow for proper public disclosures;
- training workshops for legal and financial advisors from RMCs to help strengthen their negotiating capacities in EI; and
- the provision of technical legal support during EI contract negotiations.

Furthermore, as part of its commitment to global advocacy for transparency and accountability, the Bank

- hosted the Big Table 2007 on "Managing Africa's Natural Resources for Growth and Poverty Reduction", in collaboration with the Economic Commission for Africa (ECA);
- hosted a session on "Transparent Management of EI Revenues: Making the dividends work for poverty reduction" during the Seventh Annual Conference of the Parliamentary Network in Cape Town;
- convened a high-level symposium during the 2007 AfDB Annual Meetings on "Fragile States and the Role of Extractive Industries";
- devoted the theme of the 2007 African Development Report to "Managing Natural Resources for Sustainable Development in Africa"; and

- carried out policy-based research on the impact of high oil prices the state of oil and gas in Africa and the African Petroleum Fund, to facilitate informed dialogue and decision making by RMCs.

To date, the cumulative volume of the AfDB lending to the EI sector over the last three decades stands at approximately USD 1.6 billion, and the annual growth rate of lending has averaged 20 percent since the mid-1990s.

The Bank's investments in the extractive industries have focused on direct investments through public and private sector windows to develop and enhance productive capacity (investment in mining, oil and gas extraction activities), rehabilitation and restructuring support. These operations account for 86 percent of the Bank Group's total lending to the EI sector; technical assistance for capacity building had been allocated 13 percent; and support for feasibility studies the remaining 1 percent (Figure 3.8).

Sector-wise (oil and gas versus metals, and so forth), the most significant resource in terms of Bank Group investments is the metal sub-sector, which accounts for about 38 percent of the Bank's operations in the EI sector. Bank Group support to the oil and gas sector stands at 27.6 percent, and to the "fertilizer-minerals" sector, 22.3 percent (Figure 3.9).

The Bank has financed 48 operations through its public sector window, for a total of over USD 1.1 billion. Examples of these operations include the rehabilitation of the copper industry in Zambia; the development

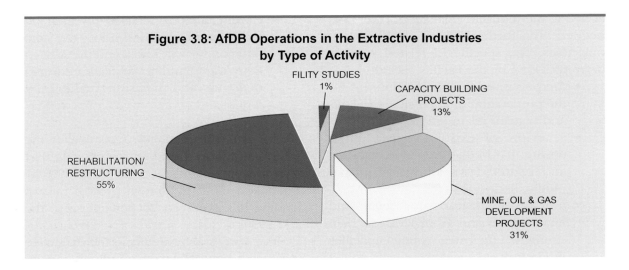

Figure 3.8: AfDB Operations in the Extractive Industries by Type of Activity

FILITY STUDIES 1%

CAPACITY BUILDING PROJECTS 13%

REHABILITATION/ RESTRUCTURING 55%

MINE, OIL & GAS DEVELOPMENT PROJECTS 31%

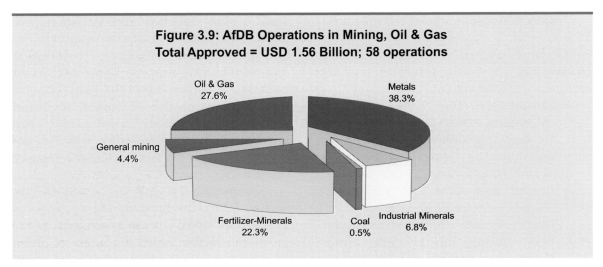

Figure 3.9: AfDB Operations in Mining, Oil & Gas
Total Approved = USD 1.56 Billion; 58 operations

Oil & Gas 27.6%

Metals 38.3%

General mining 4.4%

Fertilizer-Minerals 22.3%

Coal 0.5%

Industrial Minerals 6.8%

of an oil pipeline between Tanzania and Zambia; the modernization of the phosphate industry in Tunisia; the development of gold fields in the Democratic Republic of Congo (DRC); the expansion of the iron industry in Mauritania; and the production and transformation of bauxite in Guinea. Other projects have addressed the social and environmental aspects of the EI sector. With respect to direct lending, private sector investments in the EI sector have been increasing since the establishment of the private sector window and the granting of the first such loan in 1993. As of April 2007, ten private-sector operations had been financed for a total of USD 421 million. The volume of private sector lending to the EI sector is expected to continue to grow in coming years.

The Bank Group's non-lending activities in the EI sector are relatively new. Several studies, workshops, and seminars have recently been launched and the Bank has formerly endorsed the EITI (as mentioned above). With respect to economic and sector work, a number of studies are in their final stages (for example, the impact of high oil prices on African economies, the state of oil and gas in Africa, natural resources management in Africa).

The Bank's experience in the EI sector has been mixed. A review of project completion reports for several Bank-financed projects reveals that while the development impact of some operations has been positive, the impact of others has been rather limited. However, given the small number of operations financed by the Bank and the relatively low volume of its lending to the EI sector, it can be concluded that the Bank's contribution to the development of the sector in Africa has generally been limited and falls short of its potential. In fact, the Bank has provided only a small portion of the financing invested in the sector, and EI lending represents a very small share (3.4 percent) of the Bank's total lending. In addition, the Bank's activities in the sector have not been undertaken within the framework of a comprehensive strategy, and thus challenges posed by the sector are yet to be addressed in a comprehensive manner.

The Bank is taking steps to address this situation. These include the creation of a Governance Division and a Natural Resources and Environmental Management Division under the recent reform (restructuring) implemented at the Bank. These Divisions are now actively engaged in these issues. The most recent milestones reached in this regard include a *Task Force Report* on the Bank's engagement in the extractive industries, as well as recent proposals submitted to the Board regarding support for EITI implementation in five RMCs.

Management of Non-Renewable Natural Resources

The rest of this chapter summarizes the various approaches used by African nations to manage, conserve, and enhance their minerals and fossil fuels and the benefits and wealth they can reap from utilizing these resources. In this regard, it is important to recognize that renewable and non-renewable resources are fundamentally different in character and are thus managed differently. This applies to the extraction and utilization process itself, policies, regulations, revenues and taxation, sustainability, rehabilitation and all other key aspects.

To create and sustain wealth in the long term, mineral resources have to be converted into other forms of capital (human, financial, and manufactured) and more sustainable livelihood opportunities. Between 2000 and 2005, world trade value in minerals grew by 17 percent per year, while production rose by 2.5 percent. Mineral prices are highly volatile, but, in general, they have risen significantly over the past five years, driven in part by high demand and growth rates in China and India[61]. As outlined in detail in the previous

---

[61] OECD (2007)

sections, Africa has considerable non-renewable resources: some are currently being extracted, some are recognized reserves, and others are yet to be discovered. The growing interest in African resources is thus fundamentally about its non-renewable resources. This current scramble for African resources is gaining considerable international attention (further discussed in Chapter 4).

Overall, the management of non-renewable resources involves

- ensuring availability (exploitation and extraction) of the resources;
- allocating resources amongst competing players — may entail participation of local versus international players;
- creating an environment for resource industries to flourish;
- ensuring integrity in the management of revenues received from the extraction, mining, and processing of resources;
- developing policies to manage national ownership of non-renewable resources;
- limiting the environmental impact of the exploitation of resources;
- ensuring health and safety in the process of resource exploitation;
- converting resource use into sustainable economic development through linkages; and
- using resource rents for the development of economic and social capital and ensuring the overall creation of wealth and wellbeing in a country.

A key concern is that African governments that are major producers of fossil fuels and minerals do not receive (sufficiently) large rents or revenues from the production of these extractive products. This may stem from a number of reasons, including: fiscal regimes that are not designed to extract maximum rents; and mineral policies that are designed primarily to favor the promotion and attraction of investments and have not evolved with the changing global dynamics and national interests.

It may be time to challenge the conventional wisdom, including resource governance policies promoted by multilateral institutions in the 1970's — which are no longer appropriate because circumstances have changed. Many of these policies are pro-private sector, and, in many instances, do not ensure maximum benefits for the countries supplying the resources. A key emerging issue is tax avoidance, partly due to transfer pricing, an issue the existing mineral policies did not anticipate.

The previous sections in this chapter presented a status assessment and breakdown of non-renewable resources in Africa, as they are known and recorded at present (many resources are undoubtedly yet to be discovered). These resources have been managed with highly different results by different peoples and nations on the continent. In some countries, the resources have provided the backbone for strong economic and social growth; in others, they have directly or indirectly led to conflicts and even economic downturns. It is evident that natural resource wealth and management of minerals and fossil fuels raise unique challenges and include an element of vulnerability to "boom and bust cycles" and to the "Dutch Disease" syndrome. The paradox of natural resource wealth and the so-called "Resource Curse Syndrome" is discussed at length in Chapter 4.

Using an analytical framework, this section focuses on analyzing and presenting current management practices in Africa. The framework draws on the experiences of resource-based economies that have successfully strengthened and diversified their economies from resource capital (these include relative success stories such as Botswana and also, to a considerable extent, South Africa).

Framework for Natural Resources Management

The key feature of the framework, which is based on experience and on track records, is that a proper natural resource policy comprises a legislative framework as well as fiscal terms and policies that promote the sustainable exploitation of natural resources. The framework includes a comprehensive description of the purpose of, and characteristics of effective natural resource management — thus implying that a crucial element is *implementation or enforcement* of policies and strategies.

While most of the framework presented above is self-explanatory, some additional remarks are relevant with regard to fiscal regimes and sustainable development of non-renewable resources.

Fiscal Regimes: for fossil fuels and minerals in Africa are by no means uniform. A multitude of royalties, taxes, resource rent, incentives, state equity levels, and so on, have been developed to foster interest in

exploration and investments, on the one hand, and capture some of benefits for the state and the public, on the other hand. Tables 3.25 and 3.26 below outline key characteristics of fiscal regimes in Africa; Table 3.25 presents the fiscal petroleum regimes applied and Table 3.26 the mineral taxation used in selected countries. As clearly demonstrated, the levels and principles applied are as heterogeneous as the landscape and people in Africa.

Sustainable development: of non-renewable resources encompasses all the policies, principles, and practices that support the utilization of mineral resources in a manner that does not prevent future generations from accessing the mineral resource(s) or its benefits[62]. A key purpose is to ensure that mineral-hosting nations in Africa benefit from their mineral endowments in the short and long terms, for example, by using the revenues accrued from mineral resource developments for socio-economic development programs, the creation of manufacturing industries, and other initiatives (further discussed in Chapter 5).[63]

Mining labor inputs and direct or indirect natural resource extraction employment is an important issue that is often overlooked in Africa and that should be coordinated efficiently within a country's mining policy. A proper extraction policy should, for instance, provide guidelines for the inclusion of foreign labor coupled with a concise framework for trans-migration and local district hiring. Other issues, often lacking in

[62] UNECA and AfDB (2007)
[63] Rogers (2007)

Table 3.24: Framework for Management of Natural Resources in Africa

Criteria	Description	Purpose
Natural Resource Policy	A key document that outlines the stakeholder's objectives in the exploitation of natural resources. It addresses all issues related to the exploitation of natural resources.	— Coordinate the use of natural resources by prescribing the role of the government and that of stakeholders (those who affect or are affected by the natural resource) in relation to the exploitation of natural resources. — Enable the exploitation of natural resources in line with sustainable development practices. — Ensure the use of revenues accrued from the exploitation of natural resources for investments, e.g. infrastructure or socio-economic development programs.
Legal and Regulatory Framework	The legislative framework outlines the relevant elements of the natural resource policy in detail, setting the legal and regulatory framework, including procedures to be followed in the exploitation of natural resources.	— Provide a legislative framework that administers the exploitation of natural resources. This includes penalties for those who violate the laws governing the exploitation of natural resources. — Provide licenses, permits and rights for natural resource exploitation.
Fiscal Regime	This section of the natural resource policy illustrates fiscal terms and policies pertaining to the exploitation of natural resource.	— Provide fiscal terms that administer all commercial activities pertaining to exploitation of natural resources; for example, the imposition of taxation measures that are enforced to compel those who exploit natural resources to provide compensation. — Non renewable resources should generally have higher (and specialized) taxation levels than other resources as they cannot be replaced; i.e. so economic rents compensate for their removal.
Sustainable Development	The section of the natural resource policy that promotes sustainable exploitation of natural resources. Sustainable development entails social, economic, and environmental issues. Non-renewable natural resources and renewable natural resources are managed differently, due to the "unsustainable nature" of non-renewable resources.	— Ensure respect of sustainable development principles. If properly prepared and implemented, policies tied to sustainable development promote socio-economic and environmentally sustainable exploitation of natural resources. This also includes "derived effects" of the exploitation. For example, promoting proper co-coordination of waste management. Waste that emanates from the exploitation of natural resources should be managed effectively so that it does not surpass the capacity of the natural environment to absorb the waste products.

Source: Adapted from Otto & Cordes (2004)

Table 3.25: Key Characteristics of Fiscal Petroleum Regimes

Country	Royalties	Production sharing	Income tax rate	Resource rent tax	D.W.T. (nonres)	Investment incentives	State equity
Angola	...	15–80%(P)	50%	None	...	Yes (E)	25%
Cameroon	Negotiable	None	48.65%	None	25%	Yes (O)	50% (C)
Chad	12.5%	None	50%	None	20%	None	10%
Gabon	10–20%	65–85%(V)	Gov. Share	None	...	Yes (E)	15% (C)
Mozambique	8%	10–50%	40%	None	...	Yes (E)	None
Niger	12.5%	None	45%	None	18%	Yes (E)	...
Nigeria	0–20%	20–65%	50, 85%	None	10%	Yes (E, Cr)	Variable
Sudan	None	60–80%	None	None	None	...	None
Algeria	10–20%	60–88%(P)	Gov. Share	None	20%	None	30% (C)
Egypt	10%	70–87%(V)	Gov. Share	None	None	Yes (I)	None
Libya	16.67%	5–90%	None	None	...	...	...
Tunisia	2–15%	None	50–75%	Yes(ror)	None	Yes (E, U, I)	Negotiable

Notes: 1/ Production sharing linked to physical volume of production (V), years of production (T), or realized profitability (P)

2/ Investment incentives: tax holiday (H), accelerated depreciation (A), tax credit (Cr), current expensing of exploration and / or development cost (E), duty exemption for imports of equipment and capital goods (I), unlimited loss-carry forward (U) and other (O)

3/ The maximum equity share that the state can select to take, often on a carried basis (C)

Source: Adapted from ESMAP (2004)

Table 3.26: Mineral Taxes in Selected Countries

Country	Corporate Income Tax	Royalty/Mining License Tax	Value Added Tax (on Imported Equipment)	Typical Import Duty	Typical Export Duty
Botswana	25%	15% of realized value	n/a	n/a	n/a
Ivory Coast	35%; excess profit tax applies at profit threshold	2.5–3% of mine mouth value-rates vary by mineral	10% — exemption is possible on a case by case basis. There is no refund on VAT	0.75% exemption is possible on a case by case basis	Export duty only on diamonds, (18%)
South Africa	30%+STC (rate on dividend), but special rules for gold mines.	Rates determined by contract; 1–8% gross revenue royalty	14% — refundable within a month in case of exports	Duty applies to spares and components	None

Source: Shukla (2007)

Box 3.1: Artisanal and Small-Scale Mining in Africa

Most attention in the mining industry is focused on large operations, governments, private companies, and so forth. However, in many parts of Africa, extraction of minerals by artisanal and small-scale mining is a very important activity. It is conducted by people working with simple tools and equipment, usually in the informal sector, outside the legal and regulatory framework. The vast majority are very poor, exploiting marginal deposits in rural, harsh, and often dangerous conditions.

Artisanal mining is first and foremost a livelihood strategy, and, for many people, represents the most promising, if not the only, income opportunity available. It is certainly not without challenges and problems, including, for example, concerns about environmental damage (such as the use of mercury in gold mining); social disruption and conflicts over land and income; poor health conditions including the spread of HIV/AIDS; unsafe operations and frequent accidents; child labor; and the general unregulated nature of the activities. Artisanal miners often work seasonally (for instance, gemstone mining in Malawi in the dry season), sometimes even on an *ad hoc* day-to-day basis, which further complicates any formalization effort.

Recent research estimates that some 13 million people work directly in artisanal and small scale mining worldwide, and the livlihoods of no less than 100 million are significantly affected by related activities, but usually in appalling conditions.[64] Some very conservative estimates for workers directly engaged in Africa are: 100–200,000 in Burkina Faso; 200,000 in Ghana; 40,000 in Malawi; 200,000 in Mali; 60,000 in Mozambique; 550,000 in Tanzania; and 350,000 in Zimbabwe. The numbers are expected to increase very rapidly with the rising prices of minerals and gemstones, especially in parts of Africa where there are conflicts or where economies continue to falter (for instance, Zimbabwe). Furthermore, according to the International Labour Office, in recent years artisanal and small-scale mining have accounted for 15–20 percent of the world's non-fuel mineral production.

In most cases, governments and many others have had a very negative view of artisanal mining activities, but have often *de facto* left it alone and not attempted to optimize it in order to obtain revenue from the operations (legalize it) or to mitigate its negative consequences.

Source: Mining, Minerals and Sustainable Development Project (MMSD) (2002)

---

current regimes, include education, training, and skills development for employees as well as adherence to safety and health measures.[65] A further, often highly neglected aspect of management of resources and mining operations in Africa, is the considerable number of people engaged in artisanal and small-scale mining (Box 3.1).

The following specific principles, which are also largely absent in the majority of African countries, can improve and enhance extraction to ensure more sustainable development:[66]

— preserving strategic minerals of importance for future development (and generations),
— enforcing production quotas or caps,
— limiting the number of exploitation licenses used, the areas available for exploitation or the number of extraction sites,
— ensuring longer mine life by limiting annual capacity,

---

[64] World Bank (2007)
[65] Ibid.

[66] Otto and Cordes (2004); Rogers (2007)

— establishing a profits trust framework,

— establishing punishment and incentives to promote potential alternatives, and

— positioning current unprofitable tailings and spoils.

Case examples of Management Principles Applied in Africa

Africa's experience in natural resource management is mixed. For example, it is generally recognized that oil-rich countries in sub-Saharan Africa, in particular, have not reaped the full benefits of oil. This section focuses on the application of management principles in Africa. The analytical framework presented above is used to analyze key features and aspects of the application of management principles in selected countries in Africa (Table 3.27): Nigeria (fossil fuels); Algeria (fossil fuels); Gabon (fossil fuels, and some metals); Angola (fossil fuels and some

Table 3.27: Management Principles Applied in Africa — Case Examples

Country	Natural Resource Policy	Legal and Regulatory Framework	Fiscal Regime	Sustainable Development
Nigeria	Formulation involved stakeholders. Social, economic, and environmental aspects of mining included. Coherent and appropriate.	Mineral endowments are vested in the government, but the mining law encourages private ownership. A coherent mineral law.	Fiscal policy is comprehensive with many features and options for reductions but also requirements, which may deter some investors.	Relevant policies aimed at achieving sustainable development endorsed, but framework can be modified, e.g. to enact mining closure plans
Algeria	Unique (appropriate) method adopted in formulation of policies. Policy meets the recommended criteria. Aim is to attract foreign direct investment.	The legislative framework is coherent and, in most aspects, meets the criteria for appropriate management.	Fiscal regime is coherent and, in most aspects, meets sound management criteria. The State also has options to acquire equity stakes.	Necessary mechanisms required to promote sustainable dev. in mining industry endorsed. Responsible ministries are active, etc.
Gabon	Policy is not a rational mineral policy as it lacks a coherent fiscal framework and other key aspects.	Basic features of mineral legislation present, but not entirely coherent.	Basic features are present, but regime is not comprehensive or coherent.	Some key aspects are addressed, but strategy and approach are not entirely coherent or comprehensive.
Angola	Main objectives are clear (e.g. to reduce state-owned mining). However, policy could be more comprehensive and also target what the considerable revenues should be used for.	Adequate and relevant, but mining rights could be more descriptive in illustrating the process of acquiring and utilizing mineral rights.	Fiscal regime is substantiated by several mechanisms that regulate relevant commercial activities and taxation incentives, etc. It has sound priorities.	In principle, appropriate mechanisms developed. Plans to train local people in order to involve them in the petroleum industry.

Table 3.27: (continued)

Country	Natural Resource Policy	Legal and Regulatory Framework	Fiscal Regime	Sustainable Development
South Africa	Formulation entailed participation of all main stakeholders and a white paper was issued for public comment. In principle, addresses all key issues and is very comprehensive.	Legislation is comprehensive, concise, and stable. Several pieces of supportive legislation enacted (e.g. on social aspects).	Fiscal regime is very comprehensive, perhaps too much in some cases, as this could deter investors.	Several important mechanisms put in place to meet the social, economic and environmental impacts of mining. In other words a good example for others.
Tanzania	Formulation process heavily influenced by international donors and stakeholders, but meets the most important criteria.	Legislative framework incorporates most relevant key features, such as the right to trade in mineral rights and improved security of tenure.	Taxation and the fiscal regime are concise and, in principle, adequate.	Key principles have been developed, but further efforts needed to execute sustainable development initiatives efficiently. Mining closure needs more attention.
Ghana	Meets key criteria recommended for a coherent mineral policy	The mineral legislation clearly illustrates the framework required for proper administration of the mineral sector	Stable and concise fiscal framework	In principle, a significant number of relevant mechanisms are in place. However, resources appear to be lacking.

Sources: Assessments extracted from Campbell (2004); Mines2006 (2006); Dales (2006); USGS (2005)

metals and non-metals); Ghana (bauxite, aluminum, gold, manganese ore and silver); South Africa (gold, platinum, nickel, uranium, vanadium etc.); and Tanzania (primarily gold, nickel, iron ore and titanium).

Summarizing and Looking Forward

The overview and description of key issues and the analysis of the selected case countries reveal that all countries assessed have taken important steps to formulate policies and legislation, and incorporate fiscal terms into their strategies. However, more coherent principles, structures and, above all, due

diligence in enforcement would considerably increase benefits and sustainability for all countries. Some concrete issues related to sustainable development need to be improved. These include, incorporating environmental aspects and the full extraction cycle, including mine closure and rehabilitation. Above all, although the countries have the means and measures in place to secure significant economic and social benefits from fossil fuels and mineral exploitation, a number of key questions remain:

- Are the countries in Africa benefiting *enough* considering the resources at hand?

Box 3.2: Diamond Mining in Botswana

Botswana is a unique example in many ways and provides a striking example of how a developing country can use its mineral wealth (diamonds) for poverty reduction. It has evolved from one of the poorest countries in the world to a middle-income country. This success has been widely attributed to sound economic policies, especially in managing its large diamond resources, and to a commitment to fiscal stability.

At independence in 1966, Botswana was a country with one million people and an economy that was dependent on the cattle industry. The first government after independence made two decisions that would later prove to be crucial for growth and development. A Mines and Minerals Act gave all mineral rights to the state rather than to tribal authorities. Foreign firms were invited to engage in exploitation for minerals. It soon became apparent that the country was richly endowed with, amongst other assets, kimberlitic diamond deposits. The second crucial decision was the renegotiation of the deal with the mining firm, DeBeers in 1975, allocating half of all profits from diamond revenues to the state. The government channeled its revenues, primarily from diamond exports, into investments in education, health care, and infrastructure, while maintaining tight fiscal control. A contributing factor was the creation of a set of rules, a Sustainability Budget Index, to avoid fiscal deficits by keeping track of the ratio between consumption expenditures and non-mineral revenues. Natural resources revenues are used for investments rather than for consumption as long as the ratio remains less than one.

Furthermore, Botswana has had a well-functioning democracy and, all in all, a transparent administration (the good governance dimension). As a result, it has experienced almost three decades of high growth rates. By the late 1990s, the country had risen to the status of a middle-income country.

Source: OECD (2007)

- Is the wealth created reaching the poor and the general populations to a sufficient degree? and
- Are the resources ultimately benefiting the countries?

Africa's track record certainly varies, and policy- and decision-makers need to learn from both good (see Box 3.2 on Botswana) and bad experiences.

By and large, as demonstrated by the case examples, many countries in Africa do, in fact, have policies, legislation, and fiscal regimes in place that would ensure sustainable exploitation of natural resources and shared benefits across the society — with some relevant modifications. Unfortunately,

the implementation of the principles and the legislation is an entirely different dimension for the majority of the countries. In other words, lack of enforcement, poor institutions, limited transparency, and poor governance are the problems. Good governance is critical if the benefits from mining are to reach the poor and contribute to stable growth. Recent debates have emerged on ensuring greater development outcomes from mineral extraction. Four central issues have emerged from recent experiences: (i) fairer contracts; (ii) revenue transparency; (iii), and (iv) mining communities and beneficiation (adding value prior to export). These issues are analyzed in some detail in Chapters 4 and 5.

CHAPTER 4

Africa's Natural Resources: The Paradox of Plenty

Introduction

Africa is blessed with vast natural resources and rich environments (see Chapters 2 and 3). It is generously endowed with productive land and with valuable natural resources, which include renewable resources (such as water, forestry, and fisheries) and non-renewable resources (minerals, coal, gas, and oil). Natural resources dominate many national economies and are central to the livelihoods of the poor rural majority. These resources are the basis of income and subsistence for large segments of Africa's population and constitute a principal source of public revenue and national wealth.

Under the right circumstances, a natural resource boom can be an important catalyst for growth, development, and the transition from cottage industry to factory production. Indeed, with the right approach natural resources can be used to make the transformation from a low-value economy that relies on exports of primary commodities to one with a substantial labor-intensive manufacturing base.

It is commonly agreed that one of the avenues for getting many of the poorest African countries out of the low-income trap is to provide them with a big demand push that will generate enough demand complementarities to expand the size of markets and recover the fixed costs of industrialization. Natural resource wealth could be used to pursue this goal. Unfortunately, in many African countries natural resource booms have only to a limited extent set off a dynamic growth process (see Box 4.1). This is largely due to failure to implement the right growth-promotion policies and to ensure that strong institutions are in place — suggesting that it is very difficult to make the big push towards diversification and development of manufacturing in the resource-rich parts of Africa. The danger is that much of Africa is not industrialized and is stagnating in a staple trap, dependent on exports of a few mineral resources.[1] In particular, oil resources and other point resource-dependency could, with the wrong policies, lead to this scenario.

The failure of natural resource wealth to lead to the expected economic growth and development has been attributed to several factors, including

- the so-called "Dutch Disease" — the syndrome of rising real exchange rates and wages driving out pre-existing export and import-competing industries;
- rent-seeking by elites and others that otherwise could put their energies into profit-making activities;

---

[1] See Auty (2001); Auty (2004); and Ploeg (2007) for detailed discussion of these aspects

- volatility of prices and the "asymmetry of adjustment" (it is easier to ramp up public expenditure than to wind it down again);
- inflexibility in labor, product, and asset markets; and
- tensions between oil-producing and non-oil producing regions within countries.

What is the Resource Curse?

The resource curse refers to a situation whereby a country has an export-driven natural resources sector that generates large revenues for government but leads paradoxically to economic stagnation and political instability.[2] It is commonly used to describe the negative development outcomes associated with non-renewable extractive resources (petroleum and other minerals).[3] Essentially, the resource curse refers to the inverse association between development and natural resource abundance. It has often been asserted that petroleum, in particular, brings trouble— waste, corruption, consumption, debt over- hang, deterioration, falling apart of public services, wars, and other forms of conflicts, among others. Thus, natural resource- abundant countries tend to grow slower than expected — considering their resource wealth — and, in many cases, actually grow slower than resource-scarce countries.

A common thread in explaining the resource curse — along with the other broad explanations provided above — is the central role of government behavior. The key issue here is how governments administer resource wealth and how they use natural resource revenues.

Historical accounts indicate that natural resource booms do not always worsen economic performance, and can indeed catalyze economic transformation. A resource boom can lead to growth expansion, as demonstrated in the case of Europe (indus- trialization), the "new economies" (Australia, Canada and the United States), and tropical subsistence agricultural economies without manufacturing. Today, resource-rich coun- tries like the United Arab Emirates, Kuwait, and Qatar are using revenues from their resource wealth to construct mega-cities out of desert land, thereby also generating con- siderable down- and side-stream economic activities and additional incomes. These countries have also undertaken large-scale foreign investments, which not only promote economic development, but also foster inter- generational equity. The key point is that the often referred to "natural resource curse" can be avoided with the right knowledge, institutions and policies.

Key Questions

Drawing on an appropriate theoretical framework, and on the logic presented in the previous section, this chapter examines the *African evidence* of the paradox of plenty and the "resource curse" with a view to exploring the following issues and questions:

- Is natural resource abundance in Africa a curse or a blessing?
- Has the management of natural resources really stunted the growth

---

[2] Overseas Development Institute (ODI) (2006)
[3] Catholic Relief Services (2003)

Box 4.1: Cross-Country Evidence of the Natural Resource Curse

There are, indeed, resource-rich countries that benefit from their natural wealth, but overall, the economies of many resource-rich countries are in a surprisingly poor state. History clearly shows that natural resource wealth may harm economic performance and make citizens worse off. There are well-known examples of countries whose abundant natural resources have been accompanied by bad macroeconomic performance and growing inequality among its citizens. A dramatic example is Nigeria.

Nigeria has been a major oil exporter since 1965. Its oil revenues per capita have increased tenfold in 35 years, but its income per capita has stagnated since independence in 1960, making Nigeria one of the 15 poorest countries in the world. During this period, the country's poverty headcount ratios have almost tripled, while the rich have grabbed a much larger part of income. Huge oil exports have not benefited the average Nigerian. Despite the rapid accumulation of physical capital, Nigeria has suffered a declining Total Factor Productivity (TFP), and capacity utilization of manufacturing hovers around a third. Successive military dictatorships have plundered oil wealth and many suspect transfers of funds (of undisclosed amounts) have occurred. Oil wealth has fundamentally altered politics and governance in Nigeria. Other oil exporters such as Iran, Venezuela, Libya, Iraq, Kuwait, and Qatar have also experienced negative growth during the last few decades and OPEC as a whole has seen a decline in Gross National Product (GNP) per capita.

In contrast, Botswana has managed to beat the resource curse. Forty percent of Botswana's Gross Domestic Product (GDP) stems from diamonds. It has the second highest public expenditure on education and has enjoyed the world's highest growth rate since 1965. Its GDP per capita is ten times that of Nigeria. The Botswana experience is noteworthy, since the country started its post-colonial experience with minimal investments and substantial inequality.

The United Arab Emirates also seems to have turned the resource curse into a blessing, The UAE accounts for close to 10 percent of the world's crude oil and 4 percent of the world's natural gas reserves. The UAE's government debt is very small, inflation is low, and hydrocarbon wealth has been used to modernize infrastructure, create jobs, and establish a generous welfare system. Major strides in life expectancy and literacy have been made through universal and free access to education and health care. In anticipation of the depletion of its natural reserves, Dubai has diversified into light manufacturing, telecommunications, finance, and tourism, and the other emirates have focused on small-scale manufacturing, agriculture, quarrying, cement, and shipping services. By diversifying, the UAE is investing in sustainable growth.

Sources: Sala-i-Martin and Subramanian (2003); van der Ploeg (2007)

---

and development prospects of many resource-rich African economies?

- How does the volatility in the export value of resources contribute to volatility of growth in GDP per capita and to growth and development in general?
- What political and social factors enable some resource-abundant

countries to utilize their natural resources to promote development and prevent other resource-abundant countries from doing the same?

- How does access or non-access to the coast (that is, being a landlocked country or not) affect development parameters?

- How, or why, has the potential resource curse been avoided in some cases and how can it be overcome in the future?

Stylized Features of Africa's Resource-Rich Economies

In most of the analyses that follow, African countries are categorized as:

(1) Resource-rich (oil and mineral exporters);
(2) Resource-scarce;
(3) Land-locked (resource-rich and resource-scarce);
(4) Coastal (resource-rich and resource-scarce), and
(5) The SANE group (Africa's four largest economies: South Africa, Algeria, Nigeria and Egypt).

A complete listing is presented in Appendix 4A. Africa has 22 resource-rich countries, defined in the analysis framework for this Report as countries where fuel and mineral exports contribute over 20 percent to the GDP. These countries represented slightly more than two-thirds of Africa's GDP and half of its population in 2006 (Table 4.1). Half of these countries are oil exporters, while the other half are mineral exporters. It is worth noting that only four of the resource-rich countries are landlocked and that three of Africa's four largest economies that make up the SANE (South Africa, Algeria, and Nigeria) are both resource-rich and coastal countries. In contrast, there are 31 resource-scarce countries, accounting for 30 percent and 48 percent of regional GDP and population, respectively. One-third of these countries are land-locked.

High Export Dependence in Africa's Resource-Rich Countries

Africa's resource-rich countries continue to experience high dependence on natural resource exports for both foreign exchange and revenues (see Appendix Table 4B). For example, of the total increase in export values in African countries between 2000 and 2005, fuels accounted for 65 percent; manufactures, 24 percent; and food and raw materials about 5 percent each. Since manufactures include processed natural resources, Africa's export boom seems to be largely driven by natural resources. Since 1990, the share of fuels in the total exports of African oil-exporting countries has increased by about 12 percentage points, to almost 90 percent. The dependence of African non-fuel exports on agricultural commodities has declined, while exports of certain resource-linked manufacturing products have increased. In these countries, manufactured exports accounted for nearly 60 percent of all non-fuel exports in 2005, up from 37 percent in 1985. Within manufacturing, the major categories are precious stones (the share of which has more than trebled since 1985); and silver and platinum (the share of which has nearly doubled). Iron and aluminum are the other major product categories.[4]

High Fiscal Dependence in Africa's Resource-Rich Countries, but Improving Fiscal Performance

Before the current resource boom, resource-rich African countries had been challenged to reap the full benefits of their resource endowments. Owing to boom-bust cycles,

---

[4] IMF (2006)

Table 4.1: Macroeconomic Indicators

2006, or most recent year with available data

| | Per Capita Income (US$) | Area (Km²) | Population | | Nominal GDP | | GDP($ billions PPP) | | Annual GDP growth Rate 81–2006 | Share of Africa Export | FDI ($ millions) | |
			Million of Pop	% share of Africa	Billions US$	% share of Africa	Billions US$	% share of Africa			Millions US$	% share of Africa
Africa	838	30,323	924.3	100.0	1079.4	100.0	1886.5	100.0	3.0	100.0	30669	100.0
Resource-rich countries	991	20,975	482.5	52.2	750.9	69.6	1137.8	60.3	2.4	80.5	19587	63.9
Oil-exporting countries	935	11,537	278.2	30.1	431.0	39.9	519.6	27.5	2.4	55.1	10503	34.2
Mineral-exporting countries	1067	9,438	204.3	22.1	319.9	29.6	618.2	32.8	2.4	25.4	9084	29.6
Resource-scarce, countries	671	9,347	441.8	47.8	328.5	30.4	748.7	39.7	3.8	19.5	11082	36.1
Landlocked countries	264	7,979	225.0	24.3	82.5	7.6	202.2	10.7	3.3	6.7	2330	7.6
Resource-rich, landlocked countries	588	3,241	27.7	3.0	29.0	2.7	46.6	2.5	4.5	3.9	1316	4.3
Resource-scarce, landlocked countries	208	4,690	194.4	21.0	49.3	4.6	146.1	7.7	2.9	2.0	981	3.2
Coastal countries	1023	22,344	699.3	75.7	996.9	92.4	1684.3	89.3	2.8	93.3	28339	92.4
Resource-rich coastal countries	1016	17,734	454.8	49.2	721.9	66.9	1091.2	57.8	2.3	76.7	18271	59.6
Resource-scarce coastal countries	1132	4,017	209.4	22.7	251.9	23.3	561.2	29.7	4.1	15.6	10047	32.8
SANE	1482	5,528	290.8	31.5	593.7	55.0	1072.0	56.8	3.0	59.4	16239	52.9

Source: AfDB Statistics Department, Computed from AfDB Database, 2007.

weak institutions, poor public financial management, and weak oversight, many resource-rich African countries were saddled with unsustainable amounts of external debt as income declined, risks of violent conflicts increased, and social indicators worsened. However, a new trend seems to have emerged with the onset of the current resource boom (especially with the meteoric rise of oil prices since 2002). There are, indeed, encouraging signs that resource-rich African exporters have become more prudent in the use of natural resource revenues than in previous booms.

In the past five years, buoyant oil, gas, and mineral price increases have enabled resource-rich African countries to increase their natural resource exports and thus their revenues substantially. These increased revenues are a significant source of fiscal income for resource-rich African countries, demonstrating the importance of natural resources in output growth and capacity to generate export revenues. For example, oil revenues account for more than half of all revenues in Angola, Congo, Equatorial Guinea, Gabon, and Nigeria, and oil revenues increased in USD terms about 3½ times between 2002 and 2006. In addition to revenue upsurge, production also expanded significantly, by 45 percent on average, especially in Angola, Chad, and Equatorial Guinea.[5] Thus, oil-exporting countries, in particular, are highly fiscal dependent, implying that if the current boom cycle develops — like in the past — to a boom-*bust* cycle, prudent fiscal discipline will be required.

The available data shows that in general government expenditures have risen in recent years, but not at nearly the same rate as natural resource revenues. Before the current boom in 2002, non-oil deficits exceeded oil revenues in many resource-rich African countries (such as in Angola, Congo, and Nigeria); since then, the ratio of non-oil fiscal deficits to oil revenues has improved noticeably (Table 4.2). This reflects both the rapid rise in oil revenues and the narrowing of non-oil fiscal balances.

The relatively cautious fiscal policies in many resource-rich African countries are helping these countries reduce their macroeconomic vulnerabilities. In other words, a good number of countries have used natural resource revenues to strengthen their external positions by reducing external debt (especially Gabon and Nigeria); accumulating external reserves (Angola, Congo, Equatorial Guinea, Gabon, and Nigeria); and reducing domestic and external arrears (Angola, Equatorial Guinea, Gabon, and Nigeria). Cameroon, Angola and Congo have also improved their non-oil primary fiscal balances.[6]

Concentration of Foreign Direct Investment in Resource-Rich Countries

One major concern about Foreign Direct Investment (FDI) inflows to Africa is that the overwhelming majority of these go into natural resource exploitation. Among the top recipient countries, most of the flows to Angola, Algeria, Sudan, Nigeria, and Gabon went to oil and gas projects. Similarly, over 50 percent of the flows to South Africa and

---

[5] Ibid.

[6] IMF (2007)

Table 4.2: Fiscal Balance, Investment Rates, and Terms of Trade Changes (in %)

	1981–1985			2001–2005		
	FD	INV	TOT	FD	INV	TOT
1- Resource-rich countries	–3.6	22.6	1.6	–0.2	22.6	6.3
Oil-exporting countries	–4.4	24.5	–0.4	3.3	24.8	8.7
Mineral-exporting countries	–2.9	20.8	3.5	–3.6	20.3	3.9
2- Resource-scarce, countries	–7.9	21.9	3.2	–4.8	20.0	–1.1
3- Landlocked countries	–4.5	18.1	4.4	–3.2	20.2	1.1
Resource- rich landlocked countries	0.2	18.0	3.8	–2.7	27.5	6.1
Resource-scarce, landlocked countries	–6.1	14.6	5.9	–3.9	15.2	–1.3
4- Coastal countries	–6.8	24.0	1.8	–2.7	21.5	2.3
Resource-rich coastal countries	–4.5	23.6	1.0	0.4	21.4	6.3
Resource-scarce coastal countries	–9.3	24.4	2.2	–6.0	21.9	–1.0
5- Africa	–6.1	22.2	2.7	–2.8	21.1	2.1
SANE	–7.3	27.7	–3.4	–0.8	22.1	7.3

FD= Fiscal Deficit-GDP Ratio; INV= Domestic Investment Rate; and TOT=Change in Terms of Trade.

Source: AfDB Statistical Department. Computed from IMF (2007), and World Bank (2007b) data.

Tanzania went into gold mining. Indeed, the primary sector was the largest recipient of accumulated FDI flows to Africa, with a 55 percent share for the 1996–2000 period.[7] As shown in Table 4.1, by 2006, about 64 percent of FDI was concentrated in resource-rich countries in Africa. Furthermore, of the total FDI that came into the continent during that year, 92 percent went to coastal countries, with resource-rich countries dominating at about 60 percent.

Growth Performance of Africa's Resource-Rich Countries is Poor (compared to Resource-scarce Countries)

Before the first oil shock on the 1970s, the average oil-rich African country enjoyed favorable macroeconomic conditions: robust economic growth, moderate inflation, manageable fiscal deficits and external debt, and external current account surpluses. The pro-cyclical policies they followed during the oil booms of the 1970s and 1980s were intended to use the oil bonanza for economic and social development and to encourage economic diversification. Unfortunately, these objectives were not achieved since the actual results were economic imbalances that caused major distress when oil prices plunged in the 1980s and stayed low for over a decade. The same was true of most other mineral (metals and non-metals) exporters, with exceptions like Botswana.[8]

---

[7] See Anyanwu (2006)

[8] IMF (2006)

Indeed, as Figure 4.1 shows, resource-scarce African countries out-performed resource-rich countries in terms of real per capita GDP growth during the 1981 to 2001 period, with a reversal occurring thereafter, reflecting the current boom. It should also be noted that there were three major collapses in real per capita GDP growth during the period — in 1983, 1985, and 1993 — with the latter being the worst.

The GDP per capita of oil- and mineral-rich countries were considerably higher than that of resource-scarce countries in 1980, and it still is today (Figure 4.2), but the real per capita GDP of oil-rich African countries has remained resolutely stuck below US$1000 for more than 20 years — first dropping to US$800 in the mid 90's before rising again. On the contrary, resource-scarce countries were able to achieve real growth during nearly the whole 1980–2005 period, albeit at a modest rate, and have thus significantly narrowed the gap with resource-rich countries. Nevertheless, it is important to stress that resource-rich countries in Africa — as measured by GDP per capita — are much better off than resource-scarce countries. Besides the better

Figure 4.1: Real GDP per Capita Growth — Resource-Rich vs. Resource-Scarce Countries

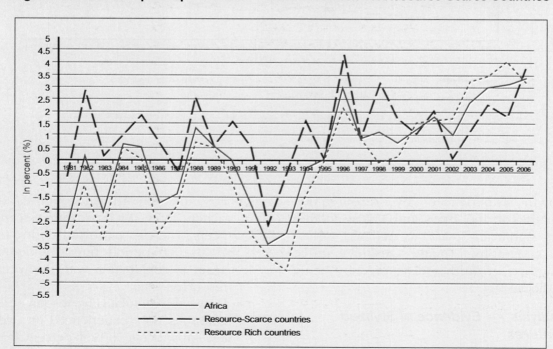

Source: AfDB Statistics Department, Computed from AfDB Database, 2007.

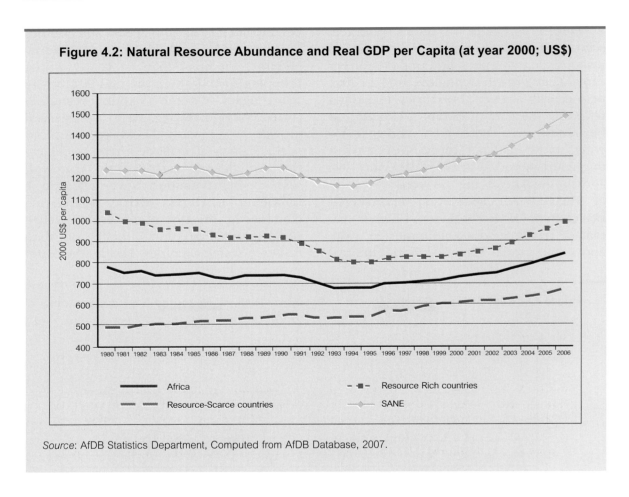

Figure 4.2: Natural Resource Abundance and Real GDP per Capita (at year 2000; US$)

Source: AfDB Statistics Department, Computed from AfDB Database, 2007.

growth experienced by resource-rich countries in the 1960s and 1970s, another very significant factor, as outlined earlier, is geography (many resource-scarce countries are further disfavored by being landlocked).

Analysis — Evidence of Stylized Features

Based on the data, tables and figures presented, the following trends and conclusions can be drawn:

- Resource-rich African countries are richer than their resource-scarce peers. The gap narrowed during the 1980–2000 period but is widening again in conjunction with the recent resource boom.
- However, cumulatively, resource-rich countries only experienced an average growth rate of 2.4 percent from 1981–2006, considerably lower than the average of 3.8 percent for resource-scarce countries.

- Resource-scarce coastal countries, which have almost a quarter of Africa's population, have experienced an average growth rate of 4.1 percent, much higher than the 2.3 percent recorded by resource-rich coastal countries. These findings indicate that being resource-rich does *not* make a significant difference for coastal countries. Indeed, resource-scarce coastal countries have a somewhat higher GDP per capita.
- The four SANE countries are by far the wealthiest in terms of GDP and have sustained a significant growth rate since 1995.
- Land-locked resource-scarce countries are the poorest, by a significant factor. These countries are five times poorer than resource-rich countries, and almost six times poorer than resource-scarce coastal countries. Furthermore, the growth rate in this group of countries only averaged 2.5 percent from 1981–2006. In other words, the most important of all factors is whether a country is land-locked or not, — more important than being resource-rich or not, or than any other aspect reviewed in this analysis.

Another feature that deserves attention is the fact that over a long-term period, both accumulation and factor productivity are significantly higher in resource-scarce countries than in resource-rich countries (see Figure 4.3).

Further analysis of the pace of productivity expansion (rate of growth in labor productivity versus rate of technical progress) in 23 diverse African countries reveal some marked differences (Figure 4.4). Countries such as Egypt, Tunisia and Mauritius have done very well — especially compared with countries such as Madagascar, Zambia, Ghana, Rwanda and Nigeria. It is thus noted that the best performing countries are all relatively resource-scarce.

Resource-Rich African Countries Have Negative Genuine Saving

One of the features of many countries endowed with abundant natural resources is that they generally save less than what is expected, considering the rents obtained from extracting and selling natural resources. Presumably, if the countries saved more, they would grow at a sustainable and faster rate. To gain a better understanding of sustainable development, it is useful to examine the concept of *genuine* saving.

Genuine saving is defined as public and private saving at home and abroad, net of depreciation, *plus* current spending on education to capture changes in intangible human capital, *minus* depletion of natural exhaustible and renewable resources, *minus* damage of stock pollutants (CO_2 and particulate matter). Genuine saving, thus defined, corresponds to an increase in the wealth of the nation. The so-called *Hartwick rule* demands that any depletion of natural resources or damage done by stock pollutants must be compensated for by increases in non-human and/or human capital. This rule of zero genuine saving can be seen as a rule of thumb or motivated by max-min egalitarianism. It requires that resource-rich countries adopt a strategy for transforming their natural

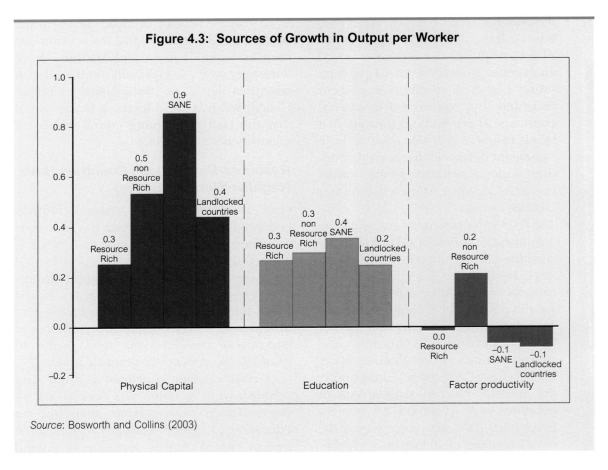

Figure 4.3: Sources of Growth in Output per Worker

Source: Bosworth and Collins (2003)

resource wealth into other forms of productive capital.[9]

Resource-rich countries in Africa therefore need credible and transparent rules for sustainable consumption and investment to ensure that exhaustible natural resources are gradually transformed into productive assets at home or abroad. Furthermore, countries with high population growth rates need *positive* rather than *zero* genuine saving rates to maintain constant consumption per head. They thus need to save more than their exhaustible resource rents — but only rarely manage to. Figure 4.5 paints a gloomy picture of resource-rich countries (worldwide analysis in this case). Countries with a large percentage of mineral and energy rents (of Gross National Income, GNI) typically have *negative* genuine saving rates. This means that many resource-rich countries become poorer each year despite their abundant natural resources[10]. Figure 4.6 suggests that

---

[9] Se i.e. World Bank (2006c) and Ploeg (2007)

[10] Ibid.

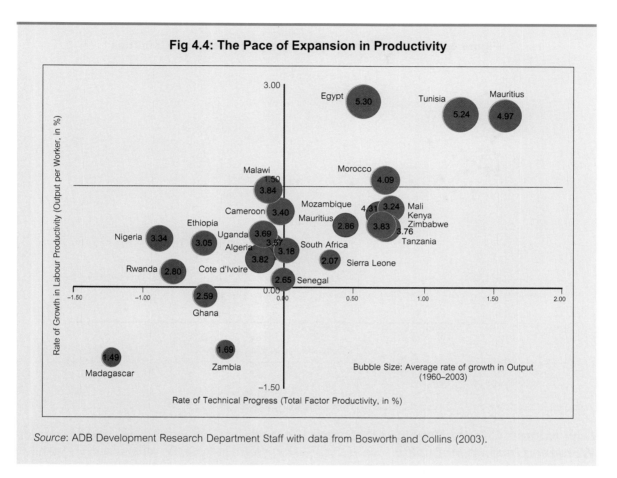

Fig 4.4: The Pace of Expansion in Productivity

Rate of Growth in Labour Productivity (Output per Worker, in %)

Rate of Technical Progress (Total Factor Productivity, in %)

Bubble Size: Average rate of growth in Output (1960–2003)

Egypt 5.30, Tunisia 5.24, Mauritius 4.97, Morocco 4.09, Malawi 1.50 / 3.84, Mozambique 4.31 / 3.24 Mali, Kenya, Cameroon 3.40, Mauritius 2.86, Zimbabwe 3.83 / 3.76, Ethiopia 3.05, Uganda 3.69, Nigeria 3.34, Algeria 3.57, South Africa 3.18 / 3.82, Tanzania, Sierra Leone 2.07, Rwanda 2.80, Cote d'Ivoire, Senegal 2.65, Ghana 2.59, Madagascar 1.49, Zambia 1.69

Source: ADB Development Research Department Staff with data from Bosworth and Collins (2003).

this may explain why a country such as Venezuela has negative economic growth rates, while countries such as Botswana and Ghana, which have positive genuine saving rates, enjoy substantial growth rates. Highly resource-dependent Nigeria and Angola have genuine saving rates of minus 30 percent, thereby impoverishing future generations on a massive scale.

The results suggest that resource-rich countries with negative genuine saving, such as Nigeria, would experience increases in productive capital by a factor of five or four,

if the Hartwick rule were applied. Effectively, for countries with negative genuine saving, the erosion of their natural resource wealth exceeds their accumulation of other assets. They effectively squander their natural resources at the expense of future generations without investing in other forms of intangible or productive wealth. This is an unfortunate feature of several resource-rich African economies (Figure 4.7).

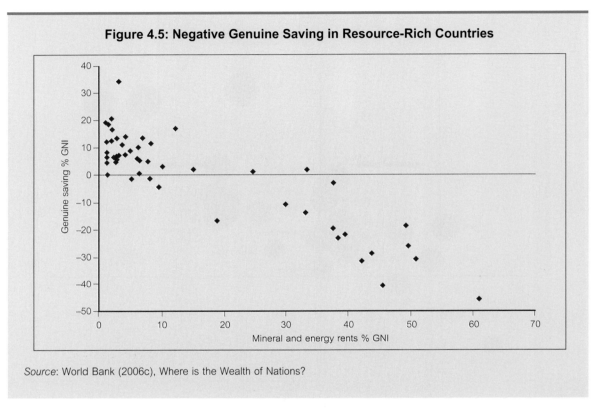

Figure 4.5: Negative Genuine Saving in Resource-Rich Countries

Source: World Bank (2006c), Where is the Wealth of Nations?

Low Human Capital Development and Worsened Income Inequality

One of the dilemmas of natural resource abundance is that it *may* pervasively cause a country to neglect human capital development — the same basic causes and effects outlined above in reference to negative genuine saving. High levels of natural resource revenues can thus divert attention from diversification and wealth creation, including from institutional and human development.[11] The logical expression of such a potential correlation between resource abundance and neglect of human

capital development would, in the medium-long term at least, be reflected in a low basic human development status. The United Nations Human Development Index (HDI), a comparative measure of life expectancy, literacy, education, and standard of living in countries worldwide, provides a standard means of measuring human well-being and country development status. As reported by the UNDP in its 2006 Human Development Report, Africa dominates the low end of the HDI (29 of the 31 countries with a low human development status). Only the Island States of Seychelles and Mauritius qualify as having a high human development status. The remaining 22 countries, including all

[11] Ibid.

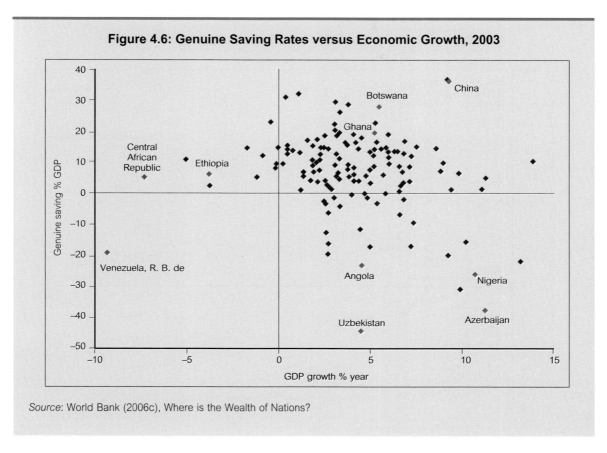

Figure 4.6: Genuine Saving Rates versus Economic Growth, 2003

Source: World Bank (2006c), Where is the Wealth of Nations?

the North African Arab states, have a middle level human development. It is also worth noting that oil-rich Norway has the highest HDI among all countries in the world.[12]

A deeper analysis of the HDI data (Table 4.3) indicates that the primary factor of the human development status seems to be *geography* and not resource abundance — that is, whether a country is landlocked or not — as landlocked countries as a group score very low in this index calculation

(average 0.42). There is no difference between resource-rich and resource-scarce countries (0.51), but it should be noted that oil-rich countries are doing considerably better in this aspect than primarily mineral-rich countries (0.55 vs. 0.46).

Another important aspect, frequently highlighted as problematic in resource-rich countries, is increased income inequality. Oil, gas, and mining industries are often characterized by their "enclave" nature, with few forward and backward linkages into the economy. During exploitation and production, such industries employ only a relatively

---

[12] UNDP (2006) — http://hdr.undp.org/hdr2006/statistics/documents/hdi2004.pdf

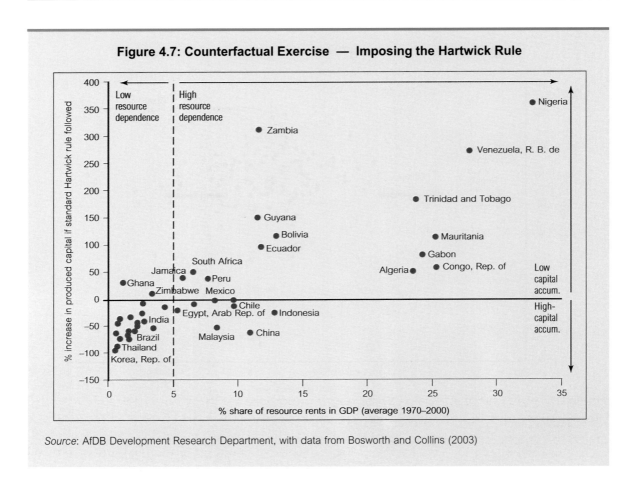

Figure 4.7: Counterfactual Exercise — Imposing the Hartwick Rule

Source: AfDB Development Research Department, with data from Bosworth and Collins (2003)

small number of highly-skilled, well-paid workers, and generally import the majority of inputs. Furthermore, there is a considerable risk that public expenditure during a resource boom may exacerbate inequality, for example, concentrating expenditure in the formal sector in towns and cities, skewing distribution (not benefiting rural households), and prioritizing the interests of the elites and wealthier classes. Because of these tendencies, society tends to identify the production and export of natural

resources with the interests of the rich.[13] As shown in Table 4.3, income inequality in resource-rich African countries is, indeed, noticeably higher (Gini Coefficient of 31.1) than in resource-scarce countries (Gini Coefficient of 26.8). Furthermore, it is worth noting that income inequality is comparatively higher in mineral-exporting countries, in landlocked countries, and in the SANE country group.

---

[13] Overseas Development Institute (2006)

Table 4.3: Resource Abundance and Social Performance

	Human Development Index **(HDI)** (Scale 0–1; Niger lowest with 0.31; Seychelles highest with 0.84)	Income Inequality (GINI Coefficient Index; scale 0–100)*
1- Resource-rich countries	0.51	31.1
Oil-exporting countries	0.55	15.3
Mineral-exporting countries	0.46	46.8
2- Resource-scarce countries	0.51	26.8
3- Landlocked countries	0.42	45.0
Resource-rich landlocked countries	0.42	41.6
Resource-scarce landlocked countries	0.40	42.8
4- Coastal countries	0.55	22.1
Resource-rich coastal countries	0.52	28.7
Resource-scarce coastal countries	0.58	14.7
5- Africa	0.51	45.9
SANE	0.63	42.8

* For the GINI Co-efficient Index; 0 corresponds to perfect equality

Sources: UNDP (2006), Human Development Report 2006; World Bank (2006d)

Stylized Features for Africa — Summary

The features and issues described and analyzed above further illustrate that resource-rich African countries have *not* fully exploited the true (potential) benefits of having significant natural resource wealth. However, geographic factors — most importantly, whether a country is landlocked or not — also play a very significant role in the present-day status as landlocked countries perform worse in nearly all aspects analyzed.

Overall, the 20-year period from 1980–2000, in particular, was disappointing for resource-rich countries in Africa. Hard lessons have been learned from the past resource boom and bust cycles and from two decades of very disappointing growth rates. These lessons need to be reviewed and used for the future, especially now that a new boom has gained traction in Africa. The following sections further explore these issues, taking into account relevant theoretical aspects and empirical data.

Explaining the Resource Curse: Main Causes, Drivers, and Sustainers

There is a large body of literature on the reasons why countries may suffer a "curse" rather than a "blessing" following large inflows of oil, gas, or mineral revenues. Some authors[14] cite three exogenous causes: (1) structuralist policies, (2) Dutch Disease, and (3) export-based theory; and three

---

[14] For example, Auty (2001)

endogenous causes: (1) policy failures, (2) inefficient investment, and (3) rent seeking. This Report further examines these causes, which, for analytical purposes, are grouped as follows[15]:

- revenue and macroeconomic volatility;
- Dutch Disease and crowding out effects;
- the role of the state; and
- socio-cultural and political impacts.

Revenue and Macroeconomic Volatility

Commodity booms are typically not permanent and prices tend to show at least some degree of mean reversion over time. As a result, countries that have experienced one or more commodity export price booms will typically also have faced high volatility of export prices. In many cases, resource booms have encouraged less prudent fiscal policies with limited control and inflation, further hampering growth, equity, and the alleviation of poverty.[16] The majority of resource-rich countries tend to have limited transparency in the management of natural resource revenues, leading to the creation of parallel budgets. As a result, price stability and budgetary discipline suffer. Thus, even as natural resource money is "pouring in", countries often have fiscal deficits, and, sometimes, double-digit inflation. Such volatility can be detrimental to growth in several respects: It is harmful to investment, income distribution, educational attainment and poverty alleviation. It also hampers exchange rate unification and trade liberalization. Furthermore, it makes invest-

ments more risky, while public spending decisions tend to become compromised, with extravagant commitments made during booms that subsequently lead to drastic cuts in vital expenditures during troughs.[17]

Evidence from recent years shows that both oil and non-fuel commodity (including metals) prices have experienced extreme volatility. Indeed, resource-rich African countries have experienced repeated boom-bust cycles over the past decades (as demonstrated in Figure 4.8). Despite recent increases, the prices of most non-fuel commodities remain below their historical peaks in real terms. Over the past five decades, commodity prices have fallen relative to consumer prices at the rate of about 1.6 percent a year[18]. This downward trend is usually attributed to large productivity gains in the agricultural and metals sectors relative to other parts of the economy.

However, compared with the prices of manufactured goods, commodity prices stopped falling in the 1990s as the growing globalization of the manufacturing sector slowed producer price inflation. Indeed, metal prices increased by over 75 percent during previous cyclical upturns, reflecting long gestation lags for increasing capacity in the industry and the low price elasticity of demand. Over the past five years, commodity prices have evolved very differently across various subgroups of the non-fuel index. For example, the prices of some non-fuel commodities have increased more than oil prices — the metals index has risen by 180 percent in real terms since 2002, while oil

---

[15] See Stevens (2003)
[16] Ploeg (2007)

[17] Ibid.
[18] See Stevens (2003)

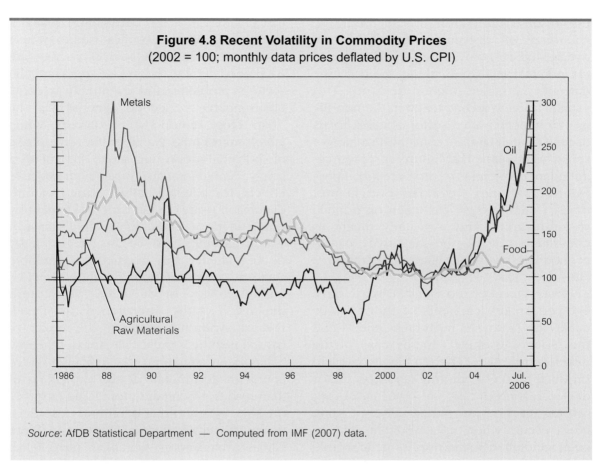

Figure 4.8 Recent Volatility in Commodity Prices
(2002 = 100; monthly data prices deflated by U.S. CPI)

Source: AfDB Statistical Department — Computed from IMF (2007) data.

prices have increased by 157 percent. The prices of food and agricultural raw materials increased much less (by 20 and 4 percent, respectively). As a result, metals have contributed almost 90 percent to the cumulative 60 percent real increase in the non-fuel commodity index since 2002.[19]

Part of the unusually strong run-up in metal prices experienced in recent years can be attributed to the low investment in the metals sector in the late 1990s and early 2000s

— following a period of earlier price declines. Some analysts have also suggested that the intensity of the price upswing in this cycle is amplified by new factors — the increasing weight of rapidly growing emerging markets (most notably China and India) in the world economy and the investment activity of financial investors in commodity markets.

Dutch Disease and Crowding Out Effects

Originally, Dutch Disease was used to refer to the appreciation of the real exchange rate:

[19] IMF (2006)

the result of inflation arising from the spending of revenues, leading to an overheated economy and an appreciation of the nominal exchange rate as the domestic currency attracted higher demand. This usually leads to a contraction in the non-oil, gas, or mineral traded sector. Some scholars use the "Dutch Disease concept" in a narrow sense to explain the failure of resource-abundant economies to promote a competitive manufacturing sector. However, in most cases, Dutch Disease has taken on a much wider meaning and is usually meant to encompass all of the negative macro-economic effects associated with "resource curses".[20]

Two effects of the Dutch Disease have evolved as key elements of the resource curse: the "resource movement effect" and the "spending effect". In the case of the resource movement effect, a higher marginal product in the booming resource sector draws resources out of other sectors[21], causing the latter to contract. The spending effect occurs when, as a result of the revenue windfall, demand rises in both tradable and non-tradable sectors of the economy. Since prices in tradable sectors are largely determined by the international market, greater demand is met by higher imports. However, prices in non-tradables rise relative to tradables and, consequently, resources shift from tradables to non-tradables.

Other dimensions of the Dutch Disease syndrome, conceptualized as the contraction of the tradable sector, have emerged. A first dimension of this detrimental development occurs when subsidies used to protect non-resource tradable sectors — that are weakened by the boom — aggravate the sector's problems and eventually become unsustainable. A second dimension is the "leap frog effect" which occurs when governments miss the labor-intensive phase of industrialization and move straight to a heavy, capital intensive phase with negative effects for the tradable sector. A third dimension relates to the issue of learning by doing in the context of Dutch Disease[22], which assumes that because learning by doing benefits only accrue from tradable sectors, a contraction in these sectors implies lower productivity. The fourth dimension of the extension of the Dutch Disease syndrome relates to the impact of natural resources on social capital, whereby it has been suggested that resource-scarce countries accumulate social capital faster than resource-rich countries.[23] The rationale for this is that limited natural resources promote early industrialization and force earlier urbanization, which, in turn, stifles entrepreneurship and allows people to escape from villages into urban environments with greater anonymity and better functioning markets. At the same time, this confers a saving dividend by reducing the dependency ratio.

Based on a series of international rankings, it is evident that private investors in Africa face more hurdles than investors in other economies. Infrastructure constraints and unfavorable business environments

---

[20] Sarraf and Jiwanji (2001)
[21] Farmanesh (1991)

[22] Gylfason et al. (1997)
[23] Woollcock et al. (2001)

impose significant costs on the private sector in terms of starting a business, the time it takes to register property, and the rigidity of labor markets, and so on. These are some of the factors that, among others, have led to low business diversification in Africa, most significantly, in oil-rich countries. As Table 4.4 clearly shows, the diversification index of resource-rich countries as a whole is much lower than that of resource-scarce African countries (see also Figure 4.9). In 2005, for example, the diversification index of resource-rich countries was only 4.1, while that of resource-scarce countries was almost double this level, at 8.4. However, it is worth noting that low diversification is primarily a problem in oil-exporting countries (with a score of only 1.9 in 2005), whereas this issue is less problematic in mineral-exporting countries (a score averaging 6.3).

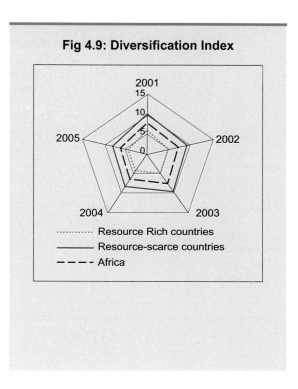

Fig 4.9: Diversification Index

Resource Rich countries
Resource-scarce countries
Africa

Table 4.4: Natural Resource Abundance and Diversification Index, 2001–2005

	2001	2002	2003	2004	2005
1- Resource-rich countries	5.5	5.1	5.1	4.5	4.1
Oil-exporting countries	2.6	2.2	2.1	2.0	1.9
Mineral-exporting countries	8.4	7.9	8.2	7.1	6.3
2- Resource-scarce countries	10.1	9.4	9.5	8.6	8.4
3- Landlocked countries	4.7	4.6	4.5	4.4	4.6
Resource-rich landlocked countries	3.9	2.3	3.0	2.3	2.2
Resource-scarce landlocked countries	4.6	4.4	3.9	4.0	3.9
4- Coastal countries	9.6	8.8	8.9	7.9	7.4
Resource-rich coastal countries	5.8	5.7	5.6	5.0	4.5
Resource-scarce coastal countries	13.0	11.5	11.7	10.2	9.8
5- Africa	8.2	7.6	7.7	6.9	6.6
SANE	16.5	15.3	15.2	13.4	12.3

Source: OECD and AfDB (2007), African Economic Outlook 2007

Table 4.5: Natural Resource Abundance and Competitiveness Index, 2007

	Overall Index	Basic requirements	Efficiency enhancers	Innovation enhancers
	Score	Score	Score	Score
1- Resource-rich countries	3.4	3.8	3.1	3.1
Oil-exporting countries	3.3	3.7	2.9	3.0
Mineral-exporting countries	3.5	3.9	3.3	3.2
2- Resource-scarce countries	3.4	3.7	3.2	3.3
3- Landlocked countries	3.1	3.3	2.9	2.9
Resource-rich landlocked countries	3.2	3.6	3.0	2.7
Resource-scarce Landlocked countries	3.0	3.2	2.9	3.0
4- Coastal countries	3.7	4.0	3.3	3.4
Resource-rich coastal countries	3.5	3.9	3.2	3.2
Resource-scarce Coastal countries	3.9	4.2	3.5	3.6
5- Africa	3.4	3.8	3.1	3.2
SANE	4.0	4.4	3.6	3.7

Source: World Bank and AfDB (2007), The African Competitiveness Report

In terms of competitiveness in African countries, Table 4.5 shows that there is little difference between the performance of resource-rich and resource-scarce African countries. While landlocked countries under-perform, the performance of mineral-exporting and resource-rich coastal countries is marginally better than that of the resource-rich group at large.

Economic Policy Failures

The effect that natural resource revenues have in exposing existing policy failures — including, on economic investment, regulatory reform, and trade — are also linked to the Dutch Disease. For example, policy decisions on economic diversification — choices governments make in supporting regulatory reform, skills development, business support, and public investment in physical infrastructure such as ports and roads — have an impact on the way in which the Dutch Disease affects the economy. At least two features have a key impact here: the effect of resource booms (through government investments and industrial policy) on tradable versus non-tradable sectors; and, the differential effect of this impact depending on whether government policy is skewed towards sectors that are "close to", or "far from", the natural resource market.[24]

Poor Industrial Policy

In the 1970s and 1980s, in particular, many resource-rich countries adopted industrial

[24] Ploeg (2007)

policies that were based on import substitution characterized by the introduction of subsidies (based on the infant industry argument) and growing protectionism. This was seen initially as the means to break out of the circle of underdevelopment — a variant of the "big-push" argument. However, these subsidies became unsustainable when revenues fell (the bust cycle). In addition, with subsidies and protection in place, continuing resource revenues reduced the incentive to create competitive manufacturing industries. Given that many development economists regard competitive manufacturing as a key source of technological progress this has had serious implications on economic progress.[25]

Thus, the relaxation of market discipline and the associated accumulation of economic distortions retards competitive diversification and lies at the heart of the general underperformance observed in many resource-rich African countries in the 1980s and 1990s. However as described and outlined through empirical evidence earlier in this chapter, there are some indications that (thanks to the lessons learned) the policies pursued today in exploiting the current resource boom are, indeed, more sustainable — or, at least, less damaging to resource-rich economies. However, any firm conclusions in this regard will have to wait for a downtrend or the full completion of a resource boom-bust cycle.

The Role of the State

In most countries and legal regimes, oil, gas, and minerals are the property of the state;

the revenues in the first instance accrue to the government, inevitably inviting government action in one way or the other to spend some of the accrued revenues. There is a recurrent debate on how or why this very often results in policy failures and poor governance. Several strands of arguments are presented below.

Bad Decision-Making

The first strand argues that large windfall revenues lead to poor general decision-making by governments. This is attributable to several factors[26]:

- Resource booms raise expectations and increase appetite for spending. The promise of natural resource wealth dramatically expands the horizons of governments in natural resource-exporting countries. A boom mentality not only affects the way governments behave — creating grandiose plans and ideas; it also shapes how people respond. Work ethics may be undermined resulting in a decline in productivity.
- The development of oil, gas, or minerals raises expectations among the population. This pressures government to "do something", thus encouraging speedy responses. This often leads to quick, inappropriate, and poorly coordinated decisions.
- Having more money to "play with" tends to weaken prudence and normal procedures of "due diligence". In particular, governments may decide on

---

[25] Ibid.

[26] Also refer to Ploeg (2007); Auty (2001); Auty (2004); Stevens (2003)

capital spending without due thought to recurrent spending implications.

- Governments often dramatically increase public spending based on unrealistic revenue projections. In resource-dependent countries, windfalls increase both public spending and the appetite for transfers by a factor that is more than proportionate to the size of the boom itself. This means that spending quickly surpasses revenues. Nonetheless, different interests and groups continue to demand even larger shares of national income when natural resource revenues go into a downtrend.

Enhanced Corruption and Rent-Seeking

Natural resource booms often decrease the quality of public spending and encourage rent seeking.[27] The centralization and, hence, concentration of fiscal resources from resource booms fosters excessive and imprudent investment. It often also leads to some level of mismanagement and misallocation of resources and in the most severe cases, massive corruption.

The key issue is that natural resource revenues tend to replace more stable and sustainable revenue streams, exacerbating problems related to development, transparency and accountability. With sizeable resource revenues, the reliance on non-resource taxes and other government incomes decreases. This tends to free natural resource-exporting governments from the types of citizen demands for fiscal transparency and accountability that arise when people pay taxes directly to the government. Thus, natural resource export earnings actually sever important links between the people and their governments that are related to popular interests and control mechanisms.

The larger the public purse, the less noticeable the leakage to interest groups. Rent-seeking is greater in resource-rich countries because wealth is concentrated in the public sector (or possibly in a small number of companies). Therefore, the bulk of the rents created in these economies are channeled by bureaucrats, the majority of whom are members of the politically dominant groups. Such rent-seeking behavior produces undesirable results for the economy. First, rent-seeking behavior imposes significant losses on many economies. Second, it distracts attention away from long-term development goals towards maximizing rent creation and capture. Third, rent seeking creates extremely powerful lobby groups that are able to block needed economic reforms. Fourth, societies face severe impediments to innovation as a result of the behavior of special interest groups. Fifth, rent seeking makes it more difficult for governments to adjust spending when faced with revenue fluctuations. Finally, rent seeking is tantamount to the creation of monopoly power in an economy and the social costs of such monopolization are higher if the costs to maintain that monopoly are added.[28]

Governance indicators such as government effectiveness, voice and accountability, political instability and violence, the rule of law, regulatory quality, and control

---

[27] Ibid.

[28] See Stevens (2003)

Table 4.6: Natural Resource Abundance and Governance Indicators

	Voice and Accountability	Political Stability	Government Effectiveness	Regulatory Quality	Rule of Law	Control of Corruption
	2006	2006	2006	2006	2006	2006
1- Resource- rich countries	−0.8	−0.7	−0.8	−0.7	−0.9	−0.8
Oil-exporting countries	−1.3	−1.0	−1.0	−1.0	−1.1	−1.0
Mineral-exporting countries	−0.4	−0.3	−0.5	−0.5	−0.6	−0.5
2- Resource-scarce countries	−0.5	−0.4	−0.7	−0.7	−0.6	−0.5
3- Landlocked countries	−0.6	−0.6	−0.7	−0.7	−0.7	−0.6
Resource-rich landlocked countries	−0.6	−0.5	−0.7	−0.6	−0.7	−0.6
Resource-scarce landlocked countries	−0.5	−0.6	−0.7	−0.6	−0.6	−0.7
4- Coastal countries	−0.6	−0.4	−0.7	−0.7	−0.7	−0.6
Resource-rich coastal countries	−0.9	−0.7	−0.8	−0.8	−0.9	−0.8
Resource-scarce coastal countries	−0.4	−0.3	−0.6	−0.7	−0.5	−0.4
5- Africa	−0.6	−0.5	−0.7	−0.7	−0.7	−0.6
SANE	−0.5	−1.0	−0.2	−0.3	−0.4	−0.4

Source: Kaufmann, D., Kraay, A and Mastruzzi, M (2007)

of corruption are markedly weaker in oil-rich African countries (see Table 4.6). Perhaps, surprisingly, mineral-rich countries actually perform much better and at the same level as resource-scarce countries, implying that this problem is by far most common in relation to oil exploration and revenue, at least at the present phase of the current resource boom.

Revenue Misallocation and Poor Investment Decisions

Relevant studies and literature emphasize the role of governments in the misallocation of resource revenues.[29] Resource booms

have adverse effects because they provide incentives for politicians to engage in inefficient redistribution of revenues and income in return for political support. However, it is important to note that the status of existing institutions (before the resource boom) is crucial, as they determine the extent to which politicians can respond to these perverse incentives. Nevertheless, regardless of the starting point, pressure from the public to raise public spending is likely to be significant — leading to inefficient redistribution in the form of public employment provisions, subsidies to farmers, labor market regulations, and protection of domestic industries from international competition.

[29] Ibid.

Socio-Cultural and Political Impacts

As outlined above, countries that have abundant point-source natural resources (such as minerals or oil) tend to have less prudent policies and poor governance. They also tend to have weaker institutional capacities. In essence, natural resources are often associated with weak institutions.[30] Some of the reasons for this relationship and reflections on how it may be avoided are discussed in the following paragraphs.

Resource rents are an invitation to non-productive lobbying and rent seeking. This problem occurs mostly in countries with "grabber-friendly" institutions, while countries with "producer-friendly" institutions generally do not suffer from the curse. In other words, countries that avoided the resource curse in previous resource booms did so because they had transparent and sound institutions and because they adopted specific policies — including institutional strengthening — to minimize the impact of and damage caused by, the resource windfalls.

It has also been argued that countries in which governance (hence transparency) is initially poor face a substantial risk of turning resource windfalls into catastrophe (see Box 4.2). Indeed, there is evidence that governance is likely to deteriorate further in a resource-boom, even from a low-start status, because of the windfalls. Governance and effective public spending are thus critical for both living standards and private activity and, since the public sector is a large part of the economy, its own productivity growth is a key component of overall growth. This in turn requires that government aspires to overall national goals and hence become accountable to citizens, regardless of its own interests and aspirations.

Poor economic performance during previous natural resource booms underscores the importance of sound macro-economic policies and strong institutions. The large public investment projects of the 1970s and 1980s, when governance and institutions were extremely weak in most of Africa, were often undertaken with little scrutiny and accountability. The return on public investment was correspondingly low. Meanwhile, poor macroeconomic management of natural resource price cycles in several African countries resulted in large exchange rate appreciation, erosion of the competitiveness of non-oil sectors, and high inflation. Given that many African countries leveraged their natural resource wealth to access credit from foreign suppliers and governments, the early 1990s witnessed a sharp rise in external debt, well above 100 percent of GDP and, in most cases, resulting in unsustainable external debt levels. These macroeconomic imbalances have eventually called for very painful policy adjustments, such as sharp fiscal contraction, trade liberalization, exchange rate adjustment, and debt rescheduling.[31]

In addition, with weak institutions and legal system dysfunctions, there is a higher return on rent seeking, and a higher occurrence of crime, corruption, unfair company take-overs, and other shady

---

[30] See Stevens (2003)

[31] Collier and Goderis (2007)

Box 4.2: Governance and Transparency

Governance remains the overarching and most critical challenge for natural resource exploitation and management. Although African governments bear prime responsibility for managing natural-resource wealth in a transparent, fair, and accountable way, they are only one part of an intricate web of interests and relationships, which include multinational extractive companies foreign governments, and regional actors. The main governance-related challenges facing resource-rich countries can be summarized as follows:

Transparency
Transparency is the key issue in establishing accountable governance structures and fighting corruption. However, this has to start with the concession contract itself, as well as with revenues accruing from the sale of the resources:
(1) Corruption in the allocation of resource concessions not only undermines governance in resource-rich countries and also entails a poor deal for their citizens. There is overwhelming evidence that concession allocation is obscure and involves a lot of corruption;
(2) Concession contracts often contain confidentiality clauses and are therefore not open to public scrutiny. Without knowing the details of the deals signed by their government, the citizens of a given country have no way of holding their politicians' accountable; and,
(3) Transparency is equally important for the revenue flows of natural-resource rents between extractive industry companies and host governments. If the companies publish what they pay and the governments publish what they earn, the revenue flows can be traced and governments can be held accountable for sustainable management of these revenues and fair distribution of the wealth.

Sources: Heinrich Boll Foundation (2007); Alley et al. (2007)

dealings. A resource bonanza thus elicits more rent seekers and reduces the number of productive entrepreneurs. In the long run, profits fall and, as a result, the economy is worse off. Weak institutions may explain the poor performance of oil-rich countries such as Angola, Nigeria, and Sudan; diamond-rich Sierra Leone, Liberia and Congo; and drug states like Columbia or Afghanistan. Thus, if institutions are weak and conditions are not favorable, dependency on oil and on other natural resources effectively hinders democracy and the quality of governance.[32]

The general recognition that many African countries have relatively weak institutions, low human development status, and poor governance raises great concern about how the current resource boom will affect development in the resource-rich parts of Africa. Current data is not all discouraging — as pointed out earlier, there are indeed resource-rich countries in Africa that have put in place strong institutions and enjoy consistent high economic and human development growth.

---

[32] Ross (1999); Ploeg (2007)

Civil Wars and Other Forms of Conflict

There is strong evidence that resource abundance increases the incidence of civil conflicts and wars and stimulates violence, theft, looting, and fighting between rival groups.[33] Over half of the conflicts listed in Table 4.7 (see also Figure 4.10) are in Africa. Since many African states are highly dependent on oil, gas, and mineral exports, they are unusually prone to resource-related conflicts (Table 4.8). Conversely, the region's mineral abundance helps explain why a significant share of the world's civil wars has taken place in Africa. Furthermore, while mineral wealth is linked to the onset of non-separatist conflicts, evidence shows that booty futures have been used to prolong conflicts and wars. Booty futures refers to advance rights granted by a rebel group (and sometimes by governments) to companies to extract natural resources in areas that the rebels hope to capture during a civil conflict. However, it should be noted that another important reason for this trend is the persistence of poverty in Africa — poverty significantly raises the risk of civil war. A downtrend has been observed in recent years, but this should not mask the fact that Africa experienced seven civil wars in the 1970s, eight in the 1980s, and fourteen in the 1990s.[34]

Altogether, between the 1960s, when most African countries became independent, and the 1990s, there were more than 80

violent changes of government in the continent. Country after country has been engaged in internal strife, conflict, or civil war.[35]

Table 4.7: Civil Wars Linked to Resource Wealth, 1990–2002

Country	Duration	Resources
Afghanistan	1978–2001	Gems, opium
Angola	1975–2002	Oil, diamonds
Angola (Cabinda)	1975–	Oil
Burma	1949–	Timber, tin, gems, opium
Cambodia	1978–97	Timber, gems
Colombia	1984–	Oil, gold, coca
Congo, Rep.	1997	Oil
Congo, Dem. Rep.	1996–97	Copper, coltan, diamonds, gold, cobalt
Congo, Dem. Rep.	1998–	Copper, coltan, diamonds, gold, cobalt
Indonesia (Aceh)	1975–	Natural gas, marijuana
Indonesia (W Papua)	1969–	Copper, gold
Liberia	1989–96	Timber, diamonds, iron, palm oil, cocoa, coffee, marijuana, rubber, gold
Morocco	1975–	Phosphates, oil
Papua New Guinea	1988–	Copper, gold
Peru	1980–1995	Coca
Sierra Leone	1991–2000	Diamonds
Sudan	1983–	Oil

Source: Ross (2004), What do we know about natural resources and civil war?

---

[33] E.g. Collier and Hoeffler (2004); (2005); Anyanwu (2002); Hodler (2006)

[34] Ross (2003); Collier and Hoeffler (2004); (2005); Hodler (2006)

[35] Adedeji (1999)

Table 4.8: Countries Ranked by Mineral Dependence, 2000

Rank	Country	Mineral Dependence	Conflict 1990–2000
1	Bahrain	63.44	0
2	Qatar	53.37	0
3	Turkmenistan	49.91	0
4	Gabon	48.83	0
5	Nigeria	48.75	3
6	Saudi Arabia	44.74	0
7	Papua New Guinea	41.52	0
8	Trinidad and Tobago	41.16	0
9	Congo, Rep.	41.07	9
10	Brunei	37.65	0
11	Kazakhstan	36.11	0
12	Libya	35.91	3
13	Algeria	35.75	27
14	Botswana	35.10	0
15	Kuwait	32.41	3
16	Azerbaijan	28.83	9
17	Angola	27.88	74
18	Zambia	27.12	0
19	Liberia	26.76	14
20	Norway	25.97	0
21	Oman	25.65	0
22	Iran, Islamic Rep.	25.55	42
23	Mongolia	25.45	0
24	Russian Federation	25.38	15
25	Venezuela, RB	23.54	0
26	Yemen, Rep.	22.32	2
27	United Arab Emirates	22.13	0

Source: Ross (2004), What do we know about natural resources and civil war?

A couple of salient characteristics distinguish the post-Cold War civil conflicts in Africa:

1) Natural resources figure as a prominent feature in the conflicts, both in situations of natural resource abundance (oil and minerals) and environmental scarcities (land). In some countries, like Sudan, conflict is related to both types of resources, oil in the South and land in Darfur; and,

2) These conflicts involve local non-state actors, non-professional fighters, or combatants often challenging the authority and legitimacy of fragile states, regional actors, and neighboring states, and trans-global forces and networks.

Nature-based conflicts, including violent conflict, civil wars and secessionist movements, have thus been commonplace in Africa. The "blood diamonds" in Sierra Leone and Angola, timber conflicts in Liberia, oil conflicts in Nigeria and Sudan, and mineral wars in the Democratic Republic of Congo are popular examples.[36] Even so, local disputes over land, water, wildlife and forests are, in fact, far more common. In many places, such conflicts overwhelm rural courts and traditional mediation platforms.[37]

The root causes of civil wars in Africa are complex and lie in a combination of factors, whether in resource-rich or resource-scarce countries. However, there is a growing body of empirical evidence that rents on natural resources and primary commodities, especially oil and other point-source natural resources, increase chances of civil conflicts

---

[36] Bannon and Collier (2003); Lind and Sturman (2002); Cilliers and Dietrich (2000); Reno (2000); Lipschutz (1987)

[37] Wolf et al. (2005); Veit and Benson (2004); LHRC (2003); Newmann (1998); Shivji (1998); Shivji and Kapinga (1998); Lane (1996)

and wars — especially in sub-Saharan Africa — by weakening the state or financing rebels. Sometimes this can even be related to engagements by multinational corporations. It is important to investigate whether civil strife and wars are the result of *grievance*, a sense of injustice about how a social group is treated (for example, systematic economic discrimination), or *greed* possibly induced by massive rents of point-source resources, as commonly highlighted in the cases of Angola, Congo, and Sierra Leone.[38]

Other studies show[39] that the largest single influence on the risk of conflict is the extent to which a country depends on primary commodity exports, and the effect is nonlinear. For instance, the probability of civil conflict in a country with no natural resources is only 0.5 percent, but it is more than 23 percent in a country with a share of natural resources (oil and minerals) of more than 25 percent in the GDP. This suggests that many conflicts are driven by greed rather than by grievance. Based on these results, the different variants of the "resource curse" theory attribute the poor resource exploitation record in resource-dependent states, either to the "predatory" inclinations of the state or to the "greed" of rebels. Apart from other empirical results pointing to the contrary, such conceptualization suggests irrational behavior by the main actors involved in the control and management of natural resources.

However, the above explanation misses the crucial point that waste and degradation of natural resources in conflict-prone countries can most commonly be traced to government policy failures. Government officials sometimes induce and engage in unsound natural-resource exploitation in order to pursue economic and political objectives that are, in principle, *unrelated* to the natural-resource sector. Even rebel groups depending on the strength or weakness of their organizational structures, often pursue various broader programmatic and political objectives.[40]

As mentioned earlier, empirical evidence also strongly suggests that conflict is more likely to erupt in countries with a low level of GDP per capita and low rate of economic growth. The three factors that determine the onset of armed conflict — natural resources, low income per capita, and low growth — are prevalent in large parts of the African continent. The literature[41] highlights other factors that may be significant, such as vertical and horizontal inequality and religion. The conflicts in Rwanda and Burundi, for instance, were not primarily driven by economic factors.

The effect of natural resources on the incidence and duration of civil wars also features strongly in the political science literature.[42] In fractionalized countries, many rival groups fighting for natural resources may well harm the quality of the legal system and thus undermine property rights. The resulting destruction of output outweighs the increase in output due to the resource boom. Fractionalization and

---

[38] Murshed (2002); Olsson and Fors (2004)
[39] Collier and Hoeffler (2004); (2005)

[40] Weinstein (2005)
[41] E.g. Stewart (2000; 2002)
[42] E.g. Ross (2004); Fearon and Laitin (2003)

Figure 4.10: Natural Resources and Conflict

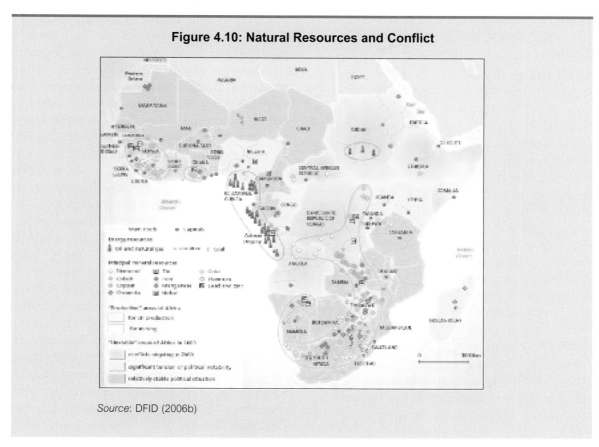

Source: DFID (2006b)

fighting for natural resource bounties can thus lead to dissipation of natural resource rents. Erosion of property rights, when there are many natural resources, can easily lead to the resource curse, especially if there are many rival fractions.[43] The "idea" is that each group manages to appropriate more natural resources if it fights more and the quality of the legal system is poor, but fighting also undermines effective property rights. There is some cross-country empirical evidence that the resource curse is more severe in countries that have many ethnic or religious fractions and many languages.

Easily lootable resources such as gemstones tend to prolong conflicts — that is, when rebel groups and rulers and their cronies fight each other over the control of point-based resources. For example, with the exception of Botswana, Namibia, and South Africa, diamond abundance on the African Continent has been shown to generally lead to depressed growth, mostly so in countries with weak institutions.[44]

[43] Hodler (2006)

[44] Ollson (2007)

Natural Resource Wealth Management in Fragile African States

Africa has a considerable number of fragile states, by far the highest number of any continent. While there are several definitions of what a fragile state is, what is most important in the context of this Report is the strong overlap between underperforming, resource-rich countries and countries widely accepted as being fragile in one form or another. It is worth noting that fragile circumstances take different forms in different countries and even within the same country at different times. There are major differences in terms of political and public security environments, institutional capacity and performance, government accountability, and commitment to progress along a credible reform path. These differences have major implications for the scope and nature of engagement by development partners. Indeed, experience has shown that a uniform approach to widely differing circumstances on the ground often fails to produce desired results and, in many circumstances, has precluded forms of selective engagement that could be both justified and effective.[45]

A stylized categorization of these different circumstances illustrates a simplified continuum along which fragile circumstances typically fall — ranging from marked deterioration to active conflict or prolonged crisis, to post-crisis and transition and, finally, to gradual improvement (Figure 4.11). The categorization also sets

out, in broad terms, strategic avenues through which governments and donors might address development in a fragile state. Needless to say, for natural resource-rich countries, the natural resource sector is an extremely important focal point, considering the whole spectrum of opportunities and challenges natural resource wealth implies (as outlined in earlier sections).

In reality, movement along this continuum (Figure 4.11) is neither automatic nor unidirectional, as countries may move back and forth between various fragile situations. The goal is to help prevent countries at risk from slippage and to help countries in post-conflict and post-crisis situations move towards more stable political and economic development. Helping countries (resource-rich as well as resource-scarce) progress along the continuum requires an internationally coordinated strategic effort that covers a country's political, security, and socio-economic domains. The key, in this regard, is a differentiated and flexible response.

Analyzing the management of mineral (and oil) resources in fragile states further reveals that it has largely been molded by four interrelated conditions that are defined by the interplay of state power, contest, and conflict over the control of mineral resources. These are (1) public policy failures; (2) state predation or "shadow state", where rent-seeking substitutes rent creation; (3) rebel-dominated war (shadow) economies; and, (4) vested interests of regional and international actors. Two of these conditions have been discussed in the earlier sections of this chapter. The following analysis thus focuses primarily on

---

[45] AfDB (2007c)

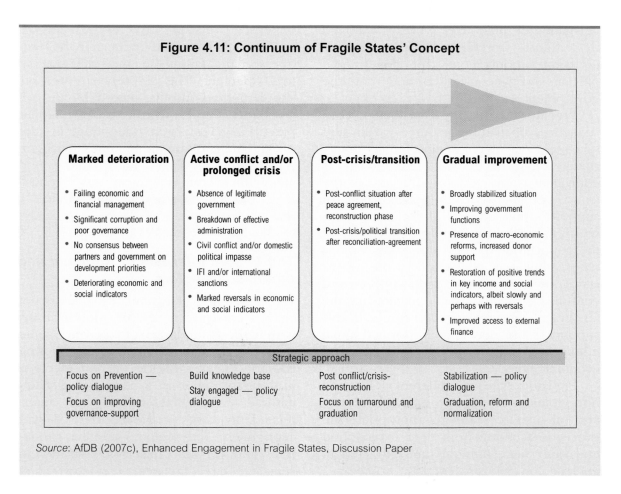

Figure 4.11: Continuum of Fragile States' Concept

Marked deterioration	**Active conflict and/or prolonged crisis**	**Post-crisis/transition**	**Gradual improvement**
• Failing economic and financial management • Significant corruption and poor governance • No consensus between partners and government on development priorities • Deteriorating economic and social indicators	• Absence of legitimate government • Breakdown of effective administration • Civil conflict and/or domestic political impasse • IFI and/or international sanctions • Marked reversals in economic and social indicators	• Post-conflict situation after peace agreement, reconstruction phase • Post-crisis/political transition after reconciliation-agreement	• Broadly stabilized situation • Improving government functions • Presence of macro-economic reforms, increased donor support • Restoration of positive trends in key income and social indicators, albeit slowly and perhaps with reversals • Improved access to external finance

Strategic approach

Focus on Prevention — policy dialogue Focus on improving governance-support	Build knowledge base Stay engaged — policy dialogue	Post conflict/crisis-reconstruction Focus on turnaround and graduation	Stabilization — policy dialogue Graduation, reform and normalization

Source: AfDB (2007c), Enhanced Engagement in Fragile States, Discussion Paper

state predation and on regional and international actors.

State Predation

The attainment of political independence did not transform the structure of a good number of African states, which remained forceful and authoritarian. Thus, instead of transforming the state and making it relevant for the satisfaction of the needs and aspirations of the people, some emerging post-colonial leaders were content with using the enormous authoritarian structures of the state to appropriate economic gains for private ends. In response to the forces of globalization, epitomized by the end of the Cold War, growing pressures for both economic and political liberalization, as well as increasing internal resistance and demands for democratization, many state regimes have resorted to repression and predation. A predatory state is characterized by the concentration of power at the top and the personalization of networks for delegation of this power, which is enforced by ruthless repression. In this context, economic inducements for government officials and generalized corruption are the government way of life.[46]

Predatory rule has two major consequences on natural resource wealth and revenue management in most fragile African states. First, access to state power is equivalent to access to wealth and to the sources of future wealth. Second, political support is built around clientele networks, which link power-holders with segments of the population. The concern of the various elites, ultimately connected to the top of state power, is how to gain support and consolidate clienteles while maximizing the amount of resources needed to obtain this support. These networks are formed along ethnic, regional, territorial, religious, and economic lines.[47]

Predatory states use different violent and non-violent strategies to manage mineral and oil resources and to appropriate the proceeds accruing from their exploitation and sale. Since minerals are extracted in enclave production centers, sometimes located off-shore, the common strategy is to negotiate royalties and other agreements directly with foreign companies. These deals are often shrouded in mystery, making it difficult, if not impossible, to track how much money is generated or how these revenues are spent. According to oil industry experts, OPEC countries on average retain some 75 percent of their oil revenues for the state budget, allowing for operating expenses. In the case of African oil producers, this proportion, even in the best-case scenario, falls in the range of 55 percent to 70 percent. The difference represents supplementary profits shared by the oil companies and African elites. Similar practices have been identified in the management of uranium mines in Niger, phosphates in Togo, and bauxite and aluminum in Guinea. Only meager revenues reach the state treasury, if at all, while the real royalties are paid directly into the foreign bank accounts of politicians.[48]

The Vested Interests of Regional and International Actors

The plundering of natural resources is not always confined to the warring factions within the boundaries of a given fragile state, but sometimes involves neighboring countries. Regional actors become involved in the exploitation of a neighboring state's natural resources through (1) the inter-related processes of proliferation of "war economies" and regional conflict formations; and, (2) direct military intervention in support of either the incumbent government or of armed insurgents.

State fragility or failure produces a number of economic ripple effects that are felt by other states in the region, with war or "shadow" economies as direct consequences. The interlinked conflict processes in Liberia and Sierra Leone, for example, have allowed huge amounts of timber and diamonds to be smuggled out by miners and shadow economic entrepreneurs.[49] An

---

[46] Castells (2000)
[47] Ibid.

[48] Hibou (1999)
[49] Humphreys (2005)

important aspect of resources and conflict is the role of third-party governments seeking to profit from resource-rich neighbors. Of all the post-Cold War civil conflicts in Africa, none reflects the complexities of the connection between natural resources and conflict more than the civil war in the DRC — referred to as "Africa's world war".

The corporate business practices of international actors are another issue. Since the end of the Cold War, foreign involvement in African conflicts has changed, giving way to the more subtle activities of non-state actors, especially private security firms, multinational corporations (MNCs), and non-governmental organizations. This foreign involvement falls into two main categories. The first, and perhaps the most controversial, is by foreign mercenary firms, euphemistically described as private security organizations (PSOs). Economic globalization has led to greater profits from investments in natural resource extraction, particularly in fragile African states, where there are impressive opportunities for profits. This has spurred increased investment by MNCs.

The second, and perhaps most important, type of external involvement in African conflicts, is by foreign multinational extractive companies (MECs), many of which have exploited situations of conflict to maximize their own profits. Unlike manufacturing or other secondary or tertiary industries, extractive industries do not divest or relocate when conflicts erupt. Given the nature and strategic importance of natural resources (especially oil and gas), the potential profits, and the capital-intensive and long-term nature of the investment,

MECs are not deterred by unpredictable or dangerous situations. Although some MECs have been known to divest in situations of instability and violence, the typical pattern of these companies is to factor in the costs of extra risks and stay on course. The business practices of MECs in African fragile states have, in various ways, contributed to conflict promotion.[50]

Transboundary Natural Resource Management

Africa faces numerous transboundary challenges, ranging from the continent's shaky political and economic spectra, to sectoral issues related to health, agriculture, natural resources management, and the environment. Regional cooperation has a fairly long history in virtually all parts of Africa, although the focus had, for a long time, been on regional economic integration schemes. While some progress has been made in this direction, new challenges related to water scarcity, deforestation, desertification, droughts, floods, and other environmental and natural resource issues have emerged in recent years.

These challenges have focused attention on regional cooperation in addressing transboundary issues to an extent that is far beyond conventional political and trade-related dimensions. Global warming, among others, requires response strategies that go far beyond national borders. In the water sector, the Nile River Basin is a very good example of a common pool of resources, which can only be harnessed through effective cooperation across countries. Another example is the

---

[50] Ballentine (2004)

observed coastal erosion in West Africa, which poses a transboundary challenge, as it is closely associated with deforestation in the tropical rainforests and in mangroves. Similar issues have emerged in East African coastal areas. Numerous examples can be provided on current *and potential* severe environmental and social impacts in Africa that are transboundary in nature (cause or effect). Some of the most important are related to *renewable* natural resources, such as water and land (described in Chapter 2). Others are related to non-renewable resources, for instance extraction of hydrocarbons (Box 4.3).

Sound "Transboundary Natural Resource Management" is essentially concerned with ensuring that goods, resources, and services of a transboundary nature — whose benefits and costs spill over national borders — are effectively managed through shared commitment and collective action, or collective efforts from all individuals or groups that benefit directly or indirectly from the goods or services. In the absence of cooperation and collective action, problems of externalities (positive or negative) arise.[51]

Addressing the Challenges

While sovereignty remains crucial in dealing with Africa's transboundary challenges, the political will of countries to perceive common challenges and to conclude binding agreements is the key determining factor. Joint strategies, policies, frameworks and subsequent commitments to address transboundary issues only yield meaningful results if the commitments are honored, or the common rules mutually respected. While mechanisms for sanctioning violators may sometimes become incentives for cooperation on transboundary issues, lack of cooperation, in most cases in Africa, is related to lack of means for honoring the commitments. This is particularly the case for many of Africa's small countries, which most often lack the technical, financial, and human resource capacity to honor transboundary commitments such as those related to river basin management, cross border trade in forest resources, conflict resources, international wildlife, and desertification. There is a clear need to strengthen African countries' capacity to implement transboundary commitments.

Box 4.3: Transboundary Cooperation in Extraction of Hydrocarbons

Hydrocarbon reserves in East Africa have been the focus of considerable attention and speculation in recent years. If not managed carefully, the potentially rich reserves in the Great Lakes region risk becoming a destabilizing factor among the nations, rather than an opportunity for joint development. In March 2007, a summit of 22 of the region's energy ministers was convened in Mozambique to discuss related issues. The hydrocarbons resources in the region have the potential to ameliorate the energy crisis significantly. However, successful exploitation of the resources will depend on security and stability, as well as on regional cooperation

Source: Oxford Analytica (2007), Africa: Middle East and Africa Executive Summary

---

[51] Bromley (1992)

Box 4.4: The African Development Bank and Transboundary Issues

As the leading development institution on the continent, the African Development Bank has long recognized its important role in helping Africa to overcome its transboundary challenges. In this regard, the Bank is actively providing support in critical areas of transboundary cooperation, which include river basin management, regional economic integration, regional cooperation on health, collaborative research (especially in agriculture), cooperation on infrastructure, and conflicts and conflict resolution. The Bank Group continues to deepen its focus on programs that provide opportunities for overcoming these challenges to improve the access of the poor to productive resources (notably water and land), technology and knowledge, and social services.

In the area of transboundary river basin management, the Bank is actively supporting river basin authorities and institutions. Examples include the Volta Basin Authority (West Africa), the Nile Basin Initiative (NBI) in Eastern and Northern Africa, and the Okavango and Limpopo Basins in Southern Africa, among others. The Bank's support is provided in the form of grants for project operations, as well as support extended through the African Water Facility.

With its current structure, which includes a "Knowledge Centre" (The Office of the Chief Economist), the Bank has further boosted its efforts in knowledge generation and dissemination, including research and training, and the provision of research and knowledge-related support to its RMCs. A key focus is transboundary issues.

Source: AfDB (2007b), Regional Cooperation: Addressing Trans-Boundary Challenges

---

Another important issue relates to the negotiation power of small and larger countries in Africa, with huge divergence in their technical, human, and financial capacities. In the case of river basin management, up-to-date technical knowledge of the short- and long-term dynamics of the water situation is required by all parties for equal bargaining power at negotiations. Thus, capacity building and technical assistance — to level the playing field — are crucial elements that should not be neglected in addressing transboundary issues. By its very nature, transboundary cooperation requires a lot of coordination and synchronization of activities, since everyone's participation and contribution are critical to minimizing externalities (positive and negative) and avoiding free riding on the efforts of others.

The New Scramble for Africa's Natural Resources

The last decade has seen a rapid increase in trade and investment flows between Africa and Asia, especially with China and India. India has a long history of trade and foreign direct investment in East Africa, in particular, given the many expatriate Indian communities in the sub-region. China's trade and investment in Africa date back decades, with heavy early investments in infrastructure such as railway systems. The basic facts about trade relations between Asia and Africa are as follows:[52]

- The volume of African exports to Asia is accelerating. It grew by 15 percent

---

[52] Broadman (2007)

between 1990 and 1995; and it has grown by 20 percent during the last five years (2000–2005).

- Since 2005, Asia's share of African exports (27 percent) has been on par with EU (32 percent) and the US (29 percent) shares.
- Asian exports to Africa are also growing rapidly. In the last five years, they have grown 18 percent more than exports from any other region, including from the European Union.
- Eighty-six (86) percent of Africa's exports to China and India are oil, metals, and agricultural raw materials.
- Five oil- and mineral-exporting African countries account for 85 percent of exports to China, while South Africa alone accounts for 68 percent of exports to India.

As illustrated in Figure 4.12, one of the most significant developments for Africa is the growing importance of capital flows from Asian countries such as China, India, South Korea, and Malaysia.

Foreign direct investment (FDI) from Asia to Africa has increased significantly in recent years. In 2005, Asian countries accounted for about 15 percent of the USD 31 billion FDI flows to Africa. Such investment contributes directly to the country's gross domestic product, generates employment, and reduces poverty. Africa is likely to benefit from Asian investments in a number of other ways:

- Asian investments facilitate the transfer of skills and technology to Africa. With their low-cost, low technology, Asian firms could create condi-

tions for facilitating competition for African domestic firms, thus enhancing productivity.

- Asian firms provide capital goods and intermediate inputs, which enable African firms to manufacture products potentially for exports, particularly to other developing countries, thereby boosting trade.
- Evidence suggests that Asian firms in Africa interact with Africa's informal business sector, thereby affecting demand and supply in the informal sector.

The discussion on the role of China and India in Africa has often highlighted the potential negative aspects of the growing demand for, and control of, natural resources by these emerging Asian powers. China and India have grown fast and have rapidly modernized their industries. As they develop and continue to grow, together with other rapidly expanding nations, the demand for natural resources, especially for oil and metals, is likely to increase even further.

The new interest in Africa, in particular, in the continent's resources, has certainly not bypassed the Western World. Systematic new efforts to tap further into this natural wealth became visible with the adoption of the African Growth and Opportunities Act by the out-going Clinton administration in the United States. Simultaneously, the European Union has sought to renegotiate its relations with the Africa, Caribbean, and Pacific countries under economic partnership agreements. These negotiations have since entered critical stages and provoked ongoing controversies, including the criticism that the

Figure 4.12: Development in Trade Relationship between Africa and Asia

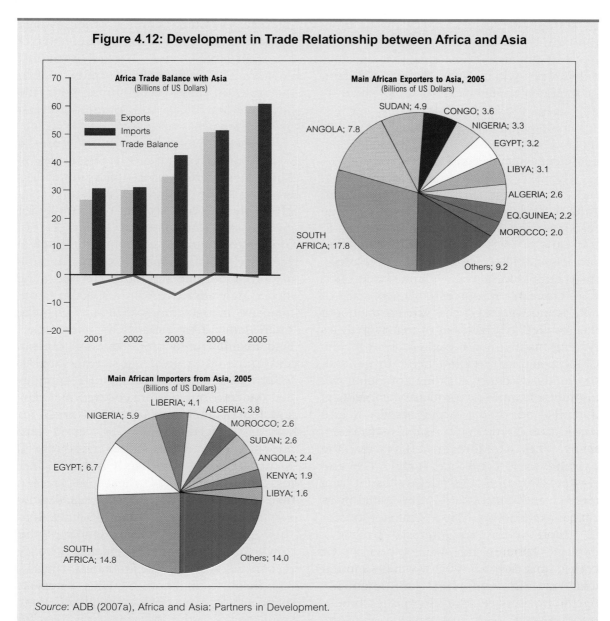

Source: ADB (2007a), Africa and Asia: Partners in Development.

EU's trade department is trying to bully through its own interests.[53] The positive news in this new scenario is that the days when Africa was considered a less important or forgotten continent — to some extent — are gone. Still, Africa remains on the "commodity supplying end", with others on the receiving end in this scramble for the continent's minerals and fossil resources.

The new offensive pursued by China, India, and others (in particular, Russia and Brazil) seeking access to fossil energy resources and other minerals and metals to fuel their own rapid industrialization processes, is likely to add further pressure to the scramble for access to limited and often non-renewable resources. This new stage of competing forces on the African continent has resulted in a plethora of recent analyses dealing mainly, if not exclusively, with the Chinese impact and practices. In general, the analyses criticize China for being yet another example of predatory capitalism, and also for being non-transparent and supportive of autocratic regimes. However, many tend to ignore the effects that the existing socio-economic imbalances and power structures (in Africa) have long created and consolidated. The criticism of China seems to be more a reflection of fear of losing one's own interests than of a genuine concern for African people. Of course, this does not whitewash the current Chinese offensive and its potentially damaging impact. The emerging Chinese track record does not suggest that the majority of African people will benefit. Nevertheless, the medium- to long-term

interests of China and of other foreign investors in Africa have to be the creation of a calculable and "investor-friendly environment". Ultimately, this must include the rule of law (in contrast with the law of the ruler) and other business-like practices.[54]

A recent World Bank study[55] uses a wealth of survey data on businesses in Africa to underline how China and India's growing trade with, and investment in, Africa presents an excellent opportunity for growth and international integration of Africa into the global economy. Although at present Africa mainly exports natural resources to China and India, it is becoming increasingly attractive with respect to labor-intensive manufacturing. There is growing Asian demand for processed commodities, light manufactured products, and tourism, and Africa has a great unused potential to fulfill this demand. The diagnosis cautions that the opportunities engendered by China and India's trade and investment in Africa will not necessarily be converted into growth and poverty reduction in the region. A critical finding of the study is that it is not just the quantity of these trades and investment flows that matters — but also the quality of the overall commercial relationships underlying as well as shaping these flows. Thus, both African and Asian policy makers need to devise appropriate policy responses to make the quality of these relationships even better. The World Bank study points to the following principles for reform (among others):

---

[53] Development Today (2007)

[54] Ibid.

[55] Broadman (2007)

At-the-Border Policy Reforms which include:
— lowering the overall level of tariffs (all countries);
— eliminating the escalating tariffs that limit Africa's leading exports (China and India);
— eliminating anti-export bias in import tariff policies, bias in investment decisions and disincentives for product diversification (for most African countries);
— eliminating trade barriers, including technical standards as protectionist measures (most countries);
— rationalizing and harmonizing existing "spaghetti bowl" bilateral and regional agreements (primarily for African countries);
— strengthening the role of investment promotion agencies and public-private investors' councils (African countries); and
— tailoring export and investment incentives to country-specific circumstances and in concert with World Trade Organization rules (African countries).

Behind-the-Border Reforms which include:
— enhancing domestic inter-enterprise competition by eliminating fundamental economic and policy barriers to entry and eliminating exit barriers (primarily for African countries);
— improving governance through greater transparency and accountability of public officials and establishing and securing efficient institutions that facilitate effective resolution of commercial disputes (primarily for African countries); and
— reducing poverty impacts from domestic price/production changes by trade flows through promotion of labor mobility, including enhancing flexibility of labor markets and improving the effectiveness of social safety nets (all African countries).

Between-the-Border Reforms which include:
— further developing trade facilitation infrastructure for integration into the global market as well as regional integration within Africa, including improvement and modernization of ports, roads, and rail transport, and modernization of telecommunications/IT (primarily for African countries);
— implementing customs reform by improving coordination among border-related agencies, simplifying customs procedures and making customs codes rule-based, transparent, and commercially-oriented and introducing the use of IT into the customs system (primarily for African countries);
— addressing imperfections in the information market for trade and investment opportunities, including technical standards (most African countries); and
— reviewing measures that restrict the movement of professionals (primarily for African countries).

The dramatic new trend in South-South economic relations is transforming traditional patterns of economic development. As outlined above, this is nowhere more evident than in African-Asian trade and investment flows. Thus, while China and

India are emerging as economic giants in Asia, Africa is coming into its own, finding a vital role in this transformation. These new South-South economic relations present real opportunities — as well as challenges — to African countries. It is important to emphasize that Africa does not need any one-size-fits-all policy reforms or approaches, since the available natural resources and the economies in Africa are highly heterogeneous. Reforms and policies should thus take into account country-specific circumstances.

Summary

This chapter presented and analyzed some stylized features of Africa's resource-rich economies, offering explanations on why natural resource wealth may stunt growth and development prospects. However, actual analysis of the data, tables and figures presented reveals the following trends and conclusions:

- Resource-rich African countries are richer (in terms of revenues, GDP and per capita GDP) than their resource-scarce peers. The gap narrowed during the 1980–2000 period, but it is widening again in conjunction with the recent resource boom.

- However, cumulatively, resource-rich countries only experienced an average growth rate of 2.4 percent from 1981–2006, considerably lower than the average 3.8 percent for resource-scarce countries.

- The group of resource-scarce coastal countries, which have almost a quarter of Africa's population, has experienced an average growth rate

of 4.1 percent, much higher than the 2.3 percent recorded by resource-rich coastal countries. Indeed, being resource-rich does *not* seem to make a significant difference for coastal countries.

- Land-locked resource-scarce countries are the poorest, by a significant factor. They are five times poorer than resource-rich countries, and almost six times poorer than resource-scarce coastal countries. Furthermore, the growth rate in this group of countries only averaged 2.5 percent from 1981 to 2006. In other words, the most important factor is whether a country is land-locked or not — this is even more important than being resource-rich or resource poor, or than any other aspect reviewed in this analysis.

- Available evidence also strongly suggests that the three factors that determine the onset of armed conflict — natural resources, low income per capita and low growth — are prevalent in large parts of the African continent. The literature also highlights other significant factors such as vertical and horizontal inequality, religion, and policy failures.

- The management of mineral (and oil) resources in fragile states has largely been molded by four interrelated conditions defined by the interplay of state power, contest, and conflict over the control of mineral resources. These conditions are public policy failures; state predation or 'shadow state', where rent-seeking substitutes rent creation; rebel-dominated war (shadow) economies; and, vested interests of regional and international actors.

The analysis further illustrates that the true potential benefits of having significant natural resource wealth has *not* been fully exploited by resource-rich African countries. Overall, the performance of resource-rich countries in Africa has been disappointing, especially from 1980 to 2000. Hard lessons learned from past resource boom and bust cycles and from the disappointing growth rates of the two-decade period need to be reviewed and lessons drawn for future use, especially now that a new boom has gained traction in Africa.

The last part of this chapter reviewed two key aspects of future development in Africa: (1) transboundary natural resource management, and (2) the new scramble for Africa's resources. The former calls for cooperation especially at the regional level, while the latter calls for a number of key reforms if Africa is to benefit from the scramble.

In conclusion, despite the challenges and issues involved, a natural resource boom can, under the right circumstances, be an important catalyst for growth and development. The often referred to "natural resource curse" can be avoided with the right knowledge, institutions, and policies. Several countries in Africa have demonstrated this, and there is some reason for cautious optimism that more countries have learned hard lessons from the past resource booms, and, in future, will pursue strategies and policies that will allow them to fully reap the benefits of natural resource wealth.

Appendix Table 4A: List of Country Classifications

Resource-Rich Countries	Resource-Scarce Countries	Landlocked Countries	Coastal Countries		SANE
			Resource-Rich	*Resource-Scarce*	
Oil-Exporting Countries	Benin	*Resource-Rich*	Algeria	Benin	South Africa
Algeria	Burkina Faso	Botswana	Angola	Cape Verde	Algeria
Angola	Burundi	Central African Republic	Cameroon	Comoros	Nigeria
Cameroon	Cape Verde	Chad	Congo	Djibouti	Egypt
Chad	Comoros		Congo, Dem. Rep.	Egypt	
Congo	Djibouti	*Resource-Scarce*	Côte d'Ivoire	Eritrea	
Côte d'Ivoire	Egypt	Burkina Faso	Equatorial Guinea	Gambia	
Equatorial Guinea	Eritrea	Burundi	Gabon	Ghana	
Gabon	Ethiopia	Ethiopia	Guinea	Guinea Bissau	
Libya	Gambia	Lesotho	Libya	Liberia	
Nigeria	Ghana	Malawi	Mauritania	Madagascar	
Sudan	Guinea Bissau	Mali	Mozambique	Mauritius	
	Kenya	Niger	Namibia	Morocco	
Mineral-Exporting Countries	Lesotho	Rwanda	Nigeria	Sao Tome & Principe	
Botswana	Liberia	Swaziland	Sierra Leone	Senegal	
Central African Republic	Madagascar	Uganda	South Africa	Seychelles	
Congo, Democratic Republic	Malawi	Zimbabwe	Sudan	Somalia	
Guinea	Mali	Zambia	Tanzania	Togo	
Mauritania	Mauritius			Tunisia	
Mozambique	Morocco				
Namibia	Niger				
Sierra Leone	Rwanda				
South Africa	Sao Tome & Principe				
Tanzania	Senegal				
	Seychelles				
	Somalia				
	Swaziland				
	Togo				
	Tunisia				
	Zimbabwe				
	Zambia				

Appendix Table 4B: African Exports, 2005

	Three main exports, with their share in total exports* (in %)			No of products accounting for more than 75 percent of exports
	Product I	Product II	Product III	
Algeria	Crude petroleum (67.2)	Natural gas, liquefied (13.2)	Natural gas, gaseous (5.6)	2
Angola	Crude petroleum (95.8)			1
Benin	Cotton, not carded, combed (55.3)	Edible nuts fresh, dried (16.5)	Oth. non-ferr. metal waste (6.4)	3
Botswana	Diamonds. excl. industrial (88.2)	Nickel mattes, sintrs. etc (8.1)		1
Burkina Faso	Cotton, not carded, combed (84.5)			1
Burundi	Coffee, not roasted (88)			1
Cameroon	Crude petroleum (48.8)	Wood, non-conifer, sawn (14.1)	Bananas, fresh or dried (8.7)	4
Cape Verde	Fish, frozen ex. f illets (61.4)	Trousers, breeches, etc. (6.3)	Gas turbines, nes (4)	4
Central African Republic	Diamonds. excl. industrial (40)	Wood, non-conif, rough, unt (33.8)	Cotton, not carded, combed (8.9)	3
Chad	Crude petroleum (94.9)			1
Comoros	Spices, ex. pepper, pimento (57.9)	Essential oils (14.2)	Fish, frozen ex.f illets (12.7)	3
Congo	Crude petroleum (88.7)			1
Congo Democratic Republic	Diamonds. excl. industrial (42.6)	Oth. non-ferr. ore, concntr (17.2)	Crude petroleum (16.7)	3
Cote d'Ivoire	Cocoa beans (38.2)	Crude petroleum (12)	Cocoa paste (7.7)	7
Djibouti	Bovine animals, live (20)	Trousers, breeches, etc. (7.2)	Othr. ferrous waste, scrap (7)	17
Egypt	Natural gas, liquefied (15.8)	Crude petroleum. (10.3)	Portland cement, etc. (4.7)	46
Equatorial Guinea	Crude petroleum (92.6)			1
Eritrea	Natural gums, resins, etc (17.3)	Sesame (sesamum) seeds (8.7)	Molluscs (7.6)	14

Appendix Table 4B (continued)

	Three main exports, with their share in total exports* (in %)			No of products accounting for more than 75 per cent of exports
	Product I	Product II	Product III	
Ethiopia	Coffee, not roasted (47.8)	Sesame (sesamum) seeds (20.2)		5
Gabon	Crude petroleum (76.7)	Wood, non-conif, rough, unt (10.6)	Manganese ores, concentrs (6.9)	1
Gambia	Edible nuts fresh, dried (43.5)	Mech.shovel etc.s-propld (9.9)	Groundnuts (peanuts) (7.7)	6
Ghana	Cocoa beans (46.1)	Manganese ores, concentrs (7.2)	Wood, non-conifer, sawn (6.7)	8
Guinea	Aluminum ore, concentrat (50.9)	Alumina (aluminum oxide) (17.2)	Copper ores, concentrates (7.8)	3
Guinea Bissau	Edible nuts fresh, dried (93.5)			1
Kenya	Tea (16.8)	Cut flowers and foliage (14.2)	Oth. frsh, chll. vegetables (8.1)	27
Lesotho	Jersys, pullovrs, etc. knit (29.2)	Trousers, breeches, etc. (22)	Diamonds. excl. industrial (15)	4
Liberia	Ships, boats, other. vessels (73.9)	Spec. purpose vessels etc (8.9)	Natural rubber latex (8)	2
Libya	Crude petroleum (95.3)			1
Madagascar	Jersys, pullovrs, etc. knit (19.4)	Crustaceans, frozen (13.2)	Spices, ex. pepper, pimento (9)	14
Malawi	Tobacco, stemmed, stripped (59.2)	Tea (7.6)	Sugars, beet or cane, raw (5.3)	4
Mali	Cotton, not carded ,combed (81.8)			1
Mauritania	Iron ore, concntr. not agg (51.3)	Molluscs (24)	Fish, frozen ex. fillets (13.5)	2
Mauritius	Sugars, beet or cane, raw (21.4)	T-shirts, other. vests knit (18.7)	Shirts (7.6)	10
Morocco	Inorganic acid, oxide etc (7.2)	Insultd wire, etc. condctr. (6.8)	Natural calc. phosphates (5.6)	32
Mozambique	Alum., alum. alloy, unwrght (73.4)	Crustaceans, frozen (4.7)		2

Appendix Table 4B (continued)

Namibia	Diamonds. excl .industrial (39.1)	Radio-active chemicals (11.4)	Zinc, zinc alloy, unwrght. (9.7)	5
Niger	Radio-active chemicals (79.5)			1
Nigeria	Crude petroleum (92.2)			1
Rwanda	Coffee, not roasted (51.9)	Ore etc. molybdn. niob. etc (19)	Tin ores, concentrates (9.8)	3
Sao Tome and Principe	Cocoa beans (55.2)	Vessels, oth. float. struct	Drawing, measurg. instrmnt (7.6) (10.9)	4
Senegal	Inorganic acid, oxide etc (38.8)	Molluscs (9.8)	Fish, fresh, chilled, whole (6.4)	8
Seychelles	Fish, prepard, presrvd, nes (44.1)	Fish, frozen ex.f fillets (27.5)	Ships, boats, othr. vessels (11)	3
Sierra Leone	Diamonds. excl. industrial (62.7)	Cocoa beans (7.2)	Cultivating machinery. etc (4.1)	4
Somalia	Sheep and goats, live (34.6)	Bovine animals, live (19.7)	Fish, frozen ex. fillets (7.8)	5
South Africa	Platinum (12.5)	Oth. coal, not agglomeratd (8)	Gold, nonmontry excl ores (7.9)	39
Sudan	Crude petroleum (89.2)			1
Swaziland	Sugars, beet or cane, raw (14.1)	Food preparations, nes (9.3)	Flavours, Industrial use (9)	20
Tanzania	Gold, nonmontry excl ores (10.9)	Fish fillets, frsh, chilld (9.7)	Copper ores, concentrates (8.6)	15
Togo	Cocoa beans (22.4)	Natural calc. phosphates (19.8)	Cotton, not carded, combed (18.6)	8
Tunisia	Crude petroleum (9)	Trousers, breeches, etc. (8.7)	Insultd wire, etc. condctr (6.7)	36
Uganda	Coffee, not roasted (31.1)	Fish fillets, frsh, chilld (24.3)	Tobacco, stemmed, stripped (7.5)	5
Zambia	Copper; anodes; alloys (55.8)	Cobalt, cadmium, etc. unwrt (7)	Cotton, not carded, combed (5.7)	5
Zimbabwe	Tobacco, stemmed, stripped (13.9)	Nickel, nckl. alloy, unwrgt (12.6)	Nickel ores, concentrates (12.3)	16
Africa	Crude petroleum (49.2) [18]	Diamonds. excl. industrial (3.7) [12.6]	Nickel ores, concentrates (2.8) [17.5]	26

Notes: * Products are reported when accounting for more than 4 percent of total exports.
** Figures in [ ] represent the share of Africa in the World export for each product.

ADB Statistics Department; PC-TAS 2001–2005 International Trade Center UNCTAD/WTO–UN Statistics Division

CHAPTER 5
Making Natural Wealth Work for the Poor

This chapter examines the linkages between natural resource wealth and poverty in Africa. The linkages are complex and a number of strategies aimed at using resources directly or indirectly for poverty reduction have been implemented most recently with the overall goal of achieving the Millennium Development Goals (MDGs). This Chapter analyses the strategies, core issues, and results achieved in selected cases. In particular, it provides a platform for pursuing the best opportunities to fully harness natural resource wealth in the future.

Nature-Wealth-Power Framework

The United Nations Millennium Declaration, which led to the formulation of the MDGs, is a worldwide pledge to eradicate extreme poverty and inequality in the world. Nowhere is this more needed than in Africa. Achieving the two goals of eradicating extreme poverty and hunger (MDG 1) and ensuring environmental sustainability (MDG 7) depends on making natural capital, along with other productive capital, work for the poor. Achieving the MDGs and development in Africa is, to a large extent, about making sure that poor rural people benefit more from local natural resources. Today, more than 400 million Africans live in poverty. Twenty-two of the world's 25 poorest countries (and 33 of the poorest 50), based on gross national income, are in Africa[1], as are 29 of the 31 least developed countries as measured by the

United Nation's Human Development Index.[2] In addition, Africa now matches Latin America in inequity along many social and economic dimensions: South Africa and Namibia, for instance, are among the world's most inequitable nations.[3]

The urbanization growth rate is considerable in many African countries, but overall, the population in Africa will remain predominantly rural-based for many decades. In 2005, a total of 460 million people lived in rural areas. By 2025, the number is expected to climb to almost 560 million. Moreover, in most countries, the rural sector accounts for more than 50 percent of national employment and income (in some countries, more than 85 percent). Small-scale agriculture is the largest single source of income for most rural families, and many rural households are also engaged in logging, charcoal production, mining, fishing, hunting, gathering, and other nature-based economic activities. It is thus important to recognize that, while all Africans depend on natural resources, rural households are generally more dependent on the natural environment and on natural resources than urban-based families. This relationship also extends to the poorest segment of the population that tends to be the most dependent of all.[4]

---

[1] World Bank (2006b)

[2] UNDP (2006)

[3] World Bank (2006a); UNDP (2005)

[4] World Bank (2006a); World Bank (2003); WRI et al. (2005); Bass et al. (2005); Pearce (2005); UNEP and IISD (2004); Shackleton and Shackleton (2004); DFID et al. (2002); Bebbington (1999)

Figure 5.1: Linkages Between Natural Resources, Economic Growth and Governance

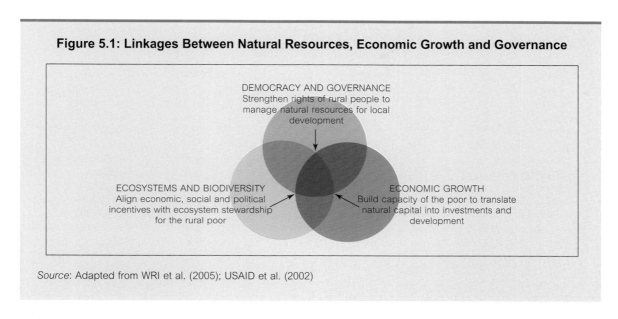

DEMOCRACY AND GOVERNANCE
Strengthen rights of rural people to
manage natural resources for local
development

ECOSYSTEMS AND BIODIVERSITY
Align economic, social and political
incentives with ecosystem stewardship
for the rural poor

ECONOMIC GROWTH
Build capacity of the poor to translate
natural capital into investments and
development

Source: Adapted from WRI et al. (2005); USAID et al. (2002)

As outlined in previous chapters, Africa is generously endowed with productive land and valuable natural resources, including renewable resources (such as timber, water, and land resources) and nonrenewable resources (minerals, gas, oil). While pockets of overexploitation and environmental degradation must be brought under management for sustainable use, much of Africa's resource base is robust, resilient, unused or underutilized, and holds great promise for development.

Making rational choices about nature is central to making natural wealth work for the poor and to maximizing the contribution that a nation's resource endowment can make to social and economic development. In Africa, the environment, economic growth, and governance are inextricably linked and are the essential elements of rural development and poverty reduction. These elements — nature, wealth, and power — and their relations provide a useful framework for understanding development and charting a path forward (see Figure 5.1). Experience in Africa and elsewhere demonstrates that investments that recognize and integrate these three elements yield positive development outcomes. As a result, a nature-wealth-power framework is defining investments in the rural development of a growing number of governments and development assistance agencies.[5]

Mobilizing all people by applying a poverty-oriented, pro-democratic and environmentally sound approach to unleash the true potential of the natural environment holds the key for the future development of Africa. This will be explored further in this chapter.

---

[5] USAID at al. (2002)

Box 5.1: Nature, Wealth and Power Principles to Guide Investments in Africa

Nature	Wealth	Power
• Improve information and knowledge management systems • Promote local land use planning and appropriate resource tenure systems • Foster innovation, social learning, and adaptive management • Build capacity and invest in human resources • Promote cost-effective technical advisory and intermediary services	• Be strategic about the economies of natural resource management • Strengthen markets and NRM market incentives • Invest in rural organizations • Create a framework for better NRM choices • Ensure that local resource managers have secure access to NRM means and benefits	• Strengthen environmental procedural rights for rural people • Improve rural input into public decisions and policy • Redistribute natural resource authority and functions • Transfer power, rights, and responsibilities to representatives and accountable authorities • Explore a minimum environmental standards approach • Promote platforms that allow for continuous and inclusive consultations

Source: Adapted from USAID et al. (2002)

Strategies for Managing Natural Resources for Sustainable Development

Implementing a nature-wealth-power framework for development in Africa requires new strategies and instruments. Africa's future economic growth and development cannot be separated from the management of its natural resources, and sound environmental management cannot be separated from the broader context of politics, political systems, and governance. Governments, civil society, and the development assistance community should recognize and capitalize on these linkages to achieve positive environment and development outcomes. There are multiple dimensions to the nature-wealth-power linkages (see Box 5.1) that collectively constitute the

principles that can guide investment for development purposes in Africa.

These nature, wealth and power principles are consistent with the features, components, and instruments of other recently developed analytical frameworks for utilizing natural endowments to foster sustainable development. These include frameworks developed from the analysis of minerals and mining by the World Bank, the United Nations Conference on Trade and Development, and the International Council on Mining and Metals[6] and by the Mining, Minerals and Sustainable Development project.[7] They are also similar to the features of new poverty reduction frameworks

---

[6] World Bank, UNCTD and ICMM (2006)
[7] MMSD (2002)

developed by the United Kingdom's Department for International Development[8] and the Poverty and Environment Partnership[9].

A common feature of the frameworks is the focus on integrating or mainstreaming natural resources into development and the important role of good governance in achieving positive development and environment outcomes. All frameworks acknowledge that sound natural resource management requires attention not only to environmental and natural resource laws and institutions, but also to the broad range of legislation, organizations, decisions, procedures and actions that influence and otherwise affect the environment. They also recognize the need to move beyond traditional approaches to natural resource management (such as command and control mechanisms) to more innovative approaches (such as economic instruments and self-audits).

Finally it is important to note that development strategies, including those that emphasize rural development and focus on making natural wealth work for the poor, are not static or final. Strategies and instruments must adjust to changing local circumstances — including changing local perceptions, interests, and priorities. Even nature-based growth and development must be seen as a stepping stone in the economic development and empowerment of the rural poor. With few opportunities for Africa in manufacturing and services, but often abundant natural resources, nature-based development is arguably the best strategy for achieving poverty reduction at present. However, in the future, Africa's environment-driven household economies may need to give way to labor-based livelihoods. Appropriate transition and exit strategies will need to be developed to sunset nature-based economic activities, in particular, to focus more on job creation and growth in sectors and regions where poor people live and work. This will include jobs in agriculture, but will increasingly emphasize non-farm activities and require new investments, such as a renewed focus on education, and labor market policies.[10]

Environmental Instruments and Policies for Natural Resources Management

Environmental policy is the body of interlocking statutes, common laws, treaties, conventions, regulations, and policies designed to protect the natural environment from activities that threaten or damage the health and welfare of people.[11] In Africa, it is even more important than elsewhere that policy makers recognize that productive ecosystems are the basis of a sustainable income stream from nature. The policies must emphasize the suite of environmental, economic, and governance policies that affect sustainable natural resource use (as opposed to protection or conservation) and, in turn, development and poverty reduction.

In most African nations, natural resource legislation has been in place since the

---

[8] DFID (2006a); (2006b); (2002)
[9] UNDP and UNEP (2007); Pearce (2005); UNEP and IISD (2004)

[10] Veit (2007)
[11] Richardson and Wood (2006)

colonial era, but many of the laws focused either on conservation, at the expense of human welfare, or on resource exploitation for export, at the expense of the environment. Laws in Africa have not, in general, promoted sustainable use or development, and environmental policies did not, in a real manner, crystallize until the late 1980s — during the general debate on sustainable development and the lead up to the 1992 United Nations Conference on Environment and Development in Rio de Janeiro, Brazil.[12]

Africa's new national environmental protection agencies were thus established quite recently — at the time governments were also downsizing, democratizing, and engaging in free market economies — and were tasked with regulation and enforcement mandates. Typically, the new environmental and natural resource laws and regulations were informed by concepts such as the precautionary and polluter pays principles, environmental impact assessments, minimum environmental standards, transparency and access to information, public participation, and environmental justice.

In much of Africa, the environmental policies enacted and the implementing institutions are inadequate and weak and, as a result, pressing environmental problems persist. Many apex environmental protection agencies lack the legal mandate and authority to coordinate, regulate, and oversee resource use by line ministries, or to address crosscutting and cross-border environmental issues. Many also remain chronically under-staffed and under-

resourced. While several environmental policy issues demand urgent attention, the two most critical issues for sustainable development are[13]

- Strengthening environmental policy and law; and
- Regulating the private sector

Strengthening environmental policy: The suite of laws and regulations that constitute environmental policy is, in general, incomplete, outdated, and poorly or selectively enforced in Africa. In some cases, new national framework environmental management acts anticipate the enactment of subsidiary legislation such as environmental impact assessment regulations and minimum environmental standards (for example, air and water quality, noise levels). Nevertheless, in many countries, this enabling legislation has yet to be developed and effectively implemented. Many natural resource laws are old, cumbersome, and irrelevant to the circumstances and concerns of today. Outdated regulations that contradict or are inconsistent with national environmental protection acts must be reformed. The legal supremacy of a national environmental act over sectoral laws, including legislation governing high-value natural resources must be recognized and systematically enforced. Apex environmental protection agencies must also have adequate authority over line ministries and natural resource departments on matters that affect the environment.[14]

---

[12] Larson and Ribot (2007); Veit (2006); Gibson (1999); Ribot (1998)

[13] Veit (2007)
[14] Ibid.

Responsibility for implementing policy and enforcing environmental laws is divided among a number of ministries, government departments, and agencies (see Box 5.2 for the case of the AfDB). For these institutions to perform their roles and functions effectively, responsibility areas must be clear and relevant government institutions strengthened with broader mandates, new authorities, and expanded capacities (human resources, funding and equipment).

Regulating the private sector: As outlined in previous chapters, recent years have seen a significant increase in the role of the private sector (forest and mining sectors, for example) in Africa with respect to the use and management of natural resources. In many cases, natural resources are being mined with little or no regard for long-term sustainability and viability issues. While all resource users have environmental management responsibilities, the commercial sector is securing rights over an increasingly larger share of productive resources and deserves special attention from regulatory agencies. Despite considerable government and donor investments in natural protection and environmental matters, many domestic and foreign corporations are not in compliance with national environmental legislation, or, for that matter, general sound extraction principles and practices. Governments must step up their efforts to conduct environmental audits, monitor the environmental effects of corporate actions, and apply sanctions on industry for non-compliance, poor performance and resource degradation.[15]

Transnational corporations and international stakeholders are responding to increasing competition and the powerful threat of global activism with new strategies. Over the past decade, a growing number of companies have more or less voluntarily adopted industry self-regulation policies, such as corporate codes of conduct, social and environmental standards, sectoral guidelines and covenants, customer or supplier requirements (value-chain demands), environmental management systems, third-party certification, and environmental auditing and monitoring systems. Such self-regulation can certainly improve environmental performance, preserve natural resources and, at times, also the bottom line for participating companies. However, relatively few industries operating in Africa have adopted such policies[16]. In other words, self-regulation must not be viewed as a substitute for government regulation. Traditional command and control regulations are still the foundation of environmental policies and play an important role in structuring and achieving positive outcomes. However, international funding mechanisms are important for sustainable livlihoods (see Box 5.3).

Natural Wealth, Economic Growth, and Poverty Reduction

Investment and Wealth Distribution Policies

Economic growth is essential for poverty reduction and, as such, is central to promoting development and improving

---

[15] Ibid.

[16] Ibid.

Box 5.2: AfDB Environmental Policies, Strategies, and Initiatives

The African Development Bank (AfDB) adopted an environmental policy in 1990, followed, in 1992, by environmental assessment guidelines aimed at guiding environmental concerns and practices in AfDB operations. The guidelines have been updated several times to accommodate growing concerns about the management of Africa's natural resources. In 1997, the Bank published its *Sectoral Environmental and Social Impact Guidelines*. In 2003, a revised environmental policy was discussed in an informal Board seminar and a revised version was finally adopted in 2004. The *2002–2004 Environment Policy* revised the sectoral approach of earlier policies and adopted a cross-sectoral approach based on the concept of sustainable development. Key to the implementation of this policy are operational strategies to mainstream environmental issues at all levels of the Bank's activities and enforce the *Environmental and Social Assessment Procedures* agreed in 2001.

In 2005, the AfDB developed an *Environmental Action Plan*, followed by the development of an Implementation Plan for 2005–2007. The plan was anchored on mainstreaming environmental issues into all Bank operations, strengthening existing environmental and social assessment procedures, and developing new environmental management tools. It was also aimed at demarcating internal responsibility for various units of the Bank, supporting institutional strengthening and capacity building for AfDB staff and regional member countries (RMCs), promoting public consultation and information disclosure, and building partnerships. This implementation plan entails a revision of the format and content of AfDB environmental guidelines to make environmental categorization an imperative for all Bank Group operations.

Furthermore, in 2005, the AfDB developed its *Strategic Environmental Assessment (SEA) Guidelines* to upstream environmental assessments from the project level to the policy, program, and plan levels. Since then, the tool has been used to screen the Bank's policy-based lending, structural adjustment lending, and sectoral adjustment lending, as well as regional projects. The main benefit of the tool is that it allows far-ranging and cumulative environmental impact assessments, compared with traditional project-specific environmental impact assessment studies. Furthermore, the SEA can help facilitate consultations with the public by identifying issues, initiating baseline data collection, and developing action programs. Environmental and social categorization is compulsory for all Bank Group operations and is based on the following categorization system:

- **Category I Projects** are operations that are likely to induce irreversible adverse environmental and social impacts or significantly affect environmental and social components considered sensitive by the Bank or the borrowing country;
- **Category II Projects** are operations that are likely to have detrimental or side-specific environmental and social impacts that are less adverse than Category I projects, and can be minimized by the application of mitigating measures or the incorporation of internationally recognized design criteria and standards;
- **Category III Projects** are operations that are not likely to have any direct and/or indirect adverse environmental and social impacts;
- **Category IV Projects** are operations related to financial intermediaries, especially Lines of Credit (LOC).

Other corporate activities implemented to improve the Bank's environmental performance include training of staff on environmental and social assessment procedures and on strategic environmental assessments.

Source: African Development Bank Annual Report (2005; 2006).

Box 5.3: The Global Environment Facility and the AfDB: A Promising Partnership to Support the African Environment and Sustainable Livelihoods

The Global Environment Facility (GEF) provides grants to developing countries for projects that benefit the global environment and promote sustainable livelihoods in local communities. GEF projects and programs address six complex global environmental issues, corresponding to the GEF focal areas: (i) biodiversity; (ii) climate change; (iii) international waters; (iv) land degradation; (v) ozone layer; and (vi) persistent organic pollutants. The GEF operates through three implementing agencies (United Nations Development Programme, United Nations Environment Programme, and World Bank) and seven executing agencies including the African Development Bank (AfDB).

The AfDB became a GEF executing agency with direct access to GEF full project resources in 2004. Direct access to GEF project resources allows the Bank to (i) identify, prepare, appraise, and implement GEF projects on behalf of GEF; (ii) submit full project proposals for GEF financing directly to GEF without going through an implementing agency; and (iii) receive project grants directly from GEF, being directly accountable for their use. The unique partnership is anchored on the recognition that the drive for global sustainability should be rooted in strong links between the environment and development — as a clean environment is essential for both sustainable development and poverty reduction.

GEF funding is intended mainly to help developing countries meet the objectives of various international environmental conventions. GEF serves as the "financial mechanism" for four conventions: the United Nations Convention on Biological Diversity, the United Nations Framework Convention on Climate Change, the United Nations Convention to Combat Desertification, and the Stockholm Convention on Persistent Organic Pollutants. Since 1991, GEF has provided funds amounting to USD 4.5 billion to more than 1,300 projects in 140 countries and generated USD 14.5 billion in co-financing from other partners for projects in developing countries and countries with economies in transition.

The partnership between GEF and AfDB provides substantial opportunities to blend Bank lending and grant resources (baseline financing) for sustainable development with GEF resources for the protection of the global environment. In 2006–07, the Bank group developed a pipeline of projects for GEF co-financing in relevant fields such as climate adaptation and sustainable land management. A number of proposals have already been approved by GEF for project preparation (grant) financing and are currently undergoing implementation preparation.

Source: Sustainable Development Division, AfDB (July 2007)

wellbeing. Across Africa, governments have implemented various economic reforms — removal of price controls, public expenditure reforms, improvement of private and cooperative banking and financial services, and marketing and input supply reforms. Economic liberalization and adoption of market systems have increased private capital investments, improved growth, and generated new public revenues and consid-erable wealth, especially for individuals and groups well-positioned with high initial assets to capitalize on the new opportunities. More natural resources are being exploited, generating more natural-based incomes. As outlined earlier in the report, this generated wealth has also yielded development outcomes and reduced poverty — albeit only on a larger scale in a limited number of countries, such as

---

Box 5.4: Gold Mining in Tanzania

Mining, especially gold mining, is a growing sector in Tanzania. The mining policy identifies three objectives: improve the national economy (GDP and foreign exchange earnings); alleviate poverty (in this case, secure employment and alternative sources of income for rural people); and ensure environmental protection and management. In 2005, Tanzania extracted more than 50 tons of gold — up from 3 tons in 1995 — and is now Africa's third largest producer, behind South Africa and Ghana. Mineral exports are the second largest contributor to foreign exchange earnings, and gold, specifically, is Tanzania's leading export. In 2003, gold accounted for 44 percent of goods sent abroad.[17]

With the economic liberalization of the late-1990s, the role of the government shifted from owning and operating mines, and favoring artisanal and small-scale mining, to providing policy guidelines, stimulating private investment, and supporting large-scale foreign investments. Large-scale mining replaced many artisanal and small-scale mining operations. This represents a very significant change in policies, with significant consequences; many people were displaced, and many have yet to be compensated for their investments and loss of livelihood opportunities. A number of activists have also claimed that significant human rights abuses occurred during the removal process.[18] In 1995, a total of 550,000 people were engaged in artisanal and small-scale gold mining, which indirectly generated up to 1.5 million jobs. Tthe average income in these mining areas was six times higher than income in the predominantly agricultural regions.[19] By some accounts, artisanal mining had contributed more to income growth for the rural poor than all development activities of the previous 30 years combined. Today, small-scale and artisanal mining employs only 20,000 people and large-scale mining employs another 8,400.[20]

Unlike in South Africa, gold can be mined at relatively shallow depths in Tanzania. The "open pit" mining technology used by large-scale mining companies has caused significant environmental damage and it is unclear whether the companies will rehabilitate the land after all the gold has been extracted. For the most part, the companies comply with national environmental laws and regulations, but they have been reluctant to go beyond minimum standards. In addition, Tanzania's environmental policy is weak and has significant gaps; and the National Environment Management Council, the institution responsible for managing EIAs, is purely advisory.[21]

Little of the government revenues from mining have trickled down to the gold mining areas or other rural regions in the country. In Tanzania, there are no specific benefit-sharing arrangements with rural communities or local governments. Moreover, local governments do not have the authority to tax the large mining companies. However, the government wants its share of mining revenue to rise to 10 percent of GDP by 2025, up from 3 percent in 2005.[22]

Botswana. Thus, history has shown that poverty remains high in many resource-rich countries, where income inequity has increased and a number of the countries may, in fact, have been better off not exploiting the resources (reference to the resource curse, etc.). One additional example of this dilemma, gold mining in Tanzania, is provided in Box 5.4.

In recent years, widespread government and donor attention has focused on promoting "pro-poor economic growth."

---

[17] Douglas Lake Minerals (DLM) (2007)
[18] Lissu (2001)
[19] Muganda (2004); Mwaipopo et al. (2004)

[20] Associated Press (2006)
[21] Lawcastles (2006)
[22] Oluoch (2007); Jomo (2007a); (2007b)

Pro-poor growth means creating opportunities that enable the poor to work their way out of poverty. It focuses on opportunities that target the assets of the poor, specifically: labor, land and local natural resources. Pro-poor growth calls for investments that improve the prospects for poor people to share in the opportunities created by economic growth — including building local capacities and providing the infrastructure that the poor need to capitalize on new opportunities.

Even with strong economic growth, poverty reduction — especially for the poorest — can be greatly enhanced by investing goods and services targeted at poor people and regions. In high-inequity, high-poverty countries, redistribution can be more effective than economic growth in reducing poverty. Even small changes in distribution can have a large effect on building the assets of the poor, enabling them to capitalize on economic opportunities and effectively compete.[23] Distribution should not be considered charity, but rather, part of a comprehensive poverty reduction strategy to speed up the participation of the poor in economic opportunities. In apartheid South Africa, when skilled labor shortages limited economic growth, the government targeted the poor with public investments in health, education, and other social services to strengthen the labor pool — with positive development outcomes.[24]

The distribution of goods and services is largely determined by government policies and practices. These distribution policies constitute powerful instruments that governments can use to provide economic, political, and other incentives in support of environmental management, poverty reduction, and other national objectives. In African countries, where the distribution of natural capital determines the overall distribution of wealth, natural resources or environmental distribution policies can be particularly effective tools for poverty reduction and development.[25] Moreover, productive land and high-value resources are not evenly distributed geographically or accessible to all citizens. In the absence of policies that facilitate fair distributions of natural and environmental benefits, resource-rich regions and people with access to productive lands may prosper, while those without valuable resources or with access to only low-value resources remain poor. Increasing benefits to the poor will also raise the value of natural resources for them, and create local incentives for sound environmental management.

Across Africa, it is common that policies promote and facilitate the concentration of many environmental goods in the hands of a privileged few, contradicting national poverty reduction and social equity objectives. History and experience show that as natural resources gain value, often through commercialization, the political and economic elite find ways to capture the benefits — by controlling the assets or markets, or by other means — while passing the associated social and environmental costs (externalities) on to

---

[23] Easterly (2002); Naschold (2002); Killick (2002)
[24] Fedderker and Mariotti (2002)

[25] Larson and Ribot (2007); Veit (2006); Ribot (1998)

the poor and disenfranchised. To counter this, poverty reduction proponents in Africa must focus their efforts on promoting pro-poor allocations of environmental goods.[26]

Two types of environmental benefits are particularly important for poverty reduction and environmental management: (1) market shares and profit margins of commercially exploited natural resource commodities; and (2) public revenues from the use of ecosystems and extraction of natural resources.

Profit Margins: In Africa, the rural poor rarely benefit in any significant manner from the commercial exploitation of natural resources. Benefits, in the form of profits, taxes, fees, or unofficial patronage of gifts, are usually concentrated in the hands of a few inter-mediaries such as money lenders, truckers, wholesalers, or state agents. Despite decen-tralization and other poverty reduction investments, there has thus been little increase in income and profit from natural commodities for rural communities.[27]

Government and donor investments are needed to promote fair distribution of bene-fits along natural product value chains. Monopolies and cartels that protect middle-men must be dismantled, and cooperatives of smallholder producers that can compete with established buyers and transporters strengthened. Profitable activities can be opened up to rural populations by increasing access to labor employment, processing, and trade opportunities both in the local arena and at higher levels in the marketing chain. Such openings can have a

dual effect on communities by increasing local benefits and revenues from the harvesting and sale of natural resources, and increasing local government revenues from an expanded nature-based tax base.[28]

Public Revenues: Natural resources and environmental rents constitute a significant percentage of the budgetary income of many African countries. Public revenues are generated from royalties, taxes, fees, fines, and other means associated with the public and private use of natural resources and ecosystems. In the absence of any meaning-ful fiscal decentralization, most environ-mental rents are captured by central or federal governments. In some cases, envir-onmental income is managed separately from other revenues, but more often nature-based revenues are placed in central coffers.

When valuable resources are not evenly distributed geographically, governments should promote poverty reduction and inter-jurisdictional equity by favoring poor people and poor regions in their budgeting and distribution of nature-based public reven-ues. Central governments can invest in social services and safety nets, issue dividend checks directly to poor people, or provide inter-governmental transfers and equalization grants to local authorities. Governments can also use environmental income to capitalize permanent savings and trust funds for the future or investment and sinking funds for more immediate needs.

In Botswana, the government relies heavily on diamond rents and has made significant investments in education and

---

[26] Veit (2007)
[27] Ibid.

[28] Larson and Ribot (2007); Ribot (1998)

health, with impressive results (see boxes in earlier chapters). In Cameroon, provincial governments receive 40 percent of the annual area tax collected on forest concessions in their jurisdiction and another 10 percent is passed on to the communities that live adjacent to the concessions. However, local authorities in Cameroon have so far not invested their shares to significantly reduce poverty or support sound environmental management[29]. In Nigeria, the federal government passes 13 percent of oil revenues to the nine oil-producing states, primarily to reduce conflict and promote local development. While this may not satisfy the local stakeholders in the Niger Delta, it is a step in the right direction and shows some will to solve the very problematic oil-related conflict in Nigeria (se full case description in Box 5.5).

The selection of the most appropriate instrument for public revenue collection and usage will vary with the circumstances. For services that local governments, rather than central governments, are better placed to provide, resource revenues can be passed to local governments or paid directly to them through fiscal decentralization.

In summary, with support from donors, governments can support rural development, poverty reduction, social equity, and natural resource management by promoting pro-poor economic growth and pro-poor distributions of environmental benefits. Creating economic opportunities that target the assets of rural people will help ensure that growth favors the poor. More attention must be paid to promoting fiscal

decentralization and pro-poor budgeting. Governments must abandon practices and repeal distribution policies that inappropriately favor the privileged and contradict national poverty reduction objectives. New laws should be enacted to provide all citizens with equal access and opportunities, and, when possible, favor poor people and regions; that is, affirmative actions for the poor — who are the majority.

Economic Instruments

In many African nations, natural resource management is governed by rules, regulations, and other command and control mechanisms that stipulate in detail what people must do and what they cannot do. Regulations place conditions and requirements on the use of local resources and other development assets, and establish sanctions — fines, fees, and other charges — for non-compliance. Regulations play an important role in rural development, but they also have limitations. They can be costly to implement and enforce, and often do not provide people and local stakeholders with the discretion they need to pursue a development path that meets local circumstances and reacts to changing conditions.

Incentive-based approaches to natural resource management and development, including the use of economic instruments, can be effective in shaping behavior and achieving desired outcomes. For example, direct payments to communities to manage private land for wildlife and ecosystem services are receiving new attention from government and development assistance agencies. Many economic instruments are

---

[29] Veit (2006)

Box 5.5: Managing Oil Resource Wealth in Nigeria — The Challenge in the Niger Delta

Oil is a major natural resource and the principal source of income for Nigeria. It accounts for as much as 95 percent of export earnings, 80 percent of government revenue, and almost 25 percent of GDP[30]. With a production level of about 2.5 million barrels per day, Nigeria is Africa's largest oil producer, the 6th largest OPEC producer and the 8th oil producer in the world[31]. The oil sector has been a major source of economic growth, an important target of foreign direct investment, and a key contributor to the build up of the country's foreign reserves. Oil — and the associated gas — is found in the Niger Delta and its adjoining coastal waters. Geographically, the Niger Delta encompasses nine states, but six of them (Akwa Ibom, Bayelsa, Cross River, Delta, Edo, and Rivers) which form the south-south geopolitical zone have traditionally provided political leadership and popular mobilization for increased resource control. Resource control is also the main source of youth agitation, which has developed in support of that cause, but has increasingly turned militant and violent.

The struggle for the control of oil wealth dates back to the 1960s. At stake has been the quintessential property rights issue: who owns the oil resources in the Niger Delta?

Through legislative enactments, most notably, the Land Use Decree of 1978, the federal government has vested ownership of all land in the country to itself, including the minerals, ores, oil and gas resources found in them. The communities where the oil resources are located argue otherwise, leading to the political and popular agitation for resource control. The communities' assertions of ownership rights have been articulated in various declarations adopted since 1990. There are three inter-related dimensions to the Niger Delta crisis: economic (resource control); environmental (the cumulative impact of oil exploitation-related damage occurring through a combination of oil spillage, gas flaring and deforestation of the mangrove forest that has led to pollution of water, air and reduction of fishing and farming activities); and social (health and human rights issues).

In recent years, several factors have intensified the conflict over the control of resources: communities' increased sense of deprivation of access to the resources they regard as theirs, growing ecological damage, lack of physical and social infrastructural facilities and deepening poverty and neglect in the region.

Possible solutions: towards a grand bargain

While resource control has historically occupied centre stage and featured prominently in recent public discourse, any comprehensive solution to the Niger Delta crisis has to address the various components described out above and should encompass new **fiscal** measures, adaptive **policy** responses and creative **programme** initiatives.

Section 162(2) of the 1999 Nigerian Constitution stipulates that not less than thirteen percent of the revenue accruing to the Federation Account should be paid to the states in which the natural resource is produced. Niger Delta leaders have argued that the share of revenue accruing to the region from the Federation Account should, at least, be double the current level. This is an area where political negotiations and decisions are required as part of a grand bargain to resolve the Niger Delta crisis.

Adaptive policy responses should reflect principles of community involvement in development of programs for the region, community empowerment, and restoration of trust between the communities, the oil companies, and the government. In practice, this calls for several initiatives: new or renewed efforts

---

[30] Financial Times (12 July 2007); Economist Intelligence Unit Country Report (Nigeria) (May 2007)

[31] Economist Intelligence Unit Country Report (Nigeria) (November 2006)

Box 5.5: (continued)

to hire indigenes for operational, managerial, and executive positions in the oil and gas sector, within the government and in the oil companies; awarding maintenance and servicing contracts to indigenes; allocating oil blocs to communities; involving communities in program design and implementation; and empowering the communities by providing them with financial resources for the development of their own businesses and for skills development, to make tem active participants in the execution and sustenance of the various programs being planned for the region.

Furthermore, a proposed new approach focuses on decentralized trusts or funds for specific programs that address the key issues in the Niger Delta. These can include a physical infrastructure fund, a social infrastructure and training trust, an environmental repair trust, and a small-medium enterprise fund. There are several advantages in the proposed new institutional arrangement. It will clearly link key programs to a funding structure. The trusts or funds will be managed by corporate governance structures that include federal (state government) and community representatives. The arrangement will also enhance government–community partnerships, stimulate competition among the various funds to produce results, and generate jobs for restive youths.

Source: Otobo (2007a, b)

consistent with rights-based and governance-first development approaches that grant citizens broad rights and authorities, develop uniform minimum standards, and establish incentives to encourage desired behavior and outcomes (for example, willing seller — willing buyer arrangements and voluntary easements).[32]

Environmental degradation resulting from the production, transport, or consumption of goods and services can cause externalities — costs to the public that are not routinely accounted for in a competitive market. Economic instruments constitute one category of policy instruments that are oriented towards improving the efficient use and allocation of resources by providing incentives for actors to modify their behavior and internalize the externalities they produce. Commonly classified as financial or market-based incentives, economic instruments are designed to affect production and consumption decisions either through pricing mechanisms or by changing the economic attractiveness of specific actions (that is, making eco-friendly and socially-responsible production profitable).[33] Economic instruments include eco-taxes, levies, user fees, pollution fees, fines and charges, marketable permits (for example, tradable emission allowances), deposit-refund schemes, performance bonds, facility or operator bonuses, subsidies, and credits.

In recent years, there has been considerable interest in finding effective methods of environmental control beyond traditional command and control regulations. Economic instruments have been applied to a variety of environmental issues — air and water pollution, deforestation, over-grazing

---

[32] Ferraro and Kiss (2002)

[33] UNEP (2007a); Robinson and Ryan (2002)

and loss of biodiversity — and have been shown to be effective policy tools for changing behavior and achieving desired outcomes.[34] These instruments are of increasing interest because they can be an effective way of inducing compliance on the part of producers and consumers, reducing implementation and enforcement costs for government and society, and raising public resources for other urgent environmental matters. Although economic instruments designed to manage environmental externalities are referred to as non-regulatory, it should be noted that they frequently require legislation to establish the incentives, reward achievements, and set and maintain minimum environmental standards.

Three economic instruments and related issues are particularly important for promoting sound natural resource management and sustainable development: (1) securing property rights; (2) creating new markets; and (3) servicing the unmet needs of the poor.

Securing Property Rights: Most land and natural resources in Africa are state-owned or public property held in trust for people by the government. Eminent domain is the only lawful means of extinguishing private land rights in a compulsory manner. The majority of poor rural people do not hold granted rights of occupancy — primarily because they lack the knowledge, capacity, and resources needed to navigate the application process and meet title conditions However, most rural people have security in their land and property — the certainty that they will be able to use and benefit from their resources — through customary rights at the individual, household, or community levels. In some countries, customary rights are recognized in law (customary or deemed rights of occupancy), but they are not always provided the same level of protection as granted rights of occupancy[35] (also refer to Chapter 2 for elaboration of land right issues).

Property arrangements that serve the needs of the poor support local environments and development. When people have secure tenure they make environmental and natural resource management investments that promote sustainable use, economic growth, and poverty reduction. Efforts are needed to protect the property rights of poor households and communities, especially from irregular acquisition by governments, corporations, external elite, and local notables (please also refer to discussion on land reform in Chapter 2). Governments must have the authority to acquire private land (and natural resources) for genuine public purposes, but this power should not be exercised for ordinary government business or pure economic development purposes. Illegal and frivolous acquisitions must be halted[36]. Moreover, open access land, including public land that is not under any effective form of management, is prone to over-exploitation and mismanagement. Thus, for improved management, open access land can be allocated or granted to a capable individual

---

[34] Ibid.

[35] DFID (2002)
[36] Veit et al. (2007)

or institution for management, such as to a community to manage as common property.

New Markets: Renewed attention to protecting property rights is welcome, but secure tenure is only one of a number of critical enabling conditions for environmental management, development, and poverty reduction. The rural poor also need new markets and market access to turn their natural assets into income and wealth. Private enterprises have a long history of developing and promoting new products, establishing markets, creating demand and bringing goods into the market place. Poor rural people generally lack the knowledge, capital, and connections to achieve such outcomes and need external assistance. Governments can assist the rural poor by creating and supporting new markets and commercial opportunities that capitalize on local environmental goods and services; such as fair-labor, organic or green products, local herbs, and medicinal plants. Similar certification applies to mineral rights. Until the rural poor gain the resources and means to effectively compete and protect their interests, governments will need to grant them special conditions, preferential access in relevant cases and shield them from private sector competitors.[37]

Recent attention has focused on developing new markets for ecosystem services to create value and generate new revenues, including income for the poor. Payment for ecosystem services (PES) is a generic term for a variety of arrangements through which the beneficiaries of ecosystem services pay the providers of those services. PES can be viewed as a complementary measure to — or the opposite of — the polluter pays principle. PES arrangements can vary: They may entail a market that brings together willing buyers and willing sellers. Private or public entities (such as a private utility or a river basin authority) may collect fees and pay ecosystem service providers, state agencies may collect public revenues and pay ecosystem managers, or international bodies may use multinational or regional funds to pay for the provision of global commons.

Rural people are well positioned to benefit from PES, especially from the ecosystem services of their common property forestlands and pastures. However, in many cases they need external assistance to establish markets, negotiate prices, develop arrangements, meet contractual obligations, and pay for the often-high transaction costs. PES arrangements promise new, regular flows of income, portfolio diversification and asset appreciation. They can also be a catalyst for adopting better environmental management practices. When natural resources gain value, people who control them often invest in their management to ensure sustainable production. In Namibia, tourist operators pay communities for wildlife and habitat conservation. In Kenya, the government pays herding communities to protect the wildlife corridors of the Nairobi National Park.[38] Moreover, Africa is generally well positioned to benefit from its intact forests that serve as carbon sinks. As with any market mechanism, for PES to support poverty reduction, arrangements

---

[37] Veit et al. (2007); Veit (2007)

[38] Ferraro and Kiss (2002)

will have to be carefully constructed to ensure that the poor benefit. If mishandled, poor people could end up paying more for the services they must purchase than they receive from the services they manage.

Servicing the unmet needs of the poor: Environmental management and poverty reduction strategies often focus on the poor as producers of natural and other commodities. Yet, these strategies must also recognize the rural poor as consumers — consumers of goods and services that will help them make better use of local environment goods and work their way out of poverty. Globally, four billion poor people or low-income consumers — the vast majority of the world's population — constitute the "base of the economic pyramid" (BOP). However, BOP markets are poorly served, are dominated by the informal economy and, as a result, are relatively inefficient and uncompetitive.[39]

Because of the inefficiencies of informal economies, poor people receive lower quality goods and pay higher prices for basic services (for example, transportation, loan fees, and transfer fees of remittances) than wealthier consumers. Addressing the unmet needs of those in poverty and lowering the high cost of being poor is essential to making more efficient use of natural resources, raising welfare, and improving productivity and income.[40]

When BOP markets are underserved, poor households and businesses lose. Engaging poor people in the formal economy must be a critical part of any envir-

onmental management, wealth-generating and inclusive growth strategy. While individually poor people have limited purchasing power, collectively they constitute a very significant global consumer market — by some estimates, at least USD 5 trillion-a-year.[41] Private enterprises and governments must think more creatively about new products and services that meet the needs of poor people and about opportunities for market-based solutions to achieve them. Because especially poor rural people are marginalized, disenfranchised, and poorly positioned to protect their rights, governments and donors will need to help ensure that businesses that service and meet the environmental and other needs of the poor do not exploit or take unfair advantage of them.

Infrastructural Policies

Infrastructure — the complex of physical structures and networks within which social and economic activities are carried out — is an essential public good and a pre-condition for economic growth and equitable development. Infrastructure can be provided through facilities and construction investments (such as roads and dams) and through policy and institutional reforms (such as demand-side management regulations for energy consumption). Infrastructure provides essential services such as water and sanitation; energy for cooking, heat, and light; employment-generating commercial activities; transportation of people and goods, including natural commodities; and transmission and communication of knowledge and envir-

---

[39] WRI and IFC (2007)
[40] Ibid.

[41] Ibid.

onmental information. Infrastructure connects people and markets; protects investments made in human, land and physical capital; and maximizes the positive effects of other development and environmental investments.[42]

The intersection of infrastructure, the environment and natural resources is multidimensional. Infrastructure is needed to exploit natural resources and generate environmental income. Infrastructure helps communities market their natural commodities, and transnational corporations need infrastructure to extract resources for export. At the same time, caution is required as construction of infrastructure can seriously affect the environment. For instance dams can inundate productive areas and roads can open up densely forested areas and pristine landscapes and lead to over-exploitation and environmental degradation.

Africa's infrastructure is significantly underdeveloped and inadequate for growth, sound environmental management, and poverty reduction. There are large gaps in services and delivery, and considerable differences in available infrastructure between urban and rural areas, and between wealthy and poor regions. The inadequate infrastructure adversely affects economic growth including natural resource exploitation, as well as environmental management and general development. Infrastructure bottlenecks constrain markets — leading to high input costs, low output prices, and other inefficiencies in the supply and demand chain.

The poor state of Africa's infrastructure reflects neglect of investment and of other factors. Public infrastructure investment in rural areas has in fact fallen in recent years in many African countries owing to fiscal pressures and to a decline in donor support. Moreover, one fifth of Africa's population is landlocked and less than one third lives within 100 kilometers of the sea. By comparison, less than 10 percent of the population in other developing regions is landlocked and over 40 percent live within 100 kilometers of the sea.[43] This further constrains development in the landlocked countries and regions of Africa, which are already seriously disfavored and "underdeveloped" (as analyzed and outlined in Chapter 4).

In general, infrastructure has two fundamental objectives: improve the quality of life and improve economic growth. Meeting these objectives in Africa requires sound environmental management. Infrastructure investments in Africa must focus on the provision of affordable and sustainable infrastructure services that contribute to local resource management and rural transformation. Rural people are the principal environmental managers in much of Africa and their efforts need to be facilitated and serviced. Priority should be given to infrastructure and investments that have the greatest impacts on the improvement of rural household incomes and on local environmental management.

Unbundling infrastructure along different criteria can help identify pro-poor and

---

[42] Bank Information Center (BIC) (2007); Bapna (2006); Cho (2005)

[43] InterAcademy Council (2004); Fan and Rao (2003)

pro-environment investments. Infrastructure can promote national growth or target enhanced access by the poor. It can be a single large project or a hundred small initiatives. It can entail high risk or low risk. Infrastructure project design and implementation can be centralized or decentralized. Infrastructure can also provide products and services for export or for domestic use. Export infrastructure is usually capital-intensive, commodity export-oriented, and requires large transport systems (for example, rail, marine and air infrastructure; or oil and gas pipelines). It also tends to have significant and adverse environmental effects. The primary development benefits to host countries of export infrastructure, including infrastructure for the exploitation and export of extractive resources, are revenues to the government. The impact of increased revenue generation on growth, poverty reduction, and the environment depends on the willingness and capacity of the government to use revenues effectively for the benefit of its people and environment. However, experience hitherto has shown that export infrastructure commonly generates few permanent jobs, creates limited spillover benefits for local businesses, and rarely succeeds in improving the livelihoods of the poor in a sustained and equitable way.[44]

Alternatively, basic service infrastructure provides primary services to users and tangible benefits to poor households and communities. Such services often provide direct and immediate pathways to poverty reduction. Basic service infrastructure includes integrated watershed development; rural water and sanitation; rural access roads; run-of-the river hydroelectric projects; wind, solar power and other renewable energy; off-grid electrification; traditional water harvesting and irrigations systems; and common property infrastructure.[45] Furthermore, wireless communication and other new technologies can provide alternatives to large-scale, expensive infrastructure.[46]

Both export and basic service infrastructure are needed for economic growth and for environmental management and development. However, in countries with high poverty and high inequity, basic service infrastructure is smart infrastructure. Basic service infrastructure is typically small in size and scale and puts communities, rural organizations, and local governments at the forefront. It uses decentralized approaches and gives users prominent roles in all stages of the project cycle — planning and design, construction, operation, management, maintenance, and monitoring.[47]

An emphasis on basic service infrastructure means a shift from centrally-controlled public sector approaches to more demand-driven, decentralized delivery models. Governments in Africa support basic service infrastructure, but they will need to increase their investments substantially to achieve realistic levels of infrastructure and rural services, and to achieve the Millennium

---

[44] Bank Information Center (BIC) (2007); Bapna (2006); Cho (2005)

[45] Ibid.
[46] InterAcademy Council (2004)
[47] Bank Information Center (BIC) (2007); Bapna (2006); Cho (2005)

Development Goals.[48] Given African fiscal budgets, donors will also need to ramp up their infrastructure investments and co-finance basic service infrastructure on a relatively larger scale than in other regions of the world.

A common instrument for infrastructure development in Africa is the inclusion of the construction of roads, railways, hospitals, schools, and other infrastructure as part of the contract and fees in concession agreements between governments and extractive industries. However, relying on extractive industries to develop the nation's export and basic service infrastructure can be problematic. The primary interest of extractive industries is extracting natural resources, not in building, maintaining, or managing infrastructure.

For obvious reasons, extractive industries prefer to focus on their main lines of business. When necessary, extractive industries construct the export infrastructure they need to market their resources. Many also construct schools, clinics, and other basic service infrastructures in their areas of operation to demonstrate social responsibility, establish good relations with local people, and reduce conflict. In many cases, however, the quality of this infrastructure is not comparable to the infrastructure developed by professional engineering companies or specialist firms.

It is also important to establish and maintain appropriate boundaries of responsibilities and operations between governments and industries. Industries must help

offset the social and environmental costs of extraction borne by local communities, but governments should be careful when using concession agreements as a principal infrastructure development instrument.

Another important aspect to be taken into account is that local governments are often well positioned to take charge of the construction and management of basic service infrastructure, while central governments may be better positioned to manage export infrastructure development.

Power, Governance, and Institutional Framework

Governance Policies

As highlighted in earlier sections, local natural resources and development flourish when the voices of the rural poor majority — who depend on a productive resource base — are heard, and when their environmental concerns are reflected in public policy and government practices. The approach to governance of natural resources can be divided into the following three areas:

- Project-based management and public participation;
- Environmental governance; and
- Good governance.

Project-based management: Many positive environmental and development outcomes are the result of community self-help initiatives, or the products of specific projects, experiments, exceptions, and pilot efforts supported by government and development assistance organizations. Experience shows that well designed and conducted projects can effectively improve the environment

---

[48] Center for Global Development (CGD) (2006); InterAcademy Council (2004); Lewis (2003)

and the lives of the direct beneficiaries.[49] Projects have certain advantages as development instruments, such as piloting new environmental management ideas — where particular innovations or technologies need to be tested before they are mainstreamed — and enabling fledgling natural commodity enterprises or programs to take root before having to compete in the market.[50]

However, project-based approaches to natural resource management (NRM), environmental management and development are not always sustainable in the long-term or manageable for scaling-up. Many projects are place-based and create artificial enabling conditions that compete with government efforts by establishing new authority systems, thus becoming alternatives to government service delivery and action. They often create their own "project law" arenas, which can conflict with national environmental law and therefore have no legal basis when the project is completed and project protection lifted. Environmental management projects often obscure the true reality and the majority of rural people are unaffected by them. These projects can become showcases of environmental management success and, in some cases, excuses for governments not to undertake needed reforms. In doing so, they can divert attention from reforming the environmental and natural resource policies that actually do affect entire nations and whole territories and populations.[51]

To protect and sustain local investments and scale up project-based natural resource management, governance systems and institutional infrastructures must be established to ensure effective environmental management. Scaling-up is the process of institutionalizing and promoting transformation in environmental management to achieve sustained, long-term results at the national or regional level. To expand and sustain impact, the curve of interest and engagement in environmental management and local development must remain high, and the leadership of activities and interventions must be magnified through national policy and an expanding set of capable organizations.[52]

In Africa, and elsewhere, government and donor investments in the environment often support participatory policy processes, facilitate public participation, and strengthen non-governmental organizations (NGOs) and other civil society groups[53]. Public participation provides direct citizen involvement in government matters, helps promote the will of the people, and can give voice to minorities and the disenfranchised.

However, direct participation in environmental matters also has shortcomings.[54] Participation can be time-consuming and expensive; it is susceptible to rushed, uninformed decision-making; and often favors the most organized and powerful independent groups in society and their positions on

[49] WRI et al. (2005); USAID et al. (2002)
[50] Ribot (2003)
[51] Ibid.

[52] Veit (2007)
[53] Waldman (2005); WRI et al. (2004); Carpini et al. (2004); Theiss-Morse and Hibbing (2004); Petkova et al. (2002); Bruch (2002); Bruch et al. (2001); Petkova and Veit (2000)
[54] Ryfe (2005); Golooba-Mutebi (2005)

the environment. History and experience show that citizens usually promote narrow private environmental interests, NGOs often peddle special environmental concerns (for instance conservation over sustainable use); and populist movements often do *not* result in broad-based inclusive decision making or actions that benefit all citizens. Many political scientists assert that scaling-up popular participation — direct democracy — is inefficient and impractical in relation to NRM and environmental management.[55]

Moreover, investments to promote and strengthen public participation around environmental matters have not led governments in Africa to institutionalize open and transparent decision-making processes or to make decisions and take actions that consistently recognize majority needs and address common societal concerns. Most environmental management projects ignore the institutional infrastructure of public participation — the procedural rights that citizens and their representatives need to realize their own development and local environmental gains, and the institutions that grant, deliver, and enforce these rights and services. When environmental projects come to an end, so do the efforts to promote citizen and NGO participation.

Environmental governance: Project-based interventions to promote citizen engagement in environmental management must not be confused with governance or even with environmental governance. Governance is the process by which

individuals, groups of people, or their designated leaders make decisions that direct their collective efforts towards various goals and purposes. Environmental governance, then, is the process of steering societies and organizations — public and private, for-profit and not-for-profit — to achieve positiveenvironmental outcomes. Governments, private corporations, NGOs, community-based groups, and other institutions have important environmental responsibilities and functions, wield considerable power and influence, and are crucial environmental governance organizations. Governance is more than management and administration, more than governments, and more than narrow environmental and natural resource laws and institutions.

While many governments in Africa have adopted more open and transparent policies meaningful power over natural resources and other matters remains centralized in the executive branch. Governments justify centralized political systems by arguing that streamlined decision-making processes are needed to respond to urgent development and natural resource management matters and that only they are willing and capable of acting in the national interest. However, as outlined earlier, public policies rarely reflect the natural resource interests of the rural majority; rather, many support the narrow interests of the powerful political and economic elite.[56]

Good governance: This is a virtuous relationship between active citizens and a strong, legitimate government based on the

---

[55] Levine et al. (2005); Ryfe (2005); Haskell (2001); Rausch (2001); Mezey (2000)

[56] Veit (2006); Gibson (1999)

Figure 5.2: The Relation between GDP per Capita and Environmental Performance and Between Human Development and Environmental Performance

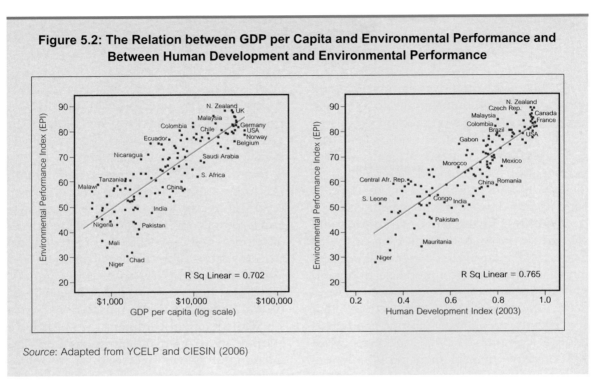

Source: Adapted from YCELP and CIESIN (2006)

representation of people's needs and aspirations in policy-making and implementation processes. Representation, the heart of a positive cyclical policy process, requires citizen voice and sanctions — the means of accountability — that can guide and discipline strong, capable and responsive governments. Accountability and responsiveness are the building blocks of representation from which good government and good governance follow.[57]

While some centralized regimes have promoted development and sound environmental policies, experience shows that democracies excel along many dimensions, including peace, security, development, and natural resources management (see Figures 5.2 and 5.3).[58]

Most governments in Africa are now based on the principle of representation, which is essential for bringing citizen inputs, including environmental concerns, into policy processes in all but the smallest of societies. Representation addresses the intellectual, time-related, and motivational obstacles to direct participation that many citizens experience.[59] When effective, representation can be "the infrastructure" for scaling up public participation and other

---

[57] Moore and Teskey (2006); Ribot (2006b); Manin et al. (1999)

[58] Ahrens and Rudolph (2006); Siegle et al. (2004)
[59] Ribot (2007); (2006a); Haskell (2001); Rosenthal et al. (2001); Mezey (2000); Przeworski et al. (1999); Rosenthal (1992); Pitkin (1967)

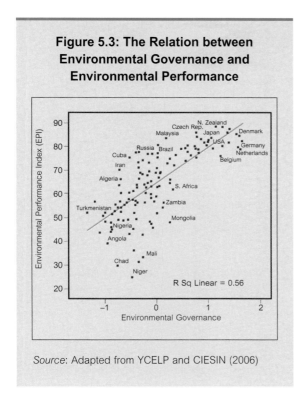

Figure 5.3: The Relation between Environmental Governance and Environmental Performance

Source: Adapted from YCELP and CIESIN (2006)

governance matters more for natural resources management and development than just for its functional value or instrumental utility in achieving desired outcomes.

A shift from project-based participation to strengthening representation of citizen environmental concerns has important implications for governments and development assistance organizations — especially in countries in which rural people with specific local environmental concerns are an electoral majority. Strengthening accountability (citizen voice and sanction) and responsiveness (government powers and capacities) can institutionalize strong state-society links and ensure that public policies reflect the environmental interests and needs of citizens. Donors and NGOs can help by working closely with governments to empower citizens and to strengthen government capacity to respond to the environmental needs of the poor rural majority (see Box 5.6 for an outline of AfDB's governance policy and initiatives).

Institutional Policies

Sound natural resources management (NRM) — initiating needed policy reforms, capitalizing on opportunities, confronting challenges. It requires the organization and structure of human interaction. Sound NRM requires attention to the range of institutions with roles, responsibilities, and powers over matters that affect natural resources. These include organizations that have specific environmental and NRM responsibilities, such as government environmental protection agencies, line ministries, and natural resource departments. They also include other institutions, such as the parliament,

forms of inclusion. Through representation, policymaking becomes a process in which professional policymakers balance competing and often contradictory interests (that is, nature conservation and sustainable use, natural wealth and development).

Sustaining and scaling up project-based and community-based environmental management requires attention to political systems and broader governance issues, not just to project management and administration. The narrow focus on promoting public participation in environmental projects has come at the expense of investments to strengthen other forms of inclusion and should be reconsidered. Investments must proceed from the firm perspective that

Box 5.6: Governance Policy of the African Development Bank

The AfDB recognizes good governance as an integral part of the development and sustainable management of natural resources. From a broader perspective, it is clear that good governance — which promotes accountability, transparency, the rule of law and participation — is central to creating and sustaining an enabling environment for development. In this regard, the Bank is committed to playing a key role in enhancing the quality of governance in individual RMCs, while articulating governance issues to the top of the region's development agenda. In response to the emerging governance challenges in RMCs, the AfDB Board of Directors approved the institution's Good Governance Policy in 1999, and Implementation Guidelines in 2001, respectively. The objective of the policy is to mainstream good governance into Bank Group operations in a manner that is consistent with the Bank's development priorities of accelerating economic growth and reducing poverty in its RMCs.

The key elements of this policy are accountability, transparency, combating corruption, stakeholder participation, and enhancement of a functional legal and judicial framework. To foster accountability — defined as the ability to account for the allocation, use, and control of public resources in accordance with legally accepted standards — the AfDB promotes public sector management focused on strengthening expenditure control mechanisms aswell as on exposure of, and sanctions against, misspending and corruption. This also extends to the monitoring and evaluation of public expenditure programs for effectiveness and performance, including public financial management, corporate governance, and civil service reform, among other key issues.

On transparency, the governance policy specifically emphasizes public access to knowledge of government policies and strategies. In particular, the Bank's governance activities are geared towards ensuring that public accounts are verifiable, providing for public participation in government policy-making and implementation, and allowing contestation over decisions that have an impact on the lives of citizens. The governance policy also places great emphasis on combating corruption and the misappropriation of public funds for private gain. The Bank Group's anti-corruption efforts in RMCs cover a wide range of areas, but focus specifically on reducing and minimizing rent-seeking and corrupt practices in the extractive industries; supporting research on the nature, origin, development, and impact of corruption on African societies; enhancing the capacity of civil society to investigate corruption; and providing assistance to the anti-corruption efforts of RMCs.

With respect to stakeholder participation, the governance policy and the supportive strategies emphasize key elements such as consultation of stakeholders over public policy decisions that affect their lives, as well as control of, and access to, natural resources or benefits from natural resource wealth, particularly those from oil and metal extractive industries. Accordingly, Bank Group interventions to enhance participation in RMCs are centered on increased stakeholder participation in policy processes; expanded co-operation with civil society; and discussion of public/private sector interface in policy dialogue with member countries.

In the context of its efforts to strengthen legal and judicial frameworks, the Bank Group regards the creation and sustenance of a predictable legal environment and an independent judiciary as essential components of good governance. The Bank Group's governance strategy therefore stresses the provision of technical assistance to RMCs to help them review existing laws and make the necessary modifications to address deficiencies and shortfalls, especially those that infringe on the rights of women, minorities, and other vulnerable social groups. Furthermore, the Bank supports reforms that affirm gender equality under the law, including property and land rights, and access of families and communities to natural resources (including land, water, forestry, and mineral wealth). Finally, the Bank Group's governance interventions are guided by selectivity, as defined by the focus of the strategy, which is adequately flexible to address the diversity of governance challenges among RMCs. The institution's governance policy is also instrumental in providing strategic guidance for it's engagement in the extractive industries and in transparency issues on the continent.

Source: African Development Bank (Policy and Operation Documents, 2007).

the judiciary, local governments, domestic companies, transnational corporations, NGOs, and community-based associations. Effective institutions have specific and clear roles and functions, and are empowered with the authorities and capacities needed to perform their tasks and meet their responsibilities. Promoting NRM in Africa thus focuses on addressing three fundamental institutional governance-related issues:[60]

- Decentralization and the distribution of power;
- Responsibilities, roles and capacity with power; and
- Accountability and the limits of power.

Decentralization and the distribution of power: Development and NRM require the delivery of various goods and services. Determining which institution to task with delivering these services can be problematic. To promote effective NRM and sustainable development, the placement of environmental roles and decision-making powers among scales of government and private institutions must ensure efficiency and equity in service delivery.[61]

The principle of subsidiarity states that decisions should be taken — and management exercised — at the lowest possible level consistent with allocative efficiency and effectiveness, and without producing negative externalities at higher levels of political, economic, or social organization (for example, the level and organization that internalizes the benefits and costs of decision-making for a particular purpose)[62].

It holds that responsibilities and power should be located at the lowest geographic scale that does not jeopardize higher-scale social and economic objectives. Subsidiarity applies to the vertical and horizontal distribution of roles and powers within a government and within private institutions (for example, corporations, political parties, NGOs, and religious bodies), including the outsourcing of traditional government roles to private groups, which are better positioned to perform those functions.

The subsidiarity principle is also applicable at the regional or international level when the action of a country is insufficient to achieve an objective and can be better accomplished at a higher level (for example, transboundary issues, as outlined in earlier parts of the report).

In much of Africa, the distribution of environmental management roles is not consistent with the principle of subsidiarity. Central governments hold responsibilities and functions over ecosystems and natural resources, and take actions which can be accomplished more effectively by local governments, NGOs, community-based organizations, private enterprises, or other local institutions. Many factors feature in the placement of environmental management roles. For example, the commercial value of a natural resource frequently influences the distribution of associated management roles, with central governments controlling high value resources and only devolving to local actors some responsibility over less valuable resources.[63]

---

[60] Summary outline provided by Veit (2007)
[61] Veit (2007)
[62] Ibid.

[63] Ibid.

Decentralization reforms are promoted to downsize and ultimately improve the performance of central government, strengthen local government, give substance to political and environmental rights by increasing local participation and democracy, and improve the efficiency and equity of local service delivery. Many central governments in Africa are passing on environmental and other responsibilities to local governments and various actors in the rural arena[64], but more efforts and new investments are needed to ensure that the placement of these roles is consistent with the principle of subsidiarity.

Responsibilities and capacity with power: Institutions must have the power and capacity needed to effectively perform their natural management responsibilities. Across Africa, central governments have downsized, decentralized and tasked a variety of local institutions with new development and NRM responsibilities. In most cases, however, central authorities have not transferred meaningful powers to local institutions or granted them sufficient autonomy and funds to play their required environmental roles. To be effective, local authorities must be granted sufficient funds and a domain of local discretion to respond to changing local circumstances and environmental interests.[65]

When institutions have NRM responsibilities, but no power, their leaders are discouraged from acting and citizens have few reasons to engage them, thus it becomes an issue of *legitimacy*. In contrast, creating or supporting empowered, accessible and responsive institutions with environmental roles can facilitate the emergence of a strong civil society and an engaged citizenry.[66]

Sound NRM requires the engagement of a large number of institutions (also refer to earlier sections and Chapter 4), including:

- Central governments;
- Private rural organizations or community-based organizations to manage local natural resources, rural cooperatives, women and youth associations, agricultural producer and rural workers' associations, rural credit unions, and other local private bodies;
- Public interest policy research, environment law, and advocacy NGOs — which conduct independent research, perform environmental monitoring, and engage in government matters;
- National environmental protection agencies, which have important regulatory and enforcement responsibilities;
- Line ministries and sectoral departments with jurisdiction over specific natural resources and ecosystems;
- Legislatures and parliamentary environmental committees, which have fundamental representation, law-making and oversight responsibilities;
- Public and private research organizations, including universities and institutions of higher education,

---

[64] Ribot (2007); (2004); Ribot and Oyono (2006); Ribot and Larson (2005)

[65] Ibid.

[66] Ribot (2003)

which conduct field work, collect environmental data and generate information for policymakers and practitioners; and

- Regional bodies and international instruments.

In addition to strengthening institutions, including regional bodies and instruments, Africa must learn to participate more effectively in global institutions and environmental policy-making processes. Africa's environmental positions and urgent needs are rarely addressed by global organizations or reflected in international environmental instruments such as the United Nations Convention to Combat Desertification, the Convention on Biological Diversity, and the Framework Convention on Climate Change. When international decisions are based on one member, one vote, it is possible for the smallest member country to have influence, although impact is often proportional to power. In recent years, other developing countries, such as Brazil, India, and China, have become effective in global negotiations. Africa can be a powerful voting block on global environmental matters, but to take advantage of its numbers, governments must be better prepared for global environmental negotiations. With its unique biological diversity and vast forests, Africa is well positioned to negotiate favorable agreements (such as carbon credits for avoided deforestation under the Framework Convention on Climate Change). Donors can help by supporting governments' efforts to find common ground, helping them establish environmental positions, and coordinating their efforts.

Accountability and the limits of power: Citizens and society could benefit considerably from government and donor investments aimed at strengthening existing accountability mechanisms and establishing new procedures to check institutions with powers over matters that affect the environment. For example, compulsory land acquisitions can be made contingent upon approval by parliament or proposed degazettement of protected areas or privatization of public lands can be presented to citizens through a ballot-box initiative. Efforts are needed to strengthen parliaments, judiciaries, advocacy NGOs, and other stakeholders and institutions with fundamental oversight mandates and roles. Staff members of public and private institutions — corporations, NGOs, political parties, traditional institutions, community-based organizations — should be encouraged and supported in their efforts to hold their leaders accountable. Legislation should be enacted to protect whistleblowers from threats and retaliation. Other checks and balances include codes of conduct, conventions of behavior, equitable legal systems, consistent enforcement of laws, citizen advocacy and oversight, and internal and independent financial and environmental performance audits.[67]

Regional and Global Dimensions
Resource Governance Policy Initiatives

The last decade has seen a growing recognition that improved transparency and accountability for the huge revenues generated by oil, gas, and mineral industries

---

[67] Veit (2007)

is vital to avoiding the "resource curse" and extending the benefits of natural resource abundance to poverty reduction. In response to these dilemmas, and to the observed environmental and socio-economic impacts of extractive industry activities, several international policy initiatives, mechanisms, and standards — aimed at improving governance and reducing negative impacts — have been launched. These include:

Transparency Initiatives:
- The Extractive Industries Transparency Initiative (EITI)
- The international Publish What You Pay (PWYP) campaign

Human Rights, Social and Environmental Standards:
- Voluntary Principles on Security and Human Rights
- International Council on Mining and Metals (ICMM)
- The United Nations Global Compact
- OECD Guidelines for Multinational Enterprises
- The Timber Certification Scheme

Conflict Resources Governance Policies:
- The Kimberley Process Certification Scheme (KPCS)

Financial Sector Governance Policies:
- The Equator Principles (social and environmental standards)
- The Wolfsberg Group (anti-money laundering principles)
- The most important of these initiatives — from an African perspective — are discussed below.

The Extractive Industries Transparency Initiative

This Initiative was launched by the UK government in 2002, against the backdrop of a general failure to transform resource wealth into sustainable development (the 'resource curse' or 'paradox of plenty') and the associated governance problems in the extractive industries sector. The EITI aims to intervene in the middle of the value chain — collection of taxes and royalties stage — but neither upstream nor downstream. It has a four-step implementation process (sign-up, preparation, disclosure, and dissemination) that is currently being pursued through three different models. These are (1) the core EITI (reconciliation of payments and revenues); (2) EITI "plus" (core EITI plus financial audits of companies and government, process audits, and public information campaigns); and (3) the sector governance program (EITI plus and institutional/regulatory reform, subnational distribution of rents, strengthening of licensing systems, and revenue management). The EITI has grown into a worldwide initiative and more than 20 countries have committed to its principles and criteria, the majority of them in Africa. See Table 5.1 below and the EITI Website for current updates (www.eitransparency.org).

Assessment of African Participation:

A considerable number of African countries have endorsed the EITI and are applying its principles to various extents (Table 5.1). However, an assessment of the status of the initiative shows that it is very much focused on the oil and gas sectors, and that its scope and mandate could be expanded, revenue transparency strengthened, and the initiative

Table 5.1: Assessment of Current Standing of EITI in African Context (July 2007)

Country	Intent to commit	Endorsement	Stakeholder engagement	Reconciler appointed	Report Published
Ghana	June 2003	Feb 2005	Yes	Yes	Yes
Nigeria	June 2003	Nov 2003	Yes	Yes	Yes
Congo, Rep.	June 2004	June 2004	Yes	No	No
Sao Tome and Principe	June 2004	Jan 2005	Yes	No	No
Sierra Leone	June 2004	Sep 2006	Yes	No	No
Gabon	July 2004	March 2005	Yes	Yes	Yes
Equatorial Guinea	Sept 2004	March 2005	Starting	No	No
Cameroon	March 2005	March 2005	Yes	Yes	Yes
Congo, DRC	March 2005	Nov 2005	Yes	No	No
Guinea	Dec 2004	April 2005	Yes	Yes	Yes
Niger	March 2005	March 2005	Starting	No	No
Mauritania	Sept 2005	Jan 2006	Yes	Yes	Yes
Mali	Aug 2006	Starting			
Cote d'Ivoire	Oct 2006	In progress			
Liberia	Oct 2006	Yes	Yes		
Madagascar	Oct 2006	In progress			
Chad	June 2004	No	No	No	No
Botswana	May 2007				

Source: Berg (2007); EITI Website (August 2007); Jourdan (2007)

extended to upstream and downstream issues and to environmental stewardship.[68]

The Nigeria Extractive Industries Transparency Initiative (NEITI), operating the EITI "plus" model, is the most advanced and comprehensive of all the initiatives of participating countries. The NEITI was launched in 2004 and has yielded the first-ever comprehensive financial, physical, and process audits of Nigeria's oil and gas sectors for the 1999–2004 period. Cameroon and Mauritania have appointed stakeholder committees at the highest levels of government, drawn action plans, and offered workshops and training for civil society. These two countries have also issued two reports.[69]

In summary, and looking ahead, the EITI has recorded some significant achievements, although it is voluntary in nature. It is increasingly being recognized as a *partial* solution to the problem of corruption in energy-rich developing countries. However, the EITI faces a number of challenges that need to be addressed[70]:

[68] Jourdan (2006)

[69] Refer to EITI Website for current updates (www.eitransparency.org)

[70] EITI Website (2007) and AfDB Memorandum on EITI (2007a)

a) Not all countries that have adhered to the EITI have started implementing it in its full extent. Several countries thus only show rhetorical commitment and have only implemented the initiative to a limited extent. At present, therefore, EITI stakeholders cannot tell who is truly implementing the EITI in letter and spirit, and who is merely going through the motions. As a result, countries and companies that are genuinely implementing EITI may not get the credit they deserve for improved governance, while free riders may claim participation in EITI as a way of evading international pressure to curb corruption.

b) Transparency at the federal level is an important first step to achieving more accountability. However, in countries where revenues flow back to the local level as part of revenue-sharing arrangements, a vertical implementation of EITI would be needed.

c) Civil society organizations play an important role in the EITI and in its implementation at the national level, where such a multi-stakeholder initiative is often difficult to realize. In Nigeria, as in many other countries, the government appoints civil society representatives for the national multi-stakeholder working group, but most members of the working group are, in fact government representatives. In other countries, records have emerged of civil society representatives being harassed.

d) The EITI does not address the core problems of corruption, mismanagement, and accountability comprehensively. This is a major concern for people in many African countries, especially those with a culture of impunity.

The success of the EITI as a concept is increasingly threatened by the lack of clarity about what it means in practice. These problems and issues must be addressed, and EITI is only a first step in the right direction. Nevertheless, one of the undeniable effects of the EITI process is that it has raised extensive international awareness that transparency in oil, gas, and mining revenues is vital to preventing corruption in countries that depend on resource revenues, and to ensuring that these revenues are used to promote growth and development. The EITI has brought together companies, investors, governments, civil society groups, and international institutions to promote this shared vision.

The International Publish What You Pay Campaign

The Publish What You Pay (PWYP) initiative is a coalition of over 300 global civil society organizations from more than 50 countries. It aims to promote full transparency in the payment, receipt, and management of revenues paid to resource-rich developing country governments by the oil, gas, and mining industries. PWYP campaigns are focused on achieving mandatory disclosure of payments made by oil, mining, and gas companies to governments and other public agencies. This is commonly accepted as a necessary first step towards a more accountable system for the management of

Box 5.7: The African Development Bank and EITI

The African Development Bank (AfDB) endorsed the Extractive Industries Transparency Initiative (EITI) in October 2006. Subsequently, the President of the AfDB, Donald Kaberuka, outlined a two-pronged approach to the institution's engagement in the EITI: (1) advocacy to create the political will among resource-rich RMCs that have not endorsed the Initiative; and (2) technical and financial assistance to RMCs that have demonstrated political will by endorsing the EITI, but lack human, financial, and institutional implementation capacity.

Five RMCs have been selected as initial candidates for EITI implementation support from the AfDB. These are Madagascar, the Central African Republic, Liberia, Botswana, and Chad. The selection process was carried out in close coordination with other supporting actors such as the World Bank and the EITI Secretariat. All the countries are at an early stage of the implementation process (sign up or preparation stage) and are preparing action plans or reforms to improve governance and extractive industry sector management. Botswana has the potential of becoming a role model for EITI implementation in the region. The other countries were selected based on their urgent need for implementation support. The support, which will include technical and financial assistance, could be crucial for the success of the EITI because, although the endorsement of EITI among African countries has been vigorous, but the resources to provided by development partners to them for the Initiative are currently inadequate.

Source: AfDB Memorandum (2007a), Support to Implementation of EITI in Resource Rich Regional Member Countries.

natural resource revenues. Such disclosures will not only allow members of civil society to draw a comparison and thus hold their governments accountable for the management of revenues; it will also strengthen the social standing of companies by demonstrating their positive contribution to society.

Assessment of African Participation:

The response of African counties to the PWYP initiative has been positive, with a considerable number of NGO's pledging their commitment. To date, NGO's from 23 African countries have joined the coalition. Nigeria has been a strong supporter of the initiative and is home to 47 PWYP coalition member NGO's.[71]

The debate on PWYP (a voluntary principle) raises the same issues highlighted above in relation to the EITI initiative.

Equator Bank Principles

Ideally, banks and financial institutions should be made accountable for oil-and mineral-backed loans and disbursements, particularly when they undermine attempts by the international community and international financial institutions to control the flow of money that involves corrupt natural-resource deals. The two most well-known global banking initiatives that target this issue are the "Equator Principles", which set social and environmental standards for project finance deals, and the "Wolfsberg Group", which has developed a set of anti-money laundering principles. However, both of these initiatives are voluntary.

---

[71] For current updates, see:
www.publishwhatyoupay.org

The Equator Principles are essentially a voluntary financial industry benchmark for determining, assessing, and managing social and environmental risks in project financing. Institutions that have adhered to the Principles (known as "Equator Principles Financial Institutions" or "EPFIs") have consequently adopted these values and principles. The initiative is currently supported by some 50 banks from 16 countries. In their current form, the Principles are based on the environmental and social safeguard policies of the International Finance Corporation (IFC). As such, they do not provide any specific guidance for extractive sector projects — a considerable limitation in itself. Nevertheless, the EPFIs have committed to not providing loans to projects where the borrower is unable to address and comply with the general principles and overall stated policies and procedures.[72]

A distinct disadvantage of the Equator Principles is that they are driven by the Western world and do not take into account developmental impacts (in the developing world).[73] It would thus be beneficial for financial institutions to look at the developmental aspects as well. Given the important role that banks play in financing private sector projects around the world, it is critical that signatories to the Equator Principles join in the global push for transparency in extractive sectors. What is further needed, to boost the effect of this and similar initiatives, is mandatory transparency in the financing of resource projects. This implies putting an end to resource-backed loans for governments, investors, and others who refuse to manage resource revenues in a transparent manner. This would also call for an amendment of money laundering regulations, recognizing that resource deals and resource-backed loans constitute a significant "yellow flag" for potential money laundering.[74]

The Kimberley Process and Governance of Conflict Minerals

The Kimberley Process Certification Scheme (KPCS) is the only significant international response to conflict resource issues. KPCS is an international, government-led scheme that was set up to prevent trade in conflict diamonds. It was negotiated by engaging relevant governments, civil-society organizations, and the diamond trade industry. The process was initiated when the nexus between diamonds and financing of conflicts in Sierra Leone, Angola, and the DRC was revealed by several NGOs and journalists. Launched in January 2003, and endorsed by the UN General Assembly and the UN Security Council, the scheme requires governments to certify the origin of shipments of rough diamonds to ensure that they are not from conflict zones. Countries that participate must pass legislation to enforce the Kimberley Process and set up control systems for the import and export of rough diamonds.

The KPCS has been relatively successful, but also has its limitations. The Scheme is currently not funded and is essentially run by those who volunteer time and resources,

---

[72] For further details see: www.equator-principles.com

[73] Jourdan (2007)

[74] Ibid.

which renders it unsustainable. At present, only two international NGOs (Global Witness and Partnership Africa-Canada) are involved. Other serious shortcomings relate to the definition of conflict diamonds by the Kimberley Process as it only applies to "rough" diamonds traded by rebel groups, though there is strong evidence that governments also use diamond resources to finance war efforts. The definition also excludes any particular focus on the diamond industry, which has the major responsibility for facilitating the entry of conflict diamonds into the legal market.[75]

Nevertheless, these issues should not cloud the fact that since the governments of diamond-producing and trading countries, NGOs, and the industry launched this unprecedented scheme to control the flow of rough diamonds, the scheme has imposed tough controls on all gem exports and imports. It is a rare example of co-operation among governments, civil society, and the private sector on a global scale. Most participants, including all African member states, have received a review visit to assess their compliance and have had to outline in detail the measures they have put in place (in an annual report). Only a few years ago, in Africa in particular, funds from illicit smuggling were being used to fuel civil wars and were a considerable factor in devastating conflicts in countries such as Angola, Cote d'Ivoire, the Democratic Republic of Congo, and Sierra Leone — KPCS has been a key factor in mitigating this illicit smuggling. The Kimberley Process comprises 45 Participants, and accounts for approximately 99.8 percent of the global production of rough diamonds.[76]

Assessment of African Participation

At present, 15 African diamond-producing countries are Kimberley Process participants. In 2004, the chair of the Kimberley Process announced that considerably less than 1 percent of diamonds were conflict diamonds, down from approximately 4 percent before the establishment of the Kimberley Process.

One of the challenges facing the Kimberly Process is the recent conflict in Cote d'Ivoire, where a significant volume of blood diamonds (from Cote d'Ivoire) is likely to have entered legitimate trade through Ghana and Mali. Apart from this, political will may be waning, as governments are blocking efforts to strengthen the Kimberly Process and the diamond industry has failed to police itself. The objective to stop the trade in blood diamonds will not be attained unless these challenges are effectively tackled.[77] An additional aspect is that KPCS only focuses on diamonds, whereas other precious minerals also require public attention (please refer to chapter 4 on relationship between natural resources and conflicts in Africa). It has thus been recommended that the KPCS be extended to other minerals such as gold.[78]

African Peer Review Mechanism (APRM)

The African Union's New Partnership for Africa's Development (NEPAD) identifies good governance as a basic requirement for

---

[75] KP website: www.kimberleyprocess.com

[76] KP website: www.kimberleyprocess.com
[77] Global Witness (2006); KP website (2007)
[78] Jourdan (2006)

peace, security, and sustainable growth and development. One of its "immediate desired outcomes" is that "Africa adopts and implements principles of democracy and good political, economic and corporate governance, and the protection of human rights becomes entrenched in every African country." For this purpose, NEPAD set up the African Peer Review Mechanism (APRM), an innovative tool aimed at peer review of governance benchmarks and design of action plans for improvement.

Participation in the system is voluntary and a panel appointed by the APRM Secretariat oversees implementation through-out Africa. The process consists of a number of stages, which are briefly outlined below:[79]

- The APRM process starts with a country self-assessment report and an action program submitted to the APRM secretariat.
- A country review team led by the responsible panel member visits the country to consult a wide range of stakeholders on the self-assessment report.
- The review team drafts a report in response to the self-assessment work, taking into account the political, economic, and corporate governance and socio-economic commitments made in the preliminary Program of Action.
- The review team reports and a final program of action is submitted to the APRM secretariat and the panel of Eminent Persons, then submitted to the APRM forum for participating Heads of States.

- The report is considered by the APRM forum and participating Heads of States and, 6 months later, tabled in key regional and sub regional structures.
- The country support mission reviews progress against the Program of Action agreed by country stakeholders.

The ultimate stated goal of the APRM is to encourage African countries to plan a way forward on governance issues and, not least, to implement relevant plans in this direction. The APRM process is designed to help participating countries develop and promote the adoption of laws, policies and practices that lead to political stability, high rates of economic growth, sustainable development, and continental economic integration. Box 5.8 provides an overview of AfDB support to the APRM.

Assessment of African Participation

At present, 27 countries have committed to the APRM and 13 of them have had reviews launched. To date, Ghana, Rwanda, and Kenya have completed the entire process, and South Africa and Algeria are nearing completion. The broad inclusiveness of the process has demonstrated the presence in countries of a strengthened culture of political dialogue and empowerment. However, implementation has posed some challenges, for instance, the establishment of an appropriate national structure, the financing of the process, and the organization of a participatory and all-inclusive self-assessment system.[80]

---

[79] See APRM website; www.aprm.org.za

[80] ARRM website and AfDB Memorandum on APRM (2007b)

Box 5.8: The African Development Bank and the APRM

The 2004 Inaugural Summit of the APRM Committee of Participating Heads of State and Government (African Peer Review (APR) Forum) designated the following four institutions as strategic partners: relevant organs and units of the African Union Commission, the African Development Bank, the United Nations Development Programme - Regional Bureau for Africa, and the United Nations Economic Commission for Africa. These strategic partners were asked to provide support and technical assistance to APR structures in the form of country profiles and technical assistance to countries, the APR Panel and the APR secretariat. More specifically, the AfDB was designated by the APR Forum as a strategic partner in the field of economic and corporate governance, including banking and financial standards. This conformed with its earlier assigned role under NEPAD.

Since 2004, the AfDB has made significant technical and financial contributions to the APRM process. In its capacity as a strategic partner, as well as a knowledge, development, and financial institution, the Bank Group has not only provided technical assistance and advisory services by participating in country reviews but also made direct financial contributions to the APRM Secretariat. In the early stages, the AfDB led the adoption and implementation of a selected number of internationally accepted standards and codes. It developed a "Framework for the Implementation of Banking and Financial Standards under NEPAD", which contributed to the design of the APRM process. It also developed instruments for economic and corporate governance assessments, which were field-tested in Senegal, Kenya, Ghana, and Cameroon and later adopted by the NEPAD. Bank Group support to the APRM since 2004 has also focused on providing technical assistance to the APRM Secretariat and Panel of Eminent Persons during country assessments. In this context, Bank staff and consultants have participated in several country missions and reviews. While the Bank is normally assigned a lead role in the area of corporate governance, its experts have also provided advice and technical support in economic governance and management.

Bank Group assistance to the APRM in the coming three years (2007–2010) will focus on the following core areas: (i) Revision of APRM methodology and process; (ii) development of a monitoring, evaluation & reporting system; (iii) continued participation in country reviews; (iv) support for implementation at the national level; and (v) continued support for international partnerships and for the overall APRM process and structures.

Source: AfDB Memorandum (2007b), Implementation Update to Bank Group Support to APRM

Voluntary participation in the APRM assessment has resulted in very high expectations, and it is imperative for RMCs and stakeholders to see the "dividends" from the APRM in terms of enhanced governance and improved living standards. The APRM is a cornerstone of NEPAD, the first African-initiated and -led instrument to take full ownership of the continent's future by addressing key governance challenges that constitute major constraints to development.

Summarizing and Looking Forward

Nature: Natural resources — such as land, forest products, fossil fuels, minerals, wildlife, and water — dominate many national economies and are central to the livelihoods of the poor rural majority in Africa. Natural resources are also a principal source of public revenues, national wealth, and power for most governments. As such, natural resources are critical to growth, development, and good governance.

The quest for economic development is focused on natural resources, in particular, high-value and commercial resources such as timber, oil, gas, gold and other minerals. However, the environment is more than just resources. A better understanding and broader view of the environment is central to maximizing its contribution to development and to the sustainable management of natural resources. Ecosystems and their full range of goods and services, including natural resources, must be mainstreamed into environment and development discourse.

A narrow natural resource approach to environmental management fails to recognize the underlying ecosystems that sustain resources, and undervalues the many other goods and services these ecosystems provide — services many people depend on for their livelihoods. An ecosystem services approach recognizes the interconnectedness and transboundary nature of environmental issues, and the importance of cooperation and collaboration for achieving positive environmental and development outcomes.

Wealth: Many African governments have dismantled their state-controlled economies, ushered in market-based systems, and engaged in the global economy. In many cases, large-scale private sector operations — commercial farms, timber and mining concessions, and other land-extensive production — are replacing government enterprises and small-scale producers. Nature-based public revenues thus pay for health, education, and other social services and, when exported, provide governments with foreign exchange to purchase essential imports and service rising debt. While a number of African countries have registered growth in per capita GDP and GNP in recent years, these national statistics mask the reality for the majority of Africans. Africa remains the only region in the world with rising poverty rates. In many cases, these gains have come at the expense of the rural poor — of rural development, poverty reduction, and other national objectives.

Africa's environmental endowment and slow growth rates in manufacturing and services means that national and household economies will likely remain resource-dependent for many decades. Improving economic growth, development, and poverty reduction will require the translation into environmental income and wealth of more of Africa's ecosystem goods and services, while maintaining a productive resource base (sustainability). NRM and environmental management are traditionally governed by rules, regulations, and other command and control mechanisms that prescribe how landscapes and resources can and cannot be used by individuals and institutions, and that levy sanctions for non-compliance. Incentive-based approaches to NRM and environmental management, including a large variety of economic instruments, are gaining momentum and are being used to shape behavior and achieve desired outcomes. A number of domestic industries and transnational corporations are also engaging themselves more comprehensively, with variable effectiveness, conducting self-audits and making production changes to improve efficiency, reduce costs, and increase profits.

To promote broad-based development and socioeconomic equity, governments must ensure that all citizens have equal opportunities to access and use natural resources and that all people benefit from Africa's natural resource endowments. Governments can promote pro-poor economic growth by helping to create new opportunities that emphasize the assets of the rural poor — land, natural resources, labor. Furthermore, government can work to secure property rights, new markets, and preferential access to these markets to ensure that poor people can compete and benefit from their land and natural resources. Governments can also support poor people by promoting pro-poor distributions of environmental goods and services. Studies show that in conditions of high poverty and high inequity, (re)distribution of environmental goods can be more effective than economic growth in reducing poverty and promoting equity.

Power and Governance: Unlocking nature's wealth for more rapid development and poverty reduction requires sound NRM and effective governance. Pro-poor governance can be defined as governance that supports multifaceted development and poverty reduction. Governance works for the poor when the poor can make government and other organizations work for them, including addressing the common high-priority environmental concerns of the rural poor. Poor rural people need secure access to productive land and valuable natural resources, information and technologies, markets for their produce, and a range of other elements to generate income and wealth from nature.

They need the means to safeguard environmental assets, ensure sustainable use, and protect critical ecosystem services. Rural people also need protection from the social and economic repercussions of environmental damage, and from the (potential) intent of local elites and external actors to alienate them from their land, natural resources, and other valuable property.

In many countries in Africa, poor rural people constitute an electoral majority, but they are not a powerful political force and, consequently, public policies and government actions frequently fail to reflect their priority environmental and other needs. Often with government support, the elite capture a disproportionately large share of environmental benefits and pass on the associated social and other costs to the marginalized and disadvantaged. Such conditions have resulted in increased competition and conflicts over natural resources. Nature-based conflicts, including violent conflict, civil wars and secessionist movements, have far too often been a normal occurrence in Africa (see Chapter 4).

Experience shows that institutional and governance failures are the root causes of underdevelopment and environmental degradation in Africa. The absence of responsive government threatens natural resource management, economic growth, and the well-being of the poor. Without addressing the failures of governance, there is little chance of harnessing the economic potential of ecosystems to reduce poverty and promote social equity.

Governance that provides adequate information to stakeholders and establishes a sound decision-making process is at the heart of sustaining healthy ecosystems and ensuring sound environmental management. Governance structures that enable the enactment, implementation, and enforcement of public policies conducive to economic growth and social development are central to achieving sustainable livelihoods and sound environmental management.[81]

Governance reforms that affect environmental management are sweeping across much of Africa. These reforms have profound implications for empowering individuals and institutions in using and managing natural resources. Fundamental democratic principles, such as accountability, participation, representation, and transparency, are key features of governance structures that foster sustainable development. History shows that democratic governance systems excel along many dimensions, including sound NRM and environmental management.

Finally, development assistance organizations, including donor agencies and international NGOs, must carefully select their partner organizations in Africa. Donor support to specific institutions can have profound effects — enhancing or undermining — on NRM, environmental management, economic growth, development, and democracy.

---

[81] Ahrens and Rudolph (2006)

CHAPTER 6
The Way Forward

Introduction

Natural resource endowment is a source of wealth and can be expected, if well managed, to support growth and development. This involves transforming the wealth into physical and human capital, increasing and sustaining economic growth, and alleviating poverty. Thus, the theoretical expectation is that resource-based economies are better placed to achieve economic transformation through a 'big push' from natural resource wealth. This expectation conforms with the long-held view of development economists that poor countries need a "big push" to propel them to economic take-off. However, with a few exceptions, the performance of resource-rich African countries has been relatively poor, in terms of economic growth and poverty reduction, and is much less than expected considering the vast amounts of resources extracted and exported. This situation poses a puzzle that some development scholars describe as the paradox of plenty, or the resource curse.

The debate on natural resources and economic growth has changed significantly over the past 40 years. The focus of natural resource-rich countries four decades ago was the potential negative impact of deteriorating terms of trade on primary agricultural products. During the next three decades, this focal point gradually shifted to the impact of resource windfalls — particularly those from oil, gas, and minerals — on fiscal management and growth and,

ultimately, to prospects for economic development. Today, the discourse has broadened even further to understanding the critical linkages between resource-endowments, fragile states, weak institutional capacity, poor governance, and civil conflicts. Moreover, recent increases in commodity prices have been accompanied by growing concerns about the impact of resource booms on African countries. Indeed, the prices of a wide range of commodities — including agricultural products, oils and minerals — have risen sharply in the last five years, driven by strong global economic growth and rising demand. Oil prices, for example, reached a historic nominal high of USD 78 as recently as August 2007.

From these trends, it is clear that the diversity of African countries in their resource endowment presents both winners and losers of high commodity prices in net terms. However, it is even more important to understand how winners and losers emerge from natural resource bonanzas. In other words, how do some countries succeed in harnessing natural resource-wealth to boost economic growth while others become trapped in the resource-curse syndrome or the paradox of plenty?

Evidence from successful resource-rich countries indicate that the successful pathway to harnessing natural resource wealth for economic growth is nested in good institutions, trade openness and high investments in exploration technology and human capital development. Sound natural resource management for economic growth therefore requires investment of resource rents in reproducible assets directly related to physical and human capital. To this end, Botswana serves as a classical example in Africa, while other countries such as Canada, Australia and Norway provide further evidence (in a global context) that it is indeed possible to escape the resource curse.

In most cases however, natural resource endowment has led to more or less severe versions of the resource curse (as outlined in Chapter 4). This is evident in the developing world, especially in Africa. Consequently, the search for practical solutions that will improve the management of Africa's natural resources for the good of the continent has become an imperative. This Chapter addresses the key issues that have emerged from the preceding chapters and highlights critical elements for the way forward, which involves turning Africa's resource curse into a blessing. The continent's natural resource endowments have a significant potential to stimulate growth and generate multiplier effects on a massive scale, but management bottlenecks have to be addressed. This hinges on:

- ensuring Africa's ownership of the development process;
- strengthening initiatives to monitor resource revenues;
- achieving a higher level of transparency;
- enhancing governance systems;
- reinforcing institutional capacity;
- investing natural resources wealth in the creation of knowledge for eco-

nomic innovation;
- negotiating better terms with external partners; and
- integrating the natural resources sector into national development frameworks.

Given the finite nature of non-renewable natural resources, it is imperative that the wealth they generate be invested in other forms of capital, particularly human capital, social services, and physical capital.

Natural Resources as Endogenous Sources of Growth

Natural resources are a major source of wealth and power in Africa and, as outlined in the Report they are fundamental for growth and development. Indeed, the quest for Africa's economic development has focused on natural resources precisely because of the central role they play in guiding the development trajectory and in enhancing the efficient accumulation of physical capital (including infrastructure) and human capital in developing economies. However, the management challenges they pose cannot be overemphasized. In addition, the context is broader than just natural resource management. Resource control, governance, transparency in the utilization of resource wealth for development, and sustainability of the resource base are critical ingredients that should be embedded in any coherent strategy for harnessing natural resource wealth for economic growth.

Abundant natural resources can be advantageous to economic development as they provide a platform for three critical elements of economic growth: (1) competitive diversification away from dependence on agricultural primary products; (2) investments in human capital development; and (3) infrastructure development. All may be critical prerequisites for investment in productive activities. The United States of America, Australia, Canada, Botswana, and Malaysia provide good examples of successful resource-based development (see case examples below). Based on these examples, there is optimism that African countries can indeed use natural resource wealth to achieve economic growth, provided they draw on the fundamental lessons that have enabled other countries to do so.

Competitive Diversification: With respect to diversification, what matters most for resource-based development is not the inherent character of the resources, but the nature of the learning process through which their economic potential is achieved. To begin with, resource-rich African countries can pursue a virtuous cycle of competitive diversification and industrialization. As indicated in Box 6.1 (the case of the United States of America), the linkages and complementarities of other economic sectors to the natural resource sector are vital to economic transformation in resource-abundant countries. In particular, African governments must pursue the diversification goal when designing strategies to best exploit their natural resources. These should range from maximizing the value of locally retained earnings and the creation of forward and backward linkages to the economy (to avoid enclave economies) to technology transfer, job creation, and minimization of environmental damage and social impact.

African countries should systematically exploit opportunities and linkages leading to

---

Box 6.1: Resource Wealth and Growth: The Case of the USA

Resource abundance is a distinguishing feature of the rise of the American economy. However, while the American economy may have been founded on resource abundance, Americans have not been rentiers living passively off their mineral royalties. The American economy has clearly made good use of its abundant resources. In the industrialization and growth of the American economy, nearly all major US manufactured goods were closely linked to the resource economy in one way or another: petroleum products, meat packing, poultry, steel works and rolling mills, coal mining, vegetable oils, grain mill products, sawmill products, and so on. The only items not conspicuously resource-oriented were various categories of machinery. Even here, however, some types of machinery serviced the resource economy (such as farm equipment), and virtually all machines were made of metal.

These observations by no means diminish the country's industrial achievements, but they confirm that American industrialization was built on natural resources. Furthermore, the abundance of American mineral resources should not be seen as merely a fortunate natural endowment. Their use demonstrates a form of collective learning, a return on large-scale investment in exploration, transportation, geological knowledge, and the technologies of mineral extraction, refining, and utilization.

Source: Wright (1990), The origins of American Industrial Success 1870–1940

competitive diversification to ensure that they grow resource economies that can service emerging industries for added downstream value and side stream supply of inputs (and emulate resource-rich Asian countries in Asia such as Malaysia; see Box 6.2).

Economic diversification, in particular the emergence of a comprehensive manufacturing sector, creates positive externalities. The manufacturing sector enhances the search for competitive advantage, which is based on the search for the development of technology, as well as for innovation benefits that come from "learning by doing processes". Unlike primary production, manufacturing is associated with the development of human capital, which, in turn, benefits the entire economy. This relationship is perhaps most

clearly demonstrated in some *resource-deficient* countries that devote their resources to the production and export of manufactured goods, which is associated with the development of high levels of skill, technology, and innovation.

Human Capital Development is another crucial mechanism for transforming natural resource wealth into economic growth. Human capital is an aggregate of the skills and knowledge of the workforce, with direct linkages to labor productivity — which can be a direct cause of economic growth. This implies that an economy that invests in human capital development, primarily through education and other forms of training that hone the skills of the workforce, is preparing itself for economic growth through

---

Box 6.2: Malaysia — Resource Wealth and Competitive Diversification

Malaysia's use of natural resources to attain economic growth through diversification is often cited as nothing less than fascinating. The Malaysian model is particularly interesting since the country adopted very restrictive trade policies in the late 1960s in order to enhance the development of its import-substituting industries. This policy was later changed in the 1980's when the country prioritized macroeconomic stability and a relatively open trade policy. Although the macroeconomic policy, centered on the Big Push, created some economic imbalances and was probably overambitious, the country was able to quickly offset the commodity price shocks of the late 1980s through rapid diversification and expansion of export-oriented manufacturing.

This strategy was nested in a political compromise that allowed the Malay majority to focus on political processes while the Chinese minority focused on business expansion opportunities. Thus, the success of the Malaysian resource-based economic transformation is also rooted in ethnic cordiality and mutual tolerance.

The Malaysian experience clearly shows how macroeconomic and fiscal discipline, coupled with high social capital (harmony among ethnic groups), can allow a resource-rich country to transform resource wealth into sustainable growth. Although there were some policy distortions in the Malaysian case, the general conclusion that resource-rich countries can achieve competitive diversification through a strong focus on sound economic policies that maintain market discipline remains valid.

Source: Auty (1998), Resource Abundance and Economic Development

improved efficiency and increased returns on investments. Thus, investment in the development of the education sector, which generates human capital, plays an integral role in economic growth. In spite of these clear linkages between human capital development and economic growth, resource-rich countries seldom invest in human capital development, at least not proportionately. There are two main reasons for this.

First, the returns on investment in human capital development accrue only over the long-term, and often do not appear attractive to resource-rich countries intent on hurriedly reaping resource benefits and spending the windfalls. Second, primary production and natural-resource-based industries (extractive industries) do not require high levels of human capital — in comparison with the manufacturing sector. Given that human capital represents one of the most important components of income creation, economies based on low human capital-demanding sectors will be characterized by low levels of economic growth. In general, it has been observed that multinational companies, to a large extent, bring their own expertise and skilled labor instead of training local people to acquire the needed skills. This leaves the local economies of resource-rich countries with little or no human capital development resulting from the activities of foreign firms.

Furthermore, in most resource-rich African countries, wealth from large natural resource endowments are managed in ways that create distortions in the economy. Primary production is often supported, as it appears particularly attractive and especially as it requires lower levels of initial investment. However, the wealth generated from these primary industries can only be sustained in the long-term if it is transformed into human, physical (including infrastructure), and social capital. These will then facilitate investments and the emergence of a vibrant private sector that will foster economic diversification and reduce resource-dependence, hence minimizing the effects of commodity shocks on the macro economy.

In some cases, resource-rich countries provide education, funded largely from resource windfalls, to appease their populations and constituencies. However, without targeting the investment to the types of skills that are relevant for economic diversification, the education qualifies as a consumption good, rather than a true creation of capital goods in the form of long-term productive human capital. In contrast, a resource-rich country that systematically plans its economy on a long-term basis and is ready to diversify and prioritize human capital development can achieve long-term growth-enhancing benefits. A case in point is Botswana, which has used its natural resource wealth to achieve economic growth through good policies, prioritized investment in human capital, infrastructure, and economic diversification (Box 6.3; also refer to Box on diamond mining in Botswana in Chapter 3).

Investing natural resource wealth in human capital development can also be considered critical from the perspective of the MDGs. Developing human capital by achieving universal primary education is a critical pillar of MDG 2. By 2005, the net enrollment rate for primary education in

Box 6.3: Botswana — Turning Natural Resources into Human Capital

Diamonds were first discovered in Botswana in 1967. Since then, the country has experienced strong economic growth, which it has sustained. Over the decades, the country has moved from being one of the poorest economies in Africa to being a model for Africa and one of the continent's rare success stories.

Since its independence, Botswana has implemented successive national development plans (NDPS), which of late have focused on the country's long-term vision of "towards prosperity for all", commonly referred to as "Vision 2016". The Vision comprises four pillars. Two of the pillars ("a prosperous, productive and innovative nation", and "an educated and informed nation"), focus on the efficient use of natural resources for human capital development. The national plans take into account all sectors of the economy and ensure efficient and effective utilization of all resources in accordance with national priorities. Human capital development is one of the country's key priorities — with great emphasis on education, health and infrastructure development — as well as the creation of a stable macroeconomic environment. In revenue allocation, Botswana has thus endeavored to achieve optimal balance between consumption and development.

The mid-term review of the current ninth National Development Plan (NDP 9) places emphasis on high budget allocation to development priorities rather than to recurrent expenditures. This should help achieve an investment level of between 30 percent and 40 percent of the GDP over the Vision 2016 period. Botswana's real GDP growth rate averaged 9.8 percent between 1966 and 2004, largely on account of the discovery of minerals and prudent management of resource revenues, which were supplemented by donor financing in the early days. Mineral resources have enabled the country to build schools, colleges and hospitals, and other requisite infrastructure. For example, there were only nine government-owned secondary schools in 1966; by 2007, this number had increased to 233. The country also plans to increase student participation in senior secondary school from 62 percent in 2007 to 100 percent in 2015.

The country has also faired well in the social sector: in 2001, a total of 97.7 percent of the population had access to safe drinking water and 77 percent to adequate sanitation. Life expectancy, however, dropped from 66 years in 1966 to 56 years in 2001, owing to the HIV/AIDS epidemic. Poverty rates, measured by the number of people living below the poverty line, declined from 47 percent in the 1993/1994 financial year to 30 percent in 2003/2004. Poverty rates are projected to fall to 23 percent in 2009.

All these achievements have placed Botswana among the highest achievers in the continent, in terms of both economic growth and of progress towards the MDGs. This achievement has not been easy, but it was made possible with careful planning, targeted and prioritized investment of resource revenues, and sound fiscal planning and management.

Source: Baledzi Gaolathe (2007)

Sub-Saharan Africa was still only 70 percent (95 percent in Northern Africa)[1]. There is thus clear room for investment in human capital development in the continent.

Infrastructure Development: In addition to developing human capital, transforming natural resources into productive capital also involves the development of infrastructure such as roads, power supply, water supply, and sanitation and communication facilities. These are critical for improving the

---

[1] UIS (UNESCO) (2007)

investment atmosphere and stimulating economic growth. In other words, achieving sustained growth from natural resources entails managing a complex portfolio of natural, human, and social capital. All of this hinges on infrastructure as a prerequisite for economic transformation — for instance, by enhancing the openness of the economy and facilitating the exploitation of trade, communications, and the movement of people.

The linkages between infrastructure and natural resources are thus multi-dimensional and comprise economic, social, and environmental perspectives. Infrastructure is needed to exploit natural resources and transform them into income and wealth. Infrastructure provides the complex of physical structures and networks within which social and economic activities are carried out, and thus serves as an essential public good. It is often a prerequisite for economic diversification, growth, and equitable development. Providing a base for economic diversification, infrastructure enhances forward linkages in the economy that provide value addition to natural resources, hence increasing wealth and supporting sectoral linkages through job creation and enhanced trade. This facilitates the full realization of the non-commodity sectors that are critical for economic diversification. As indicated in Figure 6.1, downstream value-addition, beneficiation, and export of resource-based articles can contribute significantly to job creation and diversification of income sources. Technological linkages also incorporate innovation and adaptation with other sectors that are critical for the economy and for reducing shocks associated with volatile commodity prices.

Good Governance and Management of Natural Resource Revenues

There is growing consensus on the centrality of good governance for Africa's development. African leaders, regional institutions, and all key stakeholders have stated unequivocally that good governance is a key prerequisite for development. One of the key objectives of the African Union is to promote democratic principles and institutions, popular participation and good governance. Furthermore, the African Union's New Partnership for African Development (NEPAD) identifies good governance as a basic requirement for peace, security, and sustainable growth and development. One of the desired outcomes of NEPAD is for Africa to adopt and implement principles of democracy and good political, economic, and corporate governance, and the protection of human rights. Although governance improvements face difficult challenges in Africa, it is encouraging that key institutions in Africa — and Africans themselves — are demanding better governance for the continent.

Developed countries are also committed to supporting good governance in Africa, as demonstrated by the G-8 Summits, the recent G-8 Finance Ministers Meeting in Potsdam (*Action Plan for Good Financial Governance in Africa*), as well as the Paris Declaration on Aid Effectiveness. Moreover, citizens of developed countries have expressed strong support for good governance in Africa, manifested by the continued mobilization of civil society organizations and advocacy groups.

Accountability and transparency in the management of public resources is critical in

Figure 6.1: Key Linkages — Extractive Industry, Natural Resources, and Development

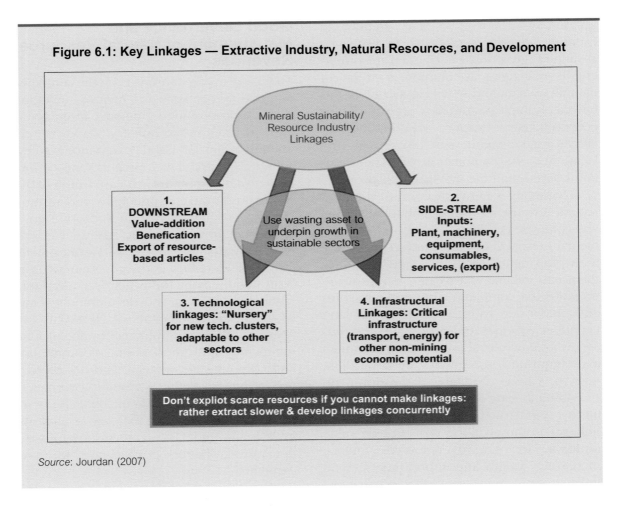

Source: Jourdan (2007)

determining the allocation and use of resources and in ensuring development impact and fiduciary risks, perhaps nowhere more so than when significant natural resource wealth is present. As outlined in this Report, the abundance of natural resources is not in itself the cause of underdevelopment or of conflicts in African countries. There are often clear linkages, but the primary causes are fragile institutions, poor policy choices and government practices, and inappropriate approaches to governance of natural resources and to utilization and investment of the wealth created.

Natural Resources and Strengthening of Institutions and States

It is commonly accepted that the "first-best strategy" for enhancing natural resource management and revenue transparency is to strengthen institutions as well as the legislative system and to insist on accountability and resource revenue transparency. Another approach is to put natural resource revenues in special funds to ensure that the interests of future generations are safeguarded. However, in countries with weak institutions, such a fund may very well be raided. An interesting alternative is to change the constitution to guarantee that resource revenues are provided directly to the public one way or the other — implying that the government has the burden of proof that resource revenues are being extended to the people. Nevertheless, whether or not such special approaches are pursued, improving governance and strengthening institutions is fundamental, and should be the first-best option.

A key recommendation is to promote the core elements of a *developmental* rather than a predatory state as a way of minimizing the risk of suffering from the "curse". Developmental states need the institutional capacity to implement the necessary policies without being controlled or captured by narrow private interests. Thus, the legitimacy of a government derives from its ability to deliver development, defined simply as an improved standard of living for the majority.

Management of Natural Resource Revenues

The objective of maximizing natural resource revenues and benefits for current and future generations can be broken down into four key issues, which correspond to different stages, from extraction through revenue flows to expenditure. The first issue concerns contracts with exploration companies and appropriate fiscal regimes; the second, the importance of transparency in natural resource payments and spending of the resulting revenues (including suggestions for more effective public sector financial management); the third deals with the timing of natural resource expenditures, in particular, how this can benefit future generations; and the fourth focuses on the core discussion about consumption and investment.

Contracting and fiscal regimes: The interaction between natural resource licensing, contracting, and taxation regimes is complex. These regimes or measures have to attain the dual objectives of achieving efficiency for the full scale of operations and securing revenue transfer to the host country. This requires sound principles to guide the design of efficient contracts and the auction and allocation of mineral and energy rights.

Achieving efficiency in the full scale of operations imposes a number of requirements. Firms should have incentives to participate, to extract efficient quantities, and to invest in exploration, extraction, production, marketing and sale. This, in turn, requires, amongst other things, that contracts be time consistent and sufficiently elaborate so that governments do not have an incentive or a need to renege and, in extreme cases, even threaten with expropriation.

Efficiency thus applies not only to the stream of output, but also to aspects such as the efficient distribution of risk — both production risk and price risk — among parties to the contract. This depends on the ability of firms and governments to bear risk and to trade risk on international capital markets. The contract may also specify environmental conditions as well as the transfer of knowledge and other tangible or intangible assets.

How can these objectives be met? An auction is an attractive option in a simple environment, since competition between firms will secure both efficiency — maximization of net revenues — and maximum net transfers to the government (see Box 6.4). Auctions also have the great merit of ensuring transparency, if conducted appropriately. However, things may become more complicated with multidimensional contracts; for example, if bidding is on a single variable,

---

Box 6.4: Auctions for Mineral Rights

African governments have been selling mineral extraction rights for decades, but the terms of these deals have often been unsatisfactory. Mineral extraction companies inevitably have better access to information on their specific business than African governments do. This information gap is sometimes compounded by an "agency" problem, which may occur when a deal is struck between the representative of a company and the representative of a country. Companies are in a better position to ensure that their representatives are acting in the interests of the company, whereas it is difficult for governments to ensure that their representatives are acting in the interests of the country. The information gap and the agency problem combine to reduce the benefits that countries derive from their resources. For example, in 2006 the government of the Democratic Republic of Congo received only USD 86,000 in royalty payments despite mineral exports in the order of USD 200 million. How can these problems be solved?

An auction of extraction rights is the institutional practice that generally maximizes government revenues from minerals. The huge advantage of an auction, compared with other ways of selling rights, is that it uses competition between companies to reveal the true value of the rights. This redresses the informational disadvantage of the government. The British government's use of an auction to sell the rights to its mobile telephone network demonstrates the superiority of an auction over attempts by civil servants to estimate the value of rights. The British Treasury, one of the most sophisticated centres of public sector financial expertise in the world, was about to sell the rights to a company for £2 billion when it was persuaded to switch to an auction. The rights were sold through the auction for £20 billion. If the British Treasury can misestimate the value of rights by a factor of ten, it is safe to assume that African civil servants are also liable to make large pricing errors. Not only does an auction bridge the information gap, it can also address the agency problem. A well-conducted auction vastly reduces the scope for government officials to put private gain before national interests.

A successful auction must follow standard procedures. In this regard, support, in the form of expertise and verification, should be provided to the official responsible for the auction. Experts provide advice on the precise design of the auction: for example, it is often advantageous to have about four serious bidders; and auctions should sometimes be conducted in phases. An external verification system demonstrates both to the government and to citizens that the auction adheres to international standards. Expertise can be hired in the market, but a verification system may need to be official to have authority. A verification system for Africa would thus be a *regional public good* — one which the African Development Bank would be well-placed to develop and supply.

Source: Collier (2007b)

such as total royalty, then other aspects of the contract (risk sharing, knowledge transfer) have to be established in some way and imposed as constraints in the auction of rights.

Revenue Transparency and Public Financial Management: Governments implementing prudent policies often choose to use resource revenues to cut government debt or to invest in useful education and infrastructure projects. Whichever strategy is chosen, all natural resource exploitation activities should be governed by the highest standards of public and corporate accountability and transparency. Accounts related to the production and export of resources should be available to journalists, financial analysts, and the general public. Open information on debts, credits, and loans, for example, should also be provided in resource-rich countries since governments may be tempted to "loot the public purse" by saddling future generations with excessive debt using natural resource reserves as collateral. Unfortunately, at present many countries affected by the natural resource curse do not make information on their export earnings or revenue expenditures available to the public.

Awareness about these issues has been growing, as have several promising responses, which include the Extractive Industries Transparency Initiative (EITI) and the African Peer Review Mechanism (APRM), reviewed in Chapter 5 of this Report.

Timing and Composition of Expenditures: Even if political economy challenges are overcome, another crucial issue that should be addressed concerns the best way *to spend accrued revenues*. In broad terms, the possible approaches include:

i) accumulation of foreign assets;
ii) domestic investment — public or private;
iii) domestic consumption — public or private; and
iv) savings or investment funds.

Making the right choice, or mix of choices, depends on income information (resource reserves, future prices, and rates of return) and the political economy in place in the country at the time, all of which are highly uncertain. One of the characteristics of most natural resources is the highly volatile nature of commodity prices and revenues, such that short-run smoothing is required to avoid boom-bust cycles. Issues such as long-term absorption and depletion rates also have to be addressed.

The first choice deals with consumption and investment — how much of the resource revenue should be consumed now and how much saved for future generations? The consumption stream that can be supported in perpetuity is the present value of the resource stock times the rate of return. The *share* of resource revenue that can be consumed in perpetuity is the expected long-run rate of growth of the resource price divided by the extraction rate. Both of these rules give steady consumption paths that do not fluctuate with short-run revenues, although they are, of course, subject to revision as information and expectations change.

The second choice concerns how the remainder (of the income) should be invested or allocated between domestic and foreign assets. A sound first criterion is that foreign assets should be used to reduce volatility and secure short- to medium-run smoothing of domestic expenditures (consumption and investment combined). Such an approach involves forming a judgment about the expected long-run revenue path and natural resource export price paths (depending on market sentiments) and using foreign assets to smooth deviations from these paths. The longer-term division of investment between foreign and domestic assets needs to be addressed. A simple criterion could be to invest wherever the social rate of return is highest, which, in a capital-scarce developing country, will often be predominantly domestic investments.

Another important priority choice concerns whether consumption or investment should be private or public. Private expenditures could be promoted by tax cuts and low levels of public debt rather than by direct public expenditures on social policies and infrastructure. Whether private expenditures are more efficient than public expenditures depends on the economic environment, in particular, access to capital markets, and on attitudes to intergenerational distribution of benefits. The efficiency of public expenditures depends on both the quality of project selection and the procurement practices used to implement projects.

Stabilization Funds versus Citizen Dividends: Since streams of natural resource revenues do not last forever and may fluctuate considerably, it is, in principle, sound practice to put a proportion of export revenues from natural resources into stabilization funds. This way the nation can spread the benefits of its natural resource wealth over a long period, protect itself against volatile commodity prices, and safeguard the interests of future generations. However, a crucial drawback is that in a regime where there is weak institutional capacity and low transparency and accountability, such a fund may be raided. Keeping natural resources under the ground may be a safer form of saving than putting it in a fund that is easily raided. In applying the concept of future funds, African countries would be well advised to look towards the lessons learned from both Africa itself and from the developed world on managing mineral rents for the benefit of future generations. Norway is a prime example of a country that manages its resources with a clear "futures perspective" (see case examples in Box 6.5 and 6.6). The need for professional management and administration of future funds is obvious.

Another approach is to distribute rents from natural resources, automatically and instantaneously, directly to the citizens of the resource-rich country.[2] Such a "citizen rent" should correspond to government revenues. The right of each citizen to an equal share of natural resource rents could even be inscribed in the constitution to establish the legal default of full direct distribution of resource revenues to the people. Given that citizenship or residence will be an eligibility criterion for receiving the resource dividend, there is a clear danger of leakage and fraud. However, the administrative costs should be manageable.

---

[2] Sala-i-Martin and Subramanian (2003)

Box 6.5: "Failure Case Study" on a Future Fund — Chad

The problematic future funds initiative of Chad's oil industry should serve as a key lesson for other African nations. The process began in 2000 with a proposal for an oil pipeline running from Doba (Chad) to the Atlantic coast (Gulf of Guinea) in Cameroon. Under the deal agreed by stakeholders, most of Chad's revenues would go toward development projects. The agreement required that Chad's 12.5 percent share of direct revenues from oil production flow be put a London-based Citibank escrow account to be monitored by an independent body created to oversee the account's management.

Another main goal was to channel Chad's revenue into poverty-reduction programs. The Future Generations Fund accounts for 10 percent of annual revenue and was created to provide Chad with reserve funds after oil reserves are exhausted.

The USD 3.7 billion project began pumping oil through the pipeline in late 2003 — ahead of schedule. In December 2004, Chad's parliament voted to modify the agreement, canceling the Future Generations Fund for Chad's post-oil future, and diverting funds away from poverty alleviation towards the purchasing of arms. A temporary agreement was reached with development partners on April 27, 2005, but experts say potential civil war, cross-border troubles with Sudan, and the weakening of the current political regime still threaten the pipeline deal, casting further doubt on prospects for transparency in future development projects in the region. Meanwhile, the Future Generations Fund (FGF) is still kept in the London-based escrow account, and is invested in an interest-bearing investment account.

Source: Zissis (2006)

Box 6.6: "Success Case Study" on a Future Fund — Norway

The Norwegian future fund was established in 1999, based on government revenues from the North Sea oil discoveries of the 1990s; it was designed specifically to meet the future pension needs of the nation. The fund holds more than USD 300 billion and is projected to rise to USD 900 billion in the next decade. Norway's population is slightly under 5 million, and its holdings could theoretically enable the entire population to "retire" on an equal payout of USD 220,000.

The fund is also a tool that ensures the transparent use of petroleum revenues. All revenue from the sale of North Sea oil is directed into the fund. This capital is invested outside Norway to counter any rise in the real exchange rate resulting from oil exports (capital outflows cause the exchange rate to depreciate). Investments are subject to ethical guidelines and an environmental sub-fund is part of the portfolio. The country's Central Bank, manages the fund.

Sources: Norway Mission to the EU (2005); Norwegian Ministry of Finance (2005)

In such cases, the government could subsequently tax its citizens to fund investment projects, reduce government debt, or transfer revenues to a fund. The resource rents could, in principle, also be used for micro-finance and housing guarantees, or tied to social targets such as the MDGs.

The great advantage of this approach is that the burden of proof lies primarily with the government, which has to explain why it wants to spend money and gain public support for its plans before it can tax its citizens. Citizens may not use their share of natural resource revenues wisely either, but less resources will be wasted on corruption and rent seeking. Other weaknesses are that it will be difficult to ensure inter-generational equity and to address the Dutch Disease syndrome (over-heating of the economy for example). A distinction can be made between an *endowment* effect, which argues that people put more pressure on the government to abide by the principles of good governance as they feel the cost of waste and corruption as an out-of-pocket cost, and an *information* effect, which stresses that people get better informed about the magnitude of the resource rents and how these are spent. Of course, a key issue once more is how to implement such a natural resource dividend *in practice* and how to address the weaknesses and overcome opposition from vested interests. Each unique case (country or resource) clearly requires further discussion and analysis.

Implications for Donors

The question of how resource windfalls can be successfully harnessed to make a significantly contribution to Africa's economic growth and development has become a central concern for the donor community in Africa. The analyses presented in this Report reveal the existence of a unique opportunity for donors and multilateral financial institutions to influence the role of resource wealth in addressing Africa's development challenges. In particular, the issues discussed below are critical in defining a donor focus.

Enhancing the Development Impact of Africa's Natural Resources: Given the inextricable linkages between natural resources and Africa's economic performance, the main challenge is how to achieve effective natural resource management that will provide sustainable growth and reduce poverty in Africa. This leaves clear room for multilateral financing institutions (MFIs) and donors. By virtue of their development activities, donors and MFIs have strong leverage that would allow them to focus on forging linkages to key areas, thus enhancing the development impact of Africa's natural resource wealth. Crucial areas include the following:

- Investing in physical and social infrastructure for future growth and development, and ensuring a holistic approach and sustainability beyond mining and other natural resource exploitation;
- Using the infrastructure developed with mineral wealth (transport, power, communication and water facilities) to systematically exploit the potential of non-commodity sectors such as agriculture, forestry, and

tourism;

- Using available raw materials (natural resources) to establish downstream industries for manufacturing and side stream sectoral linkages;
- Establishing industries to supply the natural resource sector with inputs, and achieving sectoral linkages;
- Supporting technical development and innovation by investing in research, and supporting the technological innovation to migrate to other sectors beyond mining;
- Facilitating the monitoring of natural resources and data compilation — securing regular data compilation and systematic approaches that will include the generation, maintenance, and utilization of natural resource data bases for development planning.

These areas and the highlighted linkages can serve as the starting points for various ways of linking natural resource wealth use to development operations — some of which are further described below.

Policy Dialogue and Budget Support: In recent years, aid delivery to Africa has shifted progressively from project support to more upstream, higher-level, programmatic support, sector support, and technical assistance. This shift should be embraced and taken a step further in order to enhance the development impact of natural resource wealth. For example, General Budget Support (GBS), one of the most important of these upstream aid instruments for pooling donor resources directly into national budgets, can be used to emphasize

development priorities aimed at improving the development impact of natural resources. New strategic thinking is also needed on the best way of coordinating conventional multilateral and bilateral aid to ensure that it serves as a conduit for mobilizing resource windfall revenues for the effective development of African economies. Such a strategy and dialogue could focus on the following actions and measures.

- Ensuring that General Budget Support (GBS) promotes multi-sector policy dialogue and coherence, creates a policy space for mainstreaming natural resource wealth into development, and generates economic growth;
- Making sure that GBS emphasizes and strengthens financial budgetary discipline — this discipline should be extended to the management of natural resource wealth in resource rich countries and should include relevant ministries and departments;
- Enhancing policies and programs that foster the contribution of natural resource wealth to economic growth, social equity aimed at achieving social stability, and poverty reduction;
- Facilitating economic diversification to ensure investment of resource wealth in non-resource sectors, human capital development, and infrastructure development;
- Strengthening natural resource management capacity by placing greater emphasis on internal management capacity, including on governance and democratic processes;
- Supporting the management of windfall rents, in particular, ensuring

that windfall rents are equitably appropriated. The management of large inflows should ensure that the income does not distort the economy. Options include investing in stabilization funds, citizens' funds and future funds. Some of these could be off-shore funds and committed to long-term infrastructure development;

- Using GBS to forge linkages in order to articulate issues related to transparent decision-making on natural resource matters, so that spending plans and appropriations are subject to more stringent monitoring. This can be done through initiatives such as the African Peer Review Mechanism (APRM). Oversights should be prepared and plans and implementations should increase national and citizen ownership of natural resource wealth spending priorities.

Fragile States: The management of natural resource wealth in fragile African states is important for Africa's development. The continent has more fragile states than any other continent — and many of these countries are rich in natural resources. The strong overlap between poorly performing resource-rich countries and countries that are widely accepted as being fragile is apparent from the analysis in this Report. From both spatial and temporal perspectives, circumstances that engender state fragility take different forms in different countries, and may also take different forms even within the same country. These differences have major implications for the scope and nature of engagement by development partners. In other words, a uniform approach to widely differing circumstances of state fragility may have several shortcomings on the ground, thus failing to produce results. The African Development Bank's strategic approach, which defines its engagement in fragile states — in partnership with other donors — includes:

- Focusing on prevention, policy dialogue, and support for improving governance;
- Remaining engaged and building a knowledge base (for instance, stake-holder analysis and engagement);
- Focusing on post conflict/crisis reconstruction, in particular, on turn around and graduation;
- Fostering stabilization, graduation, reform, and normalization.

The proposed framework (also refer to analysis in Chapter 4) focuses on addressing the risk from slippage (for instance, renewed conflicts) and helping weak and post conflict countries advance their political and stabilization processes. This would ensure that natural resource wealth is better harnessed and used for development.

Institutional Issues and Governance: Governance issues remain a critical challenge in the management of Africa's natural resource wealth for development. Donors and MFIs are exerting a concerted effort to use good governance principles to increase the contribution of resource wealth to Africa's development. Current institutional changes in Africa, which have led to the emergence of the African Union (AU) and associated initiatives such as the New Partnership for Africa's Development (NEPAD) and the African Peer Review Mechanism (APRM), provide a unique framework for addressing governance issues in the management of natural resources. NEPAD's identification of good governance by NEPAD as a basic requirement for peace, security, and sustainable growth and development provides an entry point from which development partners can forge linkages to natural resource sectors. To this end, donors would have to play a critical role in the following areas:

- Improving accountability and transparency in the management of natural resource wealth for Africa's development;
- Supporting central governments in effective planning and management of natural resource wealth for development;
- Shoring up relevant local institutions and civil society organizations;
- Strengthening regional bodies involved in the management of natural resources, ecosystems and related services, helping them overcome challenges stemming from political cross-border issues.

Africa-Asia Trade Partnership: The focus of the long-standing partnership between Africa and Asia, which ranges from development assistance to trade, has recently shifted to Africa's natural resources. The partnership, and the attendant challenges and opportunities, has serious implications for the management of Africa's natural resources to enhance economic growth.

Opportunities have emerged with the increase in investments and in capital flows from Asia to Africa, and the possibility that such investments entail transfer of skills, know-how, and low-cost technologies that improve efficiency. In resource-rich countries, however, the increased Asian involvement may lead to increased specialization in unprocessed commodities and to vulnerability.

For Africa's development partners, including the African Development Bank, there is a unique role to play to ensure that first, Africa clearly defines the kind of partnership that (ideally) should be pursued with China, India, and other nations scrambling to gain access to Africa's natural resources. Second, efforts are made to ensure that Asian countries (or any other countries) do not free-ride on the initiatives of other donors to reduce the debt burden of African Countries (through the Heavily Indebted Poor Countries' Initiative (HIPC) and the Multilateral Debt Relief (MDRI)), for instance, by extending new credits or loans with special conditions that may, in fact, increase Africa's debt service burden. Key areas of action in articulating Africa's benefits from the natural resource partnership with Asia (and others) include the following:

- Ensuring that foreign investments in the exploitation of Africa's natural resources are directly coupled with transfer of skills and technology to Africa. With their low-cost technologies, Asian firms can create conditions that increase productivity and improve the competitiveness of African firms in global markets.

- Ensuring that Asian firms provide capital goods and intermediate inputs, which would allow African firms to diversify and manufacture potential export products, aimed in particular at other developing countries, thereby boosting trade;
- Building capacity to strengthen Africa's technical knowledge of its resources, data, and research to increase its bargaining power during contract negotiations, and in the articulation of mining-related externalities that may need to be compensated by miners (investors); and
- Ensuring that there is no free riding that will dilute the positive effects of the HIPC and MDRI on Africa's development.

Environment and Climate Change: Climate change is expected to have a profound and irreversible impact on Africa's economic, social, and environmental systems. This is already evident in the increased frequency and intensity in the occurrence of natural imbalances and climate-related disasters on the continent — recurrent droughts, floods, and erratic rainfall. Climate change thus has a direct and important linkage to the management and sustainability of Africa's natural resources.

Because climate change affects and threatens the sustainable use of natural resources, it is critical that donor and MFI efforts integrate climate change adaptation to ensure sustainability. The bulk of renewable resources, including agricultural land, fisheries, livestock, water, tourism, natural parks, and coastal resources, are directly affected by climate change, with potentially dire consequences and increased poverty. This has a strong implication for development planning in the context of natural resource management. Donors, development partners, and African countries need to focus on the following issues to streamline climate change into natural resource management:

- The challenges and opportunities related to promoting low-carbon development. This needs considerable attention — in particular, how to finance climate change and how to mainstream it into NRM-related development assistance, including technology transfer and carbon trading;
- NRM opportunities related to climate adaptation — how natural resource wealth can be used to support climate risk management and how it can be mainstreamed into development assistance;
- The role of governments, financial institutions, donors and the private sector; and
- Bridging the financial gap for adaptation with existing or new financial instruments, and the specific challenges that these will pose for resource-rich African countries.

Overall Conclusions

Many African countries are endowed with natural resources, but this has not always been a blessing. In other countries, poor management has led to overexploitation of natural resources, resulting in environmental degradation and increased poverty. In many other countries, however, natural resources are considerably underutilized or are available in sufficient amounts to provide significant opportunities that Africa could take advantage of to propel its economies and drive its development and poverty reduction efforts. If well managed, Africa's resources could stimulate growth and multiplier effects on the continent. These issues point to the need for Africa to take the lead in its development process, and to strengthen support and initiatives aimed at ensuring that resource revenues are managed with a higher level of transparency and good governance. This can be accomplished by reinforcing institutional capacity, investing in the creation of knowledge for innovation, and integrating the natural resources sector into overall economic planning and development efforts.

The experience of African countries reveals that natural resource endowment especially in non-renewable resources, comes with opportunities but also with substantial risks. The key challenge for harnessing natural resource opportunities is achieving the right strategic choice in resource and economic policies and synchronizing their implementation in a context that supports fiscal prudence and eliminates macroeconomic distortions. This should be backed by adequate institutional capacity and national and local level participation in natural resource management. Getting the policies wrong, disregarding their sequencing and alignment with the rest of the economy, or ignoring absorptive capacity and good governance

issues may transform a natural resource boom into a curse that could effectively stall economic growth, worsen the poverty situation and become a recipe for social and political instability. With a few exceptions, notably Botswana, many resource-rich African countries have been victim to this scenario, albeit to varying degrees.

In addition, many resource-rich African countries suffer from real appreciation of their exchange rates induced by huge resource export revenues and aid flows. Consequently, Africa's pathway out of the natural resource dilemma lies primarily in sound fiscal policies and economic planning to ensure sufficient investment in productive and human capital. While the potential for such long-term investments exists, most resource-rich African countries have yet to exploit it. Although such a task (priority) is noted to be difficult, particularly in a global economy characterized by volatile commodity prices and export revenues (hence difficulty in planning public expenditures), the task is quite achievable with appropriate measures and concerted support from donors (especially in the context of budget support).

Many African governments have made concerted efforts to move away from state-controlled economies towards market-oriented systems — an important step to integrating with the global economy. This, coupled with rising commodity prices, potentially larger revenue incomes, and an increased tendency to channel natural resource revenues to expenditures on education, health, and other social services (albeit, still largely insufficient) provide some optimism for the future.

Sound environmental management and, not least, effective governance, have to be high on the agenda to ensure that Africa's natural resource wealth generates more rapid development and poverty reduction. Pro-poor governance, or governance that supports rural development and poverty reduction, should define the focus of development orientation, and the needs of the poor should be consistently reflected in development planning and in the use of natural resources. This would build a sound basis for economic growth, social equity, and stability. In the African context, these issues remain crucial for minimizing social tensions and the subsequent conflicts and wars relating directly or indirectly to natural resource wealth. The often observed situation of the elite capturing disproportionately large shares of Africa's natural resource wealth while transmitting the associated externalities and other social costs to marginalized populations is unsustainable and unacceptable. Such conditions are root causes of natural resource conflicts and the derived social and political consequences. Experience with resource-rich African countries shows that institutional and governance failures may lead to, and indeed be reinforced by, resource conflicts — leading to further underdevelopment and resource degradation. This Report has identified the fundamental elements that should underpin the use of natural resource wealth to foster development and economic progress in Africa. Essentially, this involves securing the fundamental democratic principles that ensure accountability, public participation, representation, and transparency.

BIBLIOGRAPHICAL NOTES

Introduction

The background papers and text boxes prepared specially for the Report are listed below, along with the selected bibliography used in the Report. These papers and text boxes synthesize the relevant literature. The Report has drawn on a wide range of African Development Bank reports, including on-going research and internal Bank documents. It has also drawn on outside sources, including published and unpublished works of institutions such as EIA, EITI, WRI, USAID, USGS, DFID, OECD, The World Bank, IMF, The UN and its agencies such as the ECA, FAO, IFAD, UNEP, WCED, UNICEF, UNDP, WHO, UNESCO, UNFCCC, UNCTAD, WTO, among others.

Background Papers

(i)   Collier, P (2007), Auctions for Mineral Rights — Text Box.

(ii)   Gbadegesin, A (2007), Environmental Degradation Management and the Profile, Experience and Problems of Renewable Natural Resources Management in Africa.

(iii) Kamier, E. M (2007), Experience and Problems of Natural Resources Management in Fragile States.

(iv)   MINTEK (2007), Introduction, Overview, Experience and Strategies of Natural Resources Management.

(v)   Otobo, E. E. (2007), Managing of Oil Resource Wealth: Nigeria's Challenge in the Niger Delta — Text Box.

(vi)   van der Ploeg, Rick and Venables, Tony (2007), Issues and Problems of Natural Resources Wealth Management in Africa.

(vii) Veit, P. (2007), Challenges and Harnessing of Africa's Natural Resources Potentials for Sustainable Development.

Selected Bibliography

Action Aid Ethiopia (2006), "Policies and Practices for Securing and Improving Access to and Control over Land in Ethiopia", Outcome Report and the Proceedings of Thematic Dialogue held on 17 January 2006 Addis Ababa; a process and a contribution leading to ICARRD.

Adedeji, A. (1999), "Comprehending and Mastering African Conflicts: The Search for Sustainable Peace and Good Governance", London, Zed Books.

Addison, T., P. Le Billon, and S. M. Murshed (2001a), "Conflict in Africa: The Cost of Peaceful Behaviour", *Wider Discussion Paper,* 2001/51, World Institute for Development Economics Research of the UN University (UNU/WIDER), Helsinki.

—— **(2001b),** "From Conflict to Reconstruction: Reviving the Social Contract", *WIDER Discussion Paper,* 2001/48.

AfDB (African Development Bank), (2005), "Annual Report", African Development Bank/African Development Fund.

AfDB (African Development Bank), (2006a), "Annual Report", African Development Bank/African Development Fund.

—— **(2007a),** "Africa and Asia: Partners in Development", Annual Meetings Seminars, 2007. African Development Bank/African Development Fund.

—— **(2007b),** "Regional Cooperation: Addressing Trans-Boundary Challenges: Concept Paper", African Development Bank Annual Meetings 2007, Ministerial Round Table Discussions and High Level Seminars, Shanghai, China — 15 May 2007.

—— **(2007c), "**Enhanced Engagement in Fragile States, Revised Approach", Discussion Paper for the ADF-VI Replenishment Meeting, June 2007, Tunis, Tunisia.

AfDB (African Development Bank), Memorandum (2007a), "Support to Implementation of EITI in Resource Rich Regional Member Countries", African Development Bank/African Development Fund.

—— **(2007b)**, "Implementation update to Bank Group support to APRM", African Development Bank/African Development Fund.

African Peer Review Mechanism (APRM) Homepage: http://www.aprm.org.za

Ahrens, J. and P. M. Rudolph. (2006), "The Importance of Governance in Risk Reduction and Disaster Management". *Journal of Contingencies and Crisis Management* 14, No. 4: 207–220.

Alao, A., Olonisakin, F. (2001), "Economic Fragility and Political Fluidity: Explaining Natural Resources and Conflicts". In: Adekeye Adebajo and Chandra Sriram (eds), Managing Armed Conflicts in the 21st Century, Frank Cass, London.

Algerian Ministry of Energy and Mining: http://www.mem-algeria.org/legis/index.htm

Alley, P. et al. (2007), "To Have and Have Not: Resource Governance in Africa in the 21st Century", A memorandum of the Heinrich Boll Foundation.

Anyanwu, J. C. (2002), "Economic and Political Causes of Civil Wars in Africa: Some Econometric Results", *Economic Research Papers,* No.73, December, African Development Bank.

—— **(2006),** "Promoting of Investment in Africa", *African Development Review*, 18, 1, 42–71. African Development Bank.

AOAD (1998), "Study on Suitable Modern Technologies for Forest Wealth Development in the Arab Region", Arab Organization for Agricultural Development, Khartoum.

Ascher, W. (1999), "Why Governments Waste Natural Resources: Policy Failures in Developing Countries", John Hopkins University Press, pp. 178–82.

Associated Press (2006), "Tanzania becomes Africa's third largest producer of gold; government wants larger share". *International Harold Tribune*, 26 October,

2006. Available online at: http://www.iht. com/articles/ap/2006/10/26/business/AF_F EA_FIN_Tanzania_M

AU (African Union), (2002), "Report of the AU-NEPAD Consultations on Peace and Security", Addis Ababa, 17–18 February 2002.

Auty, R. (1993), "Sustaining Development in Mineral Economics: The Resource Curse Thesis", London, Routledge.

—— **(1998),** "Resource Abundance and Economic Development: Improving the performance of Resource-Rich Countries", *UNU/WIDER Research for Action, 44.*

—— **(2001),** "Resource Abundance and Economic Development", Oxford University Press, Oxford.

—— **(2004),** "Economic and political reform of distorted oil-exporting economies", presentation at The Earth Institute, Columbia University.

Ballentine, K. (2004), "Natural Resources, Governance, Development and Conflict", *Discussion Paper,* Fafo Institute, November 2004.

Bank Information Center (2007), Infrastructure. Available online at: http://www.bicusa.org/en/Issue.7.aspx.

Bannon and Collier (eds.) (2003), "Natural Resources and Violent Conflict, Options and Actions", Washington, D.C., World Bank.

Bapna, M. (2006), "Infrastructure, Poverty, and the Role of the MDBs", Testimony before the United States Senate Committee on Foreign Relations, 12 July 2006.

Bass, S.; H. Reid; D. Satterthwaite and P. Steele (2005), "Reducing Poverty and Sustaining the Environment: The politics of local engagement", Earthscan, London.

Bebbington, A. (1999), "Capitals and Capabilities: A Framework for Analyzing Peasant Viability, Rural Livelihoods and Poverty", *World Development* 27, No. 12: 2021–2044.

Berg, A. (2007), "EITI Validation and EITI Multi-donor Trust Fund", Presentation at EITI Workshop in Dili, Timor-Leste, May 15, 2007.

Bosworth, B. and Collins, S. (2003), "The Empirics of Growth: An Update", *Brooking Papers on Economic Activity* 2003, no. 2, 113–206.

British Geological Survey (BGS) (2006), "African Mineral Production 2001–2005", Keyworth, Nottingham.

—— **(BGS) (2007),** "African Mineral Production 2002–2006". Keyworth, Nottingham.

British Petroleum (BP), (2006), "Statistical Review of World Energy 2005", London.

—— **(2007),** "Statistical Review of World Energy 2006", London, UK.

Broadman, H.G. (2007), "Africa's Silk Road — China and India's New Economic Frontier", The World Bank, Washington, D.C.

Bromley, W. B. (1992), "Making the Commons Work: Theory, Practice and Policy", ICS Press, San Francisco.

Bruce, J. W. (1993), "The variety of reform: A review of recent experience with land reform and the reform of land tenure, with particular reference to the African experience", *International Development Studies*, Occasional paper no. 9, Roskilde University, Denmark.

Bruch, Carl (2002), "The New 'Public': The Globalization of Public Participation", Environmental Law Institute, Washington, D.C.

Bruch, C., Wole, C. and VanArsdale, C. (2001), "Breathing Life into Fundamental Principles: Implementing Constitutional Environmental Protections in Africa", *Environmental Governance in Africa*, Working Paper No. 2, World Resources Institute, Washington, D.C.

Bzioui, M. (2005), "Sub Regional Report on Water Resources Development in North Africa", UN WATER-AFRICA. ECA-NA/PUB/WATER/8.

Campbell, B. (ed.) (2004), "Mining Code or Redefining the Role of the State? Regulating Mining in Africa", *Nordiska Afrikainstitutet*, Discussion Paper 26. Printed in Sweden by Elanders Info logistics Vast AB, Goteborg 2004.

Carpini, Michael X. Delli, Fay Lomax Cook and Lawrence R. Jacobs. (2004), "Public Deliberation, Discursive Participation, and Citizen Engagement: A Review of the Empirical Literature", *Annual Review of Political Science* 7: 315–344.

Caselli, F. and W.J. Coleman II (2006), "On the theory of ethnic conflict", *CEPR Discussion Paper* No. 5622, London.

Castells, M. (2000), "End of Millennium", Blackwell Publishing, UK.

Catholic Relief Services (CRS) (2003), "Bottom of the Barrel: Africa's Oil Boom and the Poor", CRS, June 2003.

Cavendish, W. (1999), "Empirical Regularities in the Poverty-Environment Relationship of African Households", *WPS 99–21.*

CEC (Commission of the European Communities) (2003), "Towards a Thematic Strategy on the Sustainable Use of Natural Resources", *1.10.2003, COM (2003) 572 final*, Brussels.

Center for Global Development (CGD) (2006), "Building Africa's Development Bank: Six Recommendations for the AfDB and its Shareholders", CGD, Washington, D.C.

Chenje M. (2000), "*State of the Environment Zambezi Basin*", SADC/IUCN/ZRA/SARDC/Sida, Maseru/Lusaka/Harare, ISBN1-77910-009-4

Cho, J. (2005), "Smart infrastructure", *UN Chronicle* Online Edition. Available online at: http://www.un.org/Pubs/chronicle/2005/issue1/0105p39.html

Chomitz, K. M. (2006), "At Loggerheads? Agricultural Expansion, Poverty Reduction, and Environment in the Tropical Forests", *World Bank Policy Research Report.*

Lund, C., R. Odgaard and E. Sjaastad (2006), "Land Rights and Land Conflicts in Africa: A review of issues and experiences", Report for the Danish Ministry of Foreign Affairs. Copenhagen, Danish Institute for International Studies, 2006, 3–4. http://www.diis.dk/graphics/Events/2006/Lund%20Odgaard%20and%20Sjaastad.pdf

Cilliers J. and Dietrich D. (eds.) (2000), "Angola's War Economy: The Role of Oil and Diamonds", Institute of Security Studies, Pretoria.

Cleaver, K.M. and G.A. Schreiber. (1994), "Reversing the Spiral", The World Bank, Washington, DC.

Collier, P. (2000), "Doing Well Out of War: An Economic Perspective", in Mats Berdal; David Malone, Greed and Grievance: Economic Agenda in Civil Wars, Lynne Rienner Publishers.

—— **(2007a),** "The Bottom Billion", Oxford University Press, Oxford.

—— **(2007b),** "Managing Commodity Booms: Lessons of International Experience", CSAE, Department of Economics, University of Oxford, Oxford.

Collier, P. and Hoeffler, A. (2004), "Greed and grievance in civil wars", *Oxford Economic Papers*, 56, 663–695.

—— **(2005),** "Resource Rents, Governance, and Conflict", Available at http://jcr.sagepub.com/cgi/content/abstract/49/4/625.

Collier, P. and B. Goderis (2007), "Commodity prices and Growth: Reconciling a Conundrum", Department of Economics, University of Oxford, January 2007.

Council for Geoscience (CGS) and Mintek, (2007), GIS Database, MESU, Randburg, South Africa.

Creamer Media's Research Channel (2005), Mining in Southern Africa 2005, Johannesburg, South Africa.

Creamer Media's Research Channel (2006), Mining in Southern Africa 2006, Johannesburg, South Africa.

Creamer Media's Research Channel (2007), Mining in Southern Africa 2007, Johannesburg, South Africa.

Dales, D (2006), "Scan Of The African Minerals Cluster". Eds.: Mudau, J; Phelane, E; Mabusela, T; Roy, R; Auchterlonie, A; Spicer, D; Toolsi, D, MESU, Mintek, 2006.

DFID (Department for International Development) (2003), "Handbook for the Assessment of Catchment Water Demand and Use", Prepared by DFID, aimed at professionals and practitioners in the southern African region.

—— **(2002),** "Better Livelihoods for Poor People: The Role of Land Policy", London: DFID.

DFID (Department for International Development) (2006a), "Eliminating World Poverty: Making Governance Work for the Poor", *DFID White Paper*, DFID, London.

—— **(2006b)**, "Eliminating World Poverty: Helping to Build States that work for Poor People", *DFID White Paper*, DFID, London.

Department for International Development (DFID), Directorate General for Development (European Commission), United Nations Development Programme and World Bank (2002), "Linking Poverty Reduction and Environmental Management: Policy challenges and opportunities", World Bank, Washington, D.C.

Department of Minerals and Energy (DME), (2007), "The South African Minerals Industry". Economic Database: http://www.dti.gov.za/econdb/

Development Today (2007), "China and the new scramble for Africa's Resources", *Development Today (DT)* 10/11/2007, July 17, 2007.

DLA (Department of Land Affairs) (1997), "White Paper on South African Land Policy", In: Prosterman, R & Riedinger, J. (1987), Land reform and democratic development. Johns Hopkins, University Press, Baltimore.

DME (2007), South African Department of Minerals and Energy, "The South African Minerals Industry 2005/2006". Available online at: http://www.dme.gov.za

Douglas Lake Minerals (DLM) (2007), "Developing Mining Opportunities in Tanzania", Investor Presentation, January 2007.

Easterly, W. (2002), "Inequality Does Cause Underdevelopment", *Working Paper, No. 1 Center for Global Development*, Washington, D.C. Available online at: http://www.cgdev.org/content/publications/detail/2789

ECA (2004), "Economic Report on Africa 2004", Economic Commission on Africa, ECA/UNECA. Available at www.un**eca**.org/publications

Economist Intelligence Unit Country Report (2007), "Report on Nigeria", May 2007, p. 5.

Economist Intelligence Unit Country Report (2006), "Report on Nigeria", Nov. 2006 p. 28.

EEA (2005), "Sustainable Use and Management of Natural resources", European Environmental Agency, *EEA Report No. 9/2005*, Copenhagen, Denmark.

EEA / EEPRI (2002), Ethiopian Economic Association / Ethiopian Economic Policy Research Institute, "A Research Report on Land Tenure and Agricultural Development in Ethiopia", October 2002, EEA/EEPRI.

EIS News (1999), "Ethiopia: Extent and Dynamics of deforestation in Ethiopia", Advisory Assistance to the Forest

Administration Study by Matthias Reusing, Addis Ababa, Ethiopia.

Energy Information Administration (EIA), (2007), "International Energy Outlook 2007", EIA.

Equator Principles Homepage: http://www.equator-principles.com

ESMAP (2004), "Petroleum Revenue Management Workshop", *ESMAP Technical Paper* 051. Joint UNDP/WB Energy Sector Management Assistance Programme (ESMAP)", WB, Washington D.C.

Eurowatch (2002), "Towards Sustainable Use of Natural Resources and Sustainable Recycling", *Eurowatch* No. 19, August 2002.

Extractive Industries Transparency Initiative (EITI) Homepage: http://www.eitransparency.org

Fan, S. and Rao, N. (2003), "Public Spending in Developing Countries: Trends, Determination and Impact", *Environment and Production Technology Division Discussion Paper No. 99,* International Food Policy Research Institute, Washington, D.C.

FAO (1995), "Forest resources assessment 1990 — Global synthesis", *FAO Forestry Paper* No. 124. Rome.

—— **(1997),** "State of the World's Forests, 1997", Food and Agriculture Organization of the United Nations, Rome.

—— **(1999)**, "State of the World's Forests 1999", FAO, Rome.

—— **(2000),** "The state of food and agriculture 2000", FAO, Rome.

—— **(2001a)**, "Forest Resources assessment 2001", FAO, Rome.

—— **(2001b)**, "State of the World's Forests 2001", FAO, Rome.

—— **(2005),** "AQUASTAT Information System on Water and Agriculture, Country Profiles", FAO, Rome. Available at: http://www.fao.org/waicent/faoinfo/agricult/agl/aglw/aquastat/countries/index.stm

—— **(2006),** "Global Forest Resources Assessment 2005", FAO, Rome.

—— **(2007),** "State of the World's Forests 2007, Forest Finance", FAO, Rome.

Farmanesh, M. (1991), "Dutch disease economics and the oil syndrome: an empirical study", *World Development*, Vol. 19, No. 6.

Fearon, J. D. and D. D. Laitin (2003), "Ethnicity, insurgency, and civil war", *American Political Science Review*, 97, 75–90.

Fedderke, J. W. and M. Mariotti (2002), "Changing Labour Market Conditions in South Africa: A Sectoral Analysis of the Period 1970–1997", *South African Journal of Economics*, 70(5), 830–864.

Ferraro, P. J. and A. Kiss (2002), "Direct Payments to Conserve Biodiversity", *Science*, Vol.298: 1718–1719.

Field, B. C. (2000), "Natural Resources Economics: An Introduction", McGraw Hill, Boston.

Financial Times Special Supplement on Nigeria, of 12 July 2007, Para 6 of THE ECONOMY Section on page 2.

Gaolathe, Baledzi (2007), "Planning For Success: Turning Natural Resources into Human Capital — Botswana Experience", The Honourable Minister of Finance and Development Planning, Botswana. 53rd Wilton Park Conference On Africa: Business, Growth And Poverty Reduction, London.

Gibson, C. (1999), "Politicians and Poachers: The Political Economy of Wildlife Policy in Africa", Cambridge: Cambridge University Press.

Global Witness (2006), "Kimberley Process Update — November 2006", Global Witness. Available online at: http://www. globalwitness.org/media_library_detail.php /474/en/kimberley_process_update_ november_2006

Golooba-Mutebi, Frederick (2005), "When Popular Participation Won't Improve Service Provision: Primary Health Care in Uganda", *Development Policy Review* 23, No. 2: 165–182.

Gylfason, T., Herbertson, T. T. and Zoega, G. (1997), "A mixed blessing: natural resources and economic growth", *CEPR Discussion Paper* No. 1668, Centre for Economic and Policy Research, London.

Hamblin (1998), "Environmental indicators for national state of the environment reporting — The Land", Australia: State of the Environment (Environmental Indicator Reports), Department of the Environment, Canberra.

Harmse, N. and B. Finca (2007), "The Role of Transnational Corporations in the extractive industry of South Africa", MESU, Mintek.

Haskell, J. (2001), "Direct Democracy or Representative Government? Dispelling the Populist Myth", Westview Press, Boulder, Colorado.

Hegazy, A.K. (1999), "Deserts of the Middle East", In Encyclopedia of Deserts (ed. Mares, M.A.), University of Oklahoma Press.

Henrich Boll Foundation (2007), "Expert Roundtable: Resource Governance in Africa in the 21st Century", Berlin, 26–28 March 2007.

Hibou, B. (1999), "The Social Capital of the State as an Agent of Deception", in (eds.), J. Bayart, S. Ellis, and B. Hibou: The Criminalization of the State in Africa, The International African Institute.

Hodler, R. (2006), "The curse of natural resources in fractionalized countries", *European Economic Review*, 50, 1367–1386.

Howard, P. and Smith, E. (2006), "Leaving two thirds out of development: Female headed households and common property resources in the highlands of Tigray, Ethiopia". Livelihood Support Programme FAO, 2006. Available at: ftp://ftp.fao.org/ docrep/fao/009/ah624e/ah624e00.pdf .

Humphreys, M. (2005), "Natural Resources, Conflict, and Conflict Resolution", *Journal of Conflict Resolution*, Vol. 49, August 2005, 508–537.

ILRI (2007), "Independent Review of Land Issues", Volume iii, Southern and Eastern Africa, June 2007. International Livestock Research Institute, ILRI.

IMF (2006), "World Economic Outlook", International Monetary Fund, Washington, DC.

—— **(2007),** "Regional and Economic Outlook: Sub-Saharan Africa", World Economic and Financial Surveys, International Monetary Fund, Washington, D.C.

InterAcademy Council (2004) "Realizing the Promise and Potential of African Agriculture", InterAcademy Council, Amsterdam.

International Copper Study Group (ICSG) (2007): Official website: http://www. icsg.org

International Fertilizer Industry Association (IFA): http://www. fertilizer.org

International Iron and Steel Institute (IISI): http://www.worldsteel.org

International Lead Zinc Study Group (ILZSG): http://www.ilzsg.org/

IOC (2005), "Report for the Commonwealth secretariat on disaster preparedness, Indian Ocean Commission, Mauritius"

IPCC (2007a), "Climate Change 2007: The Physical Science Basis Summary for Policymakers", Contribution of Working Group I to the Fourth Assessment Report of the IPCC.

—— **(2007b),** "Climate Change 2007: Climate Change Impacts, Adaptation and Vulnerability — Summary for Policymakers", Contribution of Working Group II to the Fourth Assessment Report of the IPCC.

Johnson, Mathey (2007), "Platinum 2007", London, UK.

Jomo, F. (2007a), "Tanzanian government about turn on mining royalties". *Mineweb,* 28 March 2007. Available online at: http://www.mineweb.co.za/mineweb/view/mineweb/en/page54?oid=18754&sn=Detail

—— **(2007b),** "Tanzania to remove some mining incentives to benefit more from its resources", *Mineweb,* 9 May 2007. Available online at: http://www.mineweb.co.za/mineweb/view/mineweb/en/page67?oid=20681&sn=Detail

Jourdan, P., (2006), "Regional Strategies-the case for a Resource Based Spatial Development Programme", Presentation delivered at the US-Africa Infrastructure conference. 28 September 2006.

Jourdan, P., (2007), "The Role of Extractive Industries in Fragile States in Africa", Presentation at the African Development Bank Annual Meeting, 2007.

Kalumiana, O.S. (1998), "Woodfuel Sub-Programme of the Zambia Forestry Action

Programme", Ministry of Environment & Natural Resources, Zambia, Lusaka.

Kamara, A. B. and Sally, H. (2004), "Water Management options for food security in South Africa: scenarios, simulations and policy implications", *Development Southern Africa* Vol. 21, No. 2, June 2004.

Karl, T. Lynn (1997), "The Paradox of Plenty: Oil Booms and Petro-States", Berkeley, University of California Press.

Kaufmann, D., A. Kraay, and M. Mastruzzi (2007), "Governance Matters VI: Governance Indicators for 1996–2006", World Bank Policy Research, WB, June 2007.

Killick, T. (2002), "Responding to Inequality", Inequality Briefing, Briefing Paper No. 3. London: Economists' Resource Centre.

Kimberly Process Homepage (KP/KPCS): http://www.kimberlyprocess.com

Larson, A. M. and J. C. Ribot (2007), "The Poverty of Forestry Policy: Double Standards on an Uneven Playing Field", *Journal of Sustainability Science* 2, No. 2.

Lane, C. (1996), "Pastures Lost: Barabaig Economy, Resource Tenure, and the Alienation of their Land in Tanzania". Nairobi: Initiatives Publishers.

Lawcastles (2006), "Statutory Procedure for Conducting Environmental Impact Assessment in Tanzania", *Lawcastles Technical Papers No. 2.* Available online at: http://lawcastles.com/files/Statutory%20Procedure%20for%20Conducting%20E

Levine, P. ; A. Fung and J. Gastil (2005), "Future Directions for Public Deliberation", *Journal of Public Deliberation* 1, No. 1.

Lewis, A. (2003), "Revitalizing the drive for rural infrastructure". IFPRI Forum. International Food Policy Research Institute, Washington, D.C.

LHRC (Legal and Human Rights Centre) (2003), "The Serengeti Killings: Wildlife Protection and Human Rights in the Balance", LHRC, Dar es Salaam, Tanzania.

Lind, J. and Sturman, K. (eds.) (2002), "Scarcity and Surfeit: The Ecology of Africa's Conflicts", Pretoria: Institute for Security Studies.

Lipschutz R. (1987), "Ore Wars: Access to Strategic Materials, International Conflict, and the Foreign Policies of States", University of California, Berkeley, Energy and Resources Group. PhD Dissertation, Berkeley: UC Berkeley.

Lissu, T. A. (2001), "In Gold We Trust: The Political Economy of Law, Human Rights and Environment in Tanzania's Mining Industry", *Law, Social Justice & Global Development Journal (LGD)* 2.

Lujala, P. (2003), Classification of Natural Resources, Department of Economics Norwegian University of Science and Technology, *Dragvoll No-7491*, Trondheim, Norway.

Manin, B. , A. Przeworski and S. C. Stokes (1999), "Introduction", In: Democracy, Accountability, and Representation, edited by Adam Przeworski, Susan C. Stokes and Bernard Manin. Cambridge: Cambridge University Press.

Mezey, M. L. (2000), "Representation as the Fundamental Role for Democratic Legislatures", Keynote Address at Second International Conference on Legislative Strengthening, June 5–8, 2000, Wintergreen, Virginia.

Mineral Information Institute (MII): http://www.mii.org/Minerals/

Mining Journal Online (2007): http://www.mining-journal.com/ Annual_Review.aspx

Mining, Minerals and Sustainable Development (MMSD) (2002), "Breaking New Ground: The Report of the Mining, Minerals and Sustainable Development Report". IIED, Earthscan, London.

Mining Review Africa, (2005), "Coal in Africa"; *Mining Review Africa* No. 6, 2005.

Moore, M. and G. Teskey (2006), "The CAR Framework: Capability, Accountability, Responsiveness, What Do These Terms Mean, Individually and Collectively?", A Discussion Note for Department for International Development Governance and Conflict Advisers' Retreat, 14–17 November 2006.

Moyo, S. (2000), "Land Reform under Structural Adjustment in Zimbabwe — Land–Use Change in the Mashonaland Provinces", *African Affaire*, Vol. 100, No 399, 344–346.

Mtegha, H. D (2006), "National Minerals Policies and Stakeholder Participation for broad-based development in the southern African Development community (SADC)", (eds) Cawood, F. T. Minnitt, R.C.A, School of Mining Engineering, University of the Witwatersrand, Private Bag 3, WITS 2050, 2006. Available at: www.sciencedirect.com.

Muganda, A. (2004), "Tanzania's Economic Reforms-and Lessons Learned". World Bank, Washington, D.C. Available online at: http://info.worldbank.org/etools/docs/ reducingpoverty/case/31/fullcase/Tanzania %20Country%20Study%20Full%20Case.pdf.

Murshed, S.M. (2002), "Civil war, conflict and underdevelopment", *Journal of Peace Research*, 39, 387–393.

Mwaipopo, R. , W. Mutagwaba, D. Nyange and E. Fisher (2004), "Increasing the Contribution of Artisanal and Small-Scale Mining to Poverty Reduction in Tanzania", London: Department for International Development. Available online at: www.swan.ac.uk/cds/pdffiles/TANZANIA% 20ASM%20REPORT.pdf.

Naschold, F. (2002), "Why Inequality Matters for Poverty". *Inequality Briefing, Briefing Paper No. 2*. London: Economists' Resource Centre.

NEPAD (2005b), "A Report on South Africa's First APRM Consultative Conference, 2005", NEPAD.

Newbery, D. and Stiglitz J. (1981), "The Theory of Commodity Price Stabilization", Oxford University Press, Oxford.

Neumann, R.P. (1998), "Imposing Wilderness: Struggles over Livelihood and Nature Preservation in Africa", Berkeley: University of California Press.

Ngaido, T. (2004), "Reforming Land Rights in Africa", International Food Policy Research Institute: Washington, DC 20006-1002 USA. www.ifpri.org/2020africaconference <http://www.ifpri.org/2020africaconference>. 2020 Africa Conference Brief 15.

Norway Mission of the EU (2005), "Notes on Economic and Monetary Policy". Available at: http://wwweu-norway.org/policyareas/economy+monetary/

Norwegian Ministry of Finance, (2004), "Revised National Budget for 2004", chapter 4 at http://odin.dep.no/filarkiv/209862/ch4_engelsk.pdf

Overseas Development Institute (ODI) (2006), Meeting the Challenge of the 'Resource Curse': International Experiences in Managing the Risks and Realising the Opportunities of Non-Renewable Natural Resource Revenues", ODI, London.

OECD (2007), "Natural Resources and Pro-Poor Growth: The Economics and Politics of Natural Resource Use in Developing Cooperation", Draft Paper, prepared for Meeting 23–24 May 2007, OECD.

OECD and AfDB (2007), "African Economic Outlook 2006/07**",** OECD/AfDB, 2007.

Oluoch, F. (2007), "Tanzania: De Beers Wants Overhaul of Dar Mineral Laws", East Africa (Nairobi), 31 July, 2007. Available online at: http://allafrica.com/stories/200707310594.html.

Okoth-Ogendo, HWO. (1993), "Agrarian reform in sub-Saharan Africa: An assessment of state responses to the African agrarian crisis and their implications for agricultural development", in Land in African agrarian systems, edited by TJ Bassett & DE Crummey, Madison: University of Wisconsin Press.

Olsson, O. and H.C. Fors (2004), "Congo: The prize of predation", *Journal of Peace Research*, 41, 3, 321–336.

Ollson, O. (2007), "Conflict diamonds", *Journal of Development Economics*, 82, 267–286.

Otobo, E. E. (2007a), "Managing of Oil Resource Wealth in Nigeria — The Challenge in the Niger Delta", Short paper prepared for AfDB, 2007.

Otobo, E. E. (2007b), "The Financial allocation that will be needed for Niger Delta Deal", *Financial Times*, 31 July 2007, page 8.

Otto, J. and Cordes, J. (2002), "The Regulation of Mineral Enterprises: A Global Perspective On Economics, Law and Policy", Rocky Mountain Mineral Law Foundation, Westminster, Colorado.

Otto, J. M., Cordes, J. (2004) "Regulation of Mineral Enterprises: A Global Perspective on Economics, Law and Policy", Rocky Mountain Law Foundation, 2004.

Oxford Analytica (2007), "AFRICA: Middle East and Africa Executive Summary, Cooperation Key for Great Lakes oil and gas", *Oxford Analytica,* Friday, August 3, 2007. (http://www.oxan.com/about/)

Pearce, D. (2005), "Managing Environmental Wealth for Poverty Reduction", Poverty and Environment Partnership: MDG 7 Initiative-Economics, 31 August.

Petkova, E. , C. Maurer, N. Henninger and F. Irwin with J. Coyle and G. Hoff (2002), "Closing the Gap: Information, Participation, and Justice in Decision-making for the Environment", Washington, DC: World Resources Institute.

Petkova, E. and P. Veit (2000), "Environmental Accountability Beyond the Nation-State: The Implications of the Aarhus Convention", Institutions and Governance Program, Environmental Governance Notes, April. Washington, DC: World Resources Institute.

Pitkin, H.F. (1967), "The Concept of Representation", Berkeley: University of California, Los Angeles Press.

Ploeg, F. van der (2006), "Challenges and opportunities for resource rich economies", *CEPR Discussion Paper No. 5688,* London.

—— **(2007),** "Africa and Natural Resources". Background Paper for AfDB, ADR REPORT 2007.

Prosterman & Riedinger (1987), "Land reform and democratic development",

Baltimore and London: Johns Hopkins. University Press.

Przeworski, A. , B. Manin, and S. Stokes (1999), "Democracy, accountability, and representation", Cambridge: Cambridge University Press.

Publish What You Pay homepage (PWYP): http://www.publishwhatyoupay. org

Quashie, A. Lloyd (2007), "The Case of Mineral Resources Management and Development in Sub-Saharan Africa". Available at: www.unu.edu/unupress/ unupbooks

Rausch, J.D. (2001), "Direct Democracy or Representative Government? Dispelling the Populist Myth", *Current Reviews for Academic Libraries,* Vol. 39, No. 2, pp. 388.

Reno, W. (2000), "Shadow States and the Political Economy of Civil Wars", in Mats Berdal and David Malone, Greed and Grievance: Economic Agenda in Civil Wars, Lynne Rienner Publishers.

Ribot, Jesse C. (2007), "Representation, Citizenship and the Public Domain in Democratic Decentralization." *Development* 50, No. 1: 43–49.

Ribot, Jesse C. (2006a), "Choose Democracy: Environmentalists' Socio-political Responsibility", *Global Environmental Change* 16: 115–119.

—— **(2006b),** "Representation, Citizenship and the Public Domain: The Democracy

Effects of Institutional Choice in Natural Resource Management", Presentation at Harvard Kennedy School, Cambridge, Massachusetts, 27 April.

Ribot, Jesse C. (2004), "Waiting for Democracy: The Politics of Choice in Natural Resource Decentralizations", Washington, D.C.: World Resources Institute.

—— **(2003),** "Democratic decentralization of natural resources: Institutional choice and discretionary powers in sub-Saharan Africa", *Public Administration and Development* 23:53–65.

—— **(1998),** "Theorizing Access: Forest Profits along Senegal's Charcoal Commodity Chain", *Development and Change*, Vol. 29: 307–341.

Ribot, Jesse C. and A. Larson (2005), "Decentralization through a Natural Resource Lens: Experience in Africa, Asia and Latin America", London: Frank Cass.

Ribot, Jesse C. and R. Oyono (2006), "Decentralization in Africa: An Overview," *Africa Development* Vol. 31. No. 2 in special issue "Implementing Progressive New Natural Resources Laws" (Oyono and Ribot, guest eds.). Pp. 1–19.

Richardson, B.J. and S. Wood (2006), "Environmental Law for Sustainability", Oxford: Hart Publishing.

Robinson, J. and S. Ryan (2002), "A policy framework for implementation of economic instruments for environmental management". *Coast to Coast*, pp.396–399.

Rogers, C. D (2007), "Sustainable Development, Poverty, and Livelihoods". UNECA. Available at: www.uneca.com

Rosenthal, A. (1992), "The Decline of Representative Democracy: Process, Participation, and Power in State Legislatures", Washington, D.C.: CQ Press.

Rosenthal, A. , K. T. Kurtz, J. H. and B. Loomis (2001), "The Case for Representative Democracy: What Americans Should Know About Their Legislatures", Washington, D.C.: National Conference of State Legislatures.

Ross, M.L. (1999), "The political economy of the resource curse", *World Politics, 51, 297–322.*

—— **(2002),** "Oil, Drugs, and Diamonds. 'How do Natural Resources Vary in their Impact on Civil War'", Working Paper, Dept. of Political Science, UCLA.

—— **(2003),** "Natural Resources and Civil War: An Overview", *World Bank Research Observer*, World Bank.

—— **(2004),** What do we know about natural resources and civil war?", *Journal of Peace Economics*, 41, 337–356.

Ryfe, D. M. (2005), "Does Deliberative Democracy Work?", *Annual Review of Political Science* 8: 49–71.

Sala-i-Martin, X. and A. Subramanian (2003), "Addressing the natural resource curse: An illustration from Nigeria", *NBER WP 9804*, Cambridge, Mass.

SADC (2006), "Mines 2006: Unlocking Resources in Southern Africa", Mines 2006 Conference Online: http://www.mines2006.com

Sarraf, M. and Jiwanji, M. (2001), "Beating the resource curse: the case of Botswana", *Environmental Economics Series,* Paper No. 83, October 2001.

Sengupta, S. and S. Maginnis (2005), "Forests and Development: Where do we stand?", *Forestry and Development* 2005, p. 11. Earthscan, London.

Shackleton, C. and S. Shackleton (2004), "The Importance of Non-Timber Forest Products in Rural Livelihood Security and as Safety Nets: A Review of Evidence from South Africa", *South African Journal of Science* 100: 658–664.

Shackleton, S.E., C.M. Shackleton, and B. Cousins (2000), "The economic value of land and natural resources to rural livelihoods: case studies from South Africa", Cousins, B. (ed.) (2000), pp. 35–67

Shivji, I. (1998), "Not yet Democracy: Reforming Land Tenure in Tanzania", London: International Institute for Environment and Development, HAKIARDHI and the Faculty of Law at the University of Dar es Salaam.

Shivji, I. and Kapinga, W. (1998), "Maasai Rights in Ngorongoro, Tanzania", London: International Institute for Environment and Development, HAKIARDHI and the Faculty of Law at the University of Dar es Salaam.

Shukla, G. P. (2007), "Taxation of Exhaustible Natural Resources, Mining Taxation and Legal Framework", Background Paper for World Bank Seminar, Duke University, North Carolina.

Siegle, J. T. ; M. M. Weinstein and M. H. Halperin (2004), "Why Democracies Excel", *Foreign Affairs* 83, No. 5, September/October: 57–71. Available online at: http://www.soros.org/initiatives/washington/articles_publications/articles/why_20041012/fa_whydemocracies.pdf

Steiner, G. et al. (2000), "Analysis of the Fundamental Concepts of Resource Management", Report for the European Commission, August.

Stevens, P. (2003), "Resource Impact — Curse or Blessing?: A Literature Survey", Centre for Energy, Petroleum and Mineral Law and Policy, University of Dundee, Dundee.

Stewart, F. (2000), "Crisis Prevention: Tackling Horizontal Inequalities", *Oxford Development Studies* 28(3): 245–262.

Stewart, F. (2002), "Horizontal Inequalities: A Neglected Dimension of Development", *QEH Working Paper Series* No. 81, Queen Elizabeth House, University of Oxford.

The Diamonds and Human Security Project (2006), "West Africa: Rocks in a Hard Place; The Political Economy of Diamonds and Regional Destabilization". 2006.

Theiss-Morse, E. and J. R. Hibbing (2004), "Citizenship and Civil Engagement.", *Annual Review of Political Science* 8: 227–249.

Trade Map: International Trade Database online: http://www.trademap.org

UN (2006), "Expert Group Meeting on Natural Resource and Conflict in Africa: Transforming a Peace Liability into a Peace Asset", Cairo, Egypt, 17–19 June 2006.

United Nations Commodity Trade Database Online (UN Comtrade): http://www.comtrade.un.org/db

United Nations (1992), Rio Declaration on Environment and Development. New York: UN. Available online at: http://www.un.org/documents/ga/conf151/aconf15126-1annex1.htm.

UNDP (United Nations Development Programme) (2006), "Human Development Report 2006: Beyond Scarcity: Power, Poverty and the Global Water Crisis", New York: UNDP.

—— **(2005),** "Human Development Report 2005: International Cooperation at a Crossroads: Aid, Trade and Security in an Unequal World", New York: UNDP.

UNCTAD (2006), "Boosting Africa's Growth through re-injecting 'surplus' oil revenue. An alternative to the traditional advice of save and stabilize", UNCTAD, Report number: UNCTAD/DITC/COM/2006/10

UNECA (United Nations Economic Commission for Africa) and AfDB (African Development Bank), (2007), "The 2007 Big Table: Summary Document, Managing Africa's Natural Resources For Growth And Poverty Reduction", UNECA and AfDB. February 2007.

United Nations Development Programme (UNEP) and United Nations Environment Programme (UNDP) (2007), "Mainstreaming Environment for Poverty Reduction and Pro-poor Growth: Proposal for Scaling-up the Poverty-Environment Initiative", New York: UNDP.

United Nations Environment Programme (UNEP), (2007a), "Economic instruments to promote compliance". Available online at: http://www.unep.org/DEC/OnLineManual/Enforcement/InstitutionalFrameworks/EconomicInstruments/tabid/88/Default.aspx.

United Nations Environment Programme (UNEP) and International Institute for Sustainable Development (IISD) (2004), "Exploring the Links: Human Well-Being, Poverty and Ecosystem Services", Nairobi, UNEP.

UNEP (1999), "Global Environment Outlook: United Nations Environmental Programme", UNEP, Nairobi.

—— **(2002),** "Africa Environment Outlook: Past Present and Future Perspectives", United Nations Environmental Programme, Nairobi.

—— **(2006),** "Africa Environment Outlook: Our Environment", incl. "Forests and woodlands in Africa" Encyclopedia of Earth. Eds. Cutler J. Cleveland. (http://www.eoearth.org/article/forests_and_woodlands_in_Africa.)

—— **(2007)**, "Forests and woodlands in Africa" in: Encyclopedia of Earth, Eds. Cutler J. Cleveland. (http://www.eoearth.org/article/forests_and_woodlands_in_Africa. Accessed on 06/05/2007)

UNESCO Institute for Statistics (UIS) (2007), "Mid-point progress report on the Millennium Development Goals (MDGs)", UNESCO. Available at: http://www.uis.unesco.org/ev_en.php?

UNFCCC (2006); (2007), "Climate Changes and Adaptation in Africa", Report on the Regional Workshop on Adaptation in Accra, Ghana.

United States Agency for International Development (USAID) with Center for International Forestry Research, Winrock International, World Resources Institute and International Resources Group (2002), "Nature, Wealth, and Power: Emerging Best Practices for Revitalizing Rural Africa", Washington, D.C., USAID.

United States Geological Survey (USGS) (2003), "USGS Minerals Commodity Surveys; 2002". USGS, Virginia, United States of America.

United States Geological Survey (USGS) (2005), "USGS Minerals Yearbook, Africa 2004". USGS, Virginia, United States of America.

United States Geological Survey (USGS) (2007), "USGS Minerals Commodity Surveys, 2007". USGS, Virginia, United States of America.

Veit, Peter G. and Benson, C. (2004), "When Parks and People Collide", Human Rights Dialogue. New York: Carnegie.

Veit, Peter G. (2007), "Towards Harnessing Africa's Natural Resources Potentials for Sustainable Development", Background paper written for African Development Report, 2007. AfDB.

—— **(2006),** "How African states keep their people poor: The legal issues", *South African Journal of International Affairs*, 13, 2, pp.33–52,

Veit, Peter G., R. Nshala and M. Ochieng' Odhiambo (2007), "Securing Africa's Protected Areas: Democratizing Compulsory Land Acquisition Procedures", Washington, D.C.: World Resources Institute.

Waldman, L., A. Ballance, R. Benítez Ramos, A. Gadzekpo, O. Mugyenyi, Q. Nguyen, G. Tumushabe and H. Stewart (2005), "Environment, Politics and Poverty: Lessons from a Review of PRSP Stakeholder Perspectives, Synthesis Review,Poverty and Environment Partnership.

Wass, P. (1995), "Kenya's Indigenous Forests: Status, Management and Conservation", P. Wass, (Ed), IUCN Forest Conservation Programme. IUCN, Gland & ODA, Cambridge.

Weinstein, J. (2005), "Resources and the information problem in rebel recruitment", *Journal of Conflict Resolution*, 49, 4, 598–624.

WCED (World Commission on Environment and Development) (1987), "Our Common Future", Oxford: Oxford University Press.

WHO/UNICEF (2006), "Meeting the MDG Drinking Water and Sanitation Target". WHO/UNICEF.

WMO & UNESCO (1988), "Water Resources Assessment", Handbook for Review of National Capabilities, WMO, Geneva, Switzerland.

Wolf, K., Carius and Dabelko (2005), "Managing Water Conflict and Cooperation" in State of the World 2005: Redefining Global Security, Washington, D.C.: Worldwatch Institute.

Woollcock, M., Pritchett, L. and Isham, J. (2001), "The social foundations of poor economic growth in resource-rich countries", In: Auty, R. (Ed.): Resource abundance and economic development. Oxford University Press, UK.

World Bank and AfDB (2007), "The African Competitiveness Report 2007", World Economic Forum 2007, Geneva.

World Bank (2000), "World Development Indicators", World Bank, Washington, DC. Available at: http://publications.worldbank.org.

—— **(2001),** "World Development Report 2000/2001: Attacking Poverty", New York: Oxford University Press.

—— **(2003),** "Land policies for growth and poverty reduction", Ed.: Klaus Deininger. Washington DC: World Bank and Oxford University Press.

—— **(2003b),** "World Development Report 2004: Making Services Work for Poor People", Washington, D. C.: World Bank.

—— **(2006a),** "Engaging with Fragile States: An IEG Review of World Bank Support to Low-Income Countries Under Stress", Washington D.C., The World Bank.

—— **(2006b),** "World Development Report 2006", World Bank, Washington, D.C.

—— **(2006c),** "Where is the Wealth of Nations? Measuring Capital for the 21st Century", International Bank for Reconstruction and Development/World Bank, Washington, D.C.

—— **(2006d),** "World Development Report 2006: Equity and Development", Washington, D.C.: World Bank.

—— **(2007),** "Initiative Cites Appalling Conditions for Artisanal Miners", *World Bank Weekly Update*, September 10, 2007.

—— **(2007b),** "World Development Indicators, 2007". World Bank, Washington, DC.

World Bank, United Nations Conference on Trade and Development, and International Council on Mining and Metals (2006), "The Analytical Framework: The Challenge of Mineral Wealth: Using resource endowments to foster sustainable development", World Bank, Washington D.C..

World Gold Council (2005), "Gold mining increasingly important to developing countries", *WGC, 26 May, 2005.* Available online at: http://www.invest.gold.org/sites/en/headlines/2005/05/26/story/8594853/.

WRI and IFC (World Resources Institute and International Finance Corporation (World Bank Group) (2007), "The Next 4 Billion: Market Size and Business Strategy at the Base of the Pyramid", Washington, D.C.: WRI.

WRI (World Resources Institute) (2002), "World Resources 2002–2004, An Assessment of the Resource Base that Supports the Global Economy: Decisions for the earth: Balance, voice, and power". WRI, Washington, DC.

—— **(2005),** "Earth Trends: The Environmental Information Portal", World Resources Institute. Washington, D.C. http://earthtrends.wri.org.

World Resources Institute (WRI), and United Nations Development Programme, United Nations Environment Programme and World Bank (2005), "World Resources 2005: The Wealth of the Poor—Managing Ecosystems to Fight Poverty" Washington, D.C.: WRI.

—— **(2004),** "World Resources 2002–2004: Decisions for the Earth—Balance, Voice, and Power", Washington, D.C.: WRI.

Wright (1990), "The origins of American Industrial Success 1870–1940", *In American Review*, 80, 651–68.

WWC (World Water Council) & CONAGUA (2006), "Water Resources Development in Africa: Challenges Response and Prospective", WWC and CONAGUA, Mexico.

YCELP and CIESIN (2006), "Pilot 2006 Environmental Performance Index", Yale Center for Environmental Law and Policy and Center for International Earth Science Information Network, New Haven. Available online at: http://www.yale.edu/epi/2006EPI_Report_Full.pdf.

Young, M. D. and S.A. Ryan (1995), "Using environmental indicators to promote environmentally, ecologically, and Socially-sustainable resource use: A policy orientated methodology". USAID Environmental and Natural Resources, Policy and Training Manual No. 3.

Zeeuw, A. de (2000), "Resource management: Do We Need Public Policy?", Small Study for Directorate B, European Commission (B4-3040/2000/258081/MAR/ B2).

Zissis, C. (2006), "Chad's Oil Troubles, Council on Foreign Relations", Available at: http://www.cfr.org/publication/10532

This publication was prepared by the Bank's Development Research Department (EDRE) in the Chief Economist Complex (ECON). Other publications of the Complex are:

AFRICAN DEVELOPMENT REVIEW

The African Development Review is a professional development economics journal that provides a platform for expressing analytical and conceptual views on African development challenges, published 3 times a year.

ECONOMIC RESEARCH PAPERS

A working paper series presenting preliminary research findings on topics related to African development.

COMPENDIUM OF STATISTICS

An annual publication providing statistical information on the operational activities of the Bank Group.

GENDER, POVERTY AND ENVIRONMENTAL INDICATORS ON AFRICAN COUNTRIES

A Biennial publication providing information on the broad development trends relating to gender, poverty and environmental issues in the 53 African countries.

SELECTED STATISTICS ON AFRICAN COUNTRIES

An annual publication, providing selected social and economic indicators for the 53 regional member countries of the Bank.

PRODUCT CATALOGUE FOR ICP PRICE SURVEYS IN AFRICAN COUNTRIES

This catalogue provides ICP survey information on a series of products to be priced in some Regional Member Countries.

AFRICAN ECONOMIC OUTLOOK

An annual publication jointly produced by the African Development Bank and the OECD Development Centre, which analyses the comparative economic prospects for African countries.

THE AFRICA COMPETITIVENESS REPORT

The report presents an indepth investment climate assessment for selected countries in Africa, and is published by the Bank, in colaboration with the World Economic Forum and the World Bank.

Copies of these publications may be obtained from:

Development Research Department (EDRE)
African Development Bank

Headquarters	**Temporary Relocation Agency (TRA)**
01 BP 1387 Abidjan 01,	Angle des trois rues, Avenue du Ghana,
COTE D'IVORIE	rues Pierre de Coubertin
TELEFAX (225) 20 20 49 48	et Hedi Nouira
TELEPHONE (225) 20 20 44 44	BP 323 — 1002 TUNIS BELVEDERE
TELEX 23717/23498/23263	TUNISIA
Web Site: www.afdb.org	TELEFAX (216) 71351933
EMAIL: afdb@afdb.org	TELEPHONE (216) 71333511
	Web Site: www.afdb.org
	EMAIL: afdb@afdb.org